Federal Civil Service Jobs

14th Edition

Dawn Rosenberg McKay

Michele Lipson

Kangaroo Research Mavens

THOMSON

ARCO

Australia • Canada • Mexico • Singapore • Spain • United Kingdom • United States

ACKNOWLEDGMENTS

Thanks to Janette Young and everyone at Peterson's for bringing us on board. A tremendous thank you to our husbands and families who have supported us and our efforts.

—Michele Lipson and Dawn Rosenberg McKay, Kangaroo Research Mavens
(www.rooresearch.com)

CONTENTS

INTRODUCTION

The federal government is the nation's largest source of employment for Americans. A large percentage of these government employees are members of the military, but there are also millions of civilian federal employees. Many civilian federal employees are employed through the legislative branch—the Congress itself, the General Accounting Office, the Government Printing Office, and the Library of Congress—and through the judicial branch—the Supreme Court and the U.S. Court system. But, by far, the greatest number of federal civilian employees are employees of government agencies. These include: the executive branch, executive departments, and independent agencies such as the U.S. Postal Service, the General Services Administration, the Smithsonian, the Environmental Protection Agency, and the Office of Personnel Management, to name only a few.

The executive branch includes the Office of the President, the departments with cabinet representation, and a number of independent agencies, commissions, and boards. This branch is responsible for such activities as administering federal laws, handling international relations, conserving natural resources, treating and rehabilitating disabled veterans, conducting scientific research, maintaining the flow of supplies to the armed forces, and administering other programs to promote the health and welfare of the people.

The federal government employs about three million white-collar workers. Entrance requirements for white-collar jobs vary widely. Entrants into professional occupations are required to have highly-specialized knowledge in a specified field, as evidenced by completion of a prescribed college course of study. Typical occupations in this group are attorney, physicist, and engineer.

Entrants into administrative and managerial occupations usually are not required to have specialized knowledge but rather they must indicate, by graduation from a four-year college or by responsible job experience, that they have the potential for future development. The entrant usually begins at a trainee level and learns the duties of the job after being hired. Typical jobs in this group are budget analyst, claims examiner, purchasing officer, administrative assistant, and personnel officer.

Technician, clerical, and aide/assistant jobs have entry-level positions that usually are filled by persons having a high-school diploma or the equivalent. For many of these positions, no prior experience or training is required. The entry-level position is usually that of trainee, where the duties of the job are learned and skill is improved. Persons with junior college or technical school training or those having specialized skills may enter these occupations at higher levels. Jobs typical of this group are engineering technician, supply clerk, clerk-typist, and nursing assistant.

Blue-collar jobs—service, craft, and manual labor—provide employment to over 400,000 people. The majority of these workers are in establishments such as naval shipyards, arsenals, air bases, or army depots, or they work on construction, harbor, flood-control, irrigation, or reclamation projects.

The single largest group of blue-collar workers consists of mobile equipment operators and mechanics. Among these jobs are forklift operator, chauffeur, truck driver, and automobile mechanic. The next largest group is general laborers who perform a wide variety of manual jobs.

Many skilled occupations may be entered through apprenticeship programs. Experience normally is not required to qualify, but a test may be given to indicate whether an applicant has an aptitude for the occupation.

Federal employees are stationed in all parts of the United States and its territories and in many foreign countries. Although most government departments and agencies have their headquarters in the Washington, D.C., metropolitan area, only 1 out of 9 federal workers were employed there as of 2000.

PART I

The Best Job for You in Government

CHAPTER 1

DECIDING IF A GOVERNMENT CAREER IS RIGHT FOR YOU

Getting hired by the federal government is like trying to ride an elephant. It can be a safe and rather comfortable ride—and once you're on, it's not easy to fall off. But, getting *on* the elephant? Now, that's another story.

To a job seeker, the federal government can seem as large as an elephant—and as slow and ponderous in the way it responds. This will soon become apparent to you in the amount of information you'll be asked to provide when you apply for a government job—and the time it takes for the government to respond to your application. It's not like sending in your resume to an advertisement in the Sunday paper. In fact, many people find the process of applying for a government job so complicated, so frustrating, and so time-consuming that they often throw up their hands in disgust and decide: "This is nuts. Forget about it." This is a shame because, like riding an elephant, there are real advantages to a government career, as you'll see in the following sections. In fact, you may even decide that the best possible job for you is with the federal government.

When considering any job, you're likely to go through the advantages and disadvantages of the position. You compare not only the number of pros and cons on each side, but also each one's relative importance. Not every pro equals every con. For example, a particular job might have five points listed in the pro column and only one con. But, if that single con can't be overcome—say, the job requires moving and you absolutely can't move—then the one disadvantage outweighs all the advantages.

Other disadvantages may not be stumbling blocks so much as they are trade-offs. This is especially true when the job you're considering is a government job. When you consider government employment, you go through the same process you would with any job, listing the advantages and disadvantages. Besides the obvious points on each side, keep in mind the intangibles. A government career brings with it a certain frame of mind, almost a lifestyle. For people who see this lifestyle as bringing peace of mind, this will be a definite plus; for those who see it as repetitive, bringing boredom, it will be a minus. Be honest when assessing the pros and cons and your own reactions to them.

THE ADVANTAGES OF GOVERNMENT WORK

THE GOVERNMENT IS AMERICA'S LARGEST EMPLOYER

Nearly three million Americans work for the U.S. government. That's a lot of people—and a lot of jobs. Now you can understand why the government is one employment opportunity that cannot be overlooked. With this size comes diversity. Almost every imaginable occupation has its place in government work. There's room for everyone from soldiers, special agents, and politicians to auto mechanics, pipefitters, and carpenters. There's room for satellite watchers and map readers, secretaries and file clerks, accountants and auditors, purchasing agents and contract administrators, scientists and medical doctors, teachers and law enforcement officers—well, you get the picture. Almost anyone can find a suitable job at some level of government.

THE GOVERNMENT IS ALWAYS HIRING

Roughly 10 percent of all currently filled federal jobs will become vacant and open for rehiring in any given year. This is due to turnover—attrition due to retirement and to subsequent promotions up the ladder, as lower-graded employees apply for the jobs that higher-graded employees have just left. This makes for a continual process of hiring, rehiring, and promotion throughout the entire federal government. As a result, jobs are always being filled.

But what about government budget cuts? Politicians can stand in front of the cameras and announce that they're "going to cut the bloated federal payroll," but this fact can't be changed: The government is always hiring people, even during so-called "hiring freezes." Government agencies have had more than 200 years to learn how to protect themselves from Washington politics and are very creative about protecting their payrolls. Plus, these agencies provide real services that, when cut, cause taxpayers to complain and to change their votes. This means that when push comes to shove, politicians back off.

While hiring freezes may be felt more on the lower levels, the state and municipal levels of government are also engaged in a continual process of hiring new people—and have also learned how to survive the political axe.

A GOVERNMENT JOB IS A SECURE JOB

Although it's difficult to get a government job, once you're "on the elephant," it's likely that no one will be able to get you off of it until you're good and ready. In other words, you can stay or leave according to your own schedule. Reductions In Force (RIFs) happen infrequently, and when they do, most agencies achieve their goals through early retirements—often accompanied by $25,000 incentives—and by attrition (not filling the jobs left vacant by people who have taken on other careers or retired).

A GOVERNMENT JOB PROVIDES ROOM FOR MOVEMENT AND GROWTH

While you may start out in one particular position, once you're working for the government, you'll find that you have opportunities to move upward or sideways in your field—or to change fields entirely. Advancement may not be rapid, but if you do your work well, it is almost guaranteed, as good work is generally rewarded. In addition, the security of a government position allows you to make long-term career plans. In most cases, you'll know just how to earn a promotion—as well as a raise to the next pay grade. These procedures will be clearly defined.

GOVERNMENT JOBS PROVIDE STRONG SALARIES

All civil service jobs vary in expectations, requirements, and salary, but we can look at some specific levels of government salaries to get a good sense of the general pay scales.

As an example, below you'll find the pay schedule for most white-collar federal employees. They're covered by the General Schedule, which is established by the Federal Wage System. Wages for the General Schedule originate from recommendations by the Federal Prevailing Rate Advisory Committee, which is made up of management and labor unions. The committee surveys non-federal pay for similar jobs in the same location, then advises the Director of the Office of Personnel Management on pay policy.

GENERAL SCHEDULE BASIC PAY FOR 2002

GS-1 $14,757	GS-5 $22,737	GS-9 $34,451	GS-13 $59,409
GS-2 $16,592	GS-6 $25,344	GS-10 $37,939	GS-14 $70,205
GS-3 $18,103	GS-7 $28,164	GS-11 $41,684	GS-15 $82,580
GS-4 $20,322	GS-8 $31,191	GS-12 $49,959	

Here's how the General Schedule works:

There are 15 grades, each defined by law according to work difficulty, responsibility, and the qualifications required for performance. There are 10 steps within each pay grade. Advancement through Steps one through three in each grade is scheduled after each fifty-two weeks of service; through Steps four, five, and six, after each 104 weeks of service; and through Steps seven, eight, and nine, after each 156 weeks of service. At Step 2 of each grade, compensation is based on the average going rate for private-sector employees performing the same job. So while the first step may fall below the average pay rate, it would certainly fall within the range of what an actual private-sector job might pay. At Step 5 within each grade, however, federal employees are paid 12 percent above this average private-sector rate, which demonstrates the advantage in moving through the ranks of federal employment.

Federal employees not only receive wages comparable to the same job in the private sector, but they also receive wages comparable to the same job in each particular location. This is important, as certain areas of the country have a higher cost of living and often pay employees higher salaries. This *locality pay* can be 8.64 to 19.04 percent higher than the regular General Schedule amount for jobs within the continental United States—and 10 to 25 percent higher for jobs outside the continental United States.

In addition to locality pay, certain hard-to-fill jobs in specialized scientific, technical, and medical fields begin at higher starting rates. And, as in the private sector, employees who work the night shift are paid a night differential.

GOVERNMENT EMPLOYEES RECEIVE MANY SOLID BENEFITS

Would you like paid vacations? Comprehensive health-care insurance? A secure retirement pension? Of course you would.

With health-care costs rising—and health insurance premiums skyrocketing just as quickly—a strong benefits package is one of the most important advantages of working for the federal government. In addition, a secure retirement is another major concern for many people. As the stock market rises and falls (and private-sector pension plans crumble under administration costs and poor investments), federal employees have the comfort of knowing their retirement benefits are secure.

An added plus is that this solid package of benefits is available to *all* government workers, not just a selected few. This fact, combined with a sense of job security, is often enough to sway people to find a government career.

What kinds of benefits do government workers receive? Below is a chart of the benefits offered to federal employees.

FEDERAL BENEFITS

Type of Benefits	Who Is Covered	Available Options
Health: *Federal Employees Health Benefits (FEHB)*	Federal employees and retirees and their survivors. Coverage may include: • Self only; or • Family coverage for yourself, your spouse, and unmarried dependent children under age 22	• Managed Fee for Service Plans; • Point of Service (PPO) options; or • Health Maintenance Organizations (HMOs)
Retirement: *Federal Employees Retirement System (FERS)*	Almost all new employees hired after 1983 are automatically covered. Employees who leave may still qualify for benefits. Builds on the Social Security Benefits employees may earn in the future, or may already have earned, from non-federal work.	FERS is a three-tiered retirement plan, consisting of these components: • Social Security benefits (available for those age 62 and retired) • Basic Benefits Plan (financed by a small contribution from the employee and the government) *A Special Retirement Supplement, for employees who meet the criteria, is paid as a monthly benefit until the employee reaches age 62.* • Thrift Savings Plan (tax-deferred retirement savings and investment plan; similar to 401(k) plans)
Life: The Federal Employees' Group Life Insurance Program (FEGLI)	Federal employees and retirees, as well as many of their family members are eligible for this group life insurance program.	Basic Insurance (automatic unless employee opts out; insured pays two thirds of cost and the government pays one third); plus Optional Insurance (not automatic; insured pays 100 percent of cost)
Long Term Care: Federal Long Term Care Insurance Program (FLTCIP)	Employees, annuitants, current spouses, adult children, parents, parents-in-law, and stepparents of living employees.	Employees pays premium until he or she is eligible for benefits. Insurance is portable as long as you pay your premium. Premiums vary by your age when you buy the policy and by the options you choose.

A GOVERNMENT CAREER IS A CAREER IN PUBLIC SERVICE

Working for the government can provide a level of satisfaction that few other careers offer. You are a public servant, in the best sense. As just a few examples, consider these important federal agencies: the Federal Emergency Management Administration (FEMA), the Federal Aviation Administration (FAA), the Federal Bureau of Investigations (FBI), the Small Business Administration (SBA), the Center for Disease Control (CDC), or the National Institutes of Health (NIH). Each one of these agencies—and every one of its employees—is contributing to the health and welfare of the American people. In many instances, mid-career professionals who have already succeeded in the private sector want to give something back and will choose to work for the government, precisely for this reason.

A GOVERNMENT JOB OFFERS OPPORTUNITIES FOR ADVANCED PROFESSIONAL TRAINING

Not everyone who is hired by a government agency is fully trained to begin working their first day on the job or to effectively handle an increase in job responsibility. In response to this need, both federal and state agencies see to the full training of their people. As a result, multiple training and educational opportunities are available. These opportunities may include full or partial tuition reimbursement, as well as time off—sometimes with pay—to complete the programs. This is a *major* benefit, as such training helps you do your current job better and helps prepare you for future promotions.

THE GOVERNMENT HIRES PEOPLE AT ALL STAGES OF CAREER DEVELOPMENT

This is an important fact. You can be a high school graduate with virtually no work experience, a recent college graduate, a student still in college, or a veteran who is separating or retiring from the U.S. military, and the government will have positions for which you can successfully apply. You can be a Ph.D. or a high school dropout who went back to finish the GED degree, and the government will have opportunities for you. There is almost no situation imaginable for which the federal government does not have opportunities!

THE DISADVANTAGES OF GOVERNMENT WORK

In the previous section, you were presented with several reasons to consider working for the federal government. But what about the other side of the coin: the con side? There are some very important factors you need to consider before you can make an informed decision about a career in government service.

YOU WILL HAVE TO WORK IN A LARGE BUREAUCRACY

The government is a bureaucracy, an organization with a strict hierarchy. This means several things to you, the federal employee, with regards to your ability to make a decision. First, every move you make must be approved by a rigid chain of command. Second, every action you take must have a precedent. Third, every aspect of your employment will be regulated by pre-existing guidelines and procedures (outlined in your personnel manual). These regulations protect you from being fired and protect your job from being eliminated. However, these regulations also require you to do your work according to rules and requirements that may no longer make sense.

A bureaucracy the size of the U.S. government changes slowly because many of its regulations were written long ago. The situations they were to address may have changed, but the regulations and requirements remain. That's why the government is often referred to as a "dinosaur."

THE GOVERNMENT FAVORS BUREAUCRATS OVER RISK TAKERS

A bureaucracy favors bureaucrats. It makes wonderful sense. However, if *you're* not a bureaucrat, this can become a challenge to your patience and persistence. If you're the kind of person who sees what needs to be done, wants to do it, and is accustomed to doing it on your own, you may find this aspect of government work intolerable. What *you* see as taking initiative, the bureaucracy may see as taking risks; after all, you're acting without precedent and without approval. Actions *you* think show you off as a self-starter may make you, in the bureaucracy's eyes, a loose cannon.

CHANGE IN MOST GOVERNMENT AGENCIES IS A SLOW PROCESS

It is a general rule that as an organization grows, it becomes more cumbersome. As a result, it becomes resistant to change. With an organization as large as the government, change comes about very slowly.

When we speak of the U.S. government, we're talking about a vast empire of agencies and departments—all of which are subject to regulation by the legislative and executive branches of our national government. These agencies may have huge budgets, but they are not fully their own bosses. They do "the will of the people," as expressed by Congress and the executive branch.

It all boils down to this: If you're a government worker and somewhere along the way you become dissatisfied with the status quo, you're in for a very long ride if you try to change things.

INCOMPETENCE IS EASILY HIDDEN IN LARGE ORGANIZATIONS

The larger the organization, the more dead weight it will carry. By *dead weight,* we are referring to those employees who simply go through the *motions* of working but who actually accomplish very little. These individuals rely heavily on the work ethic of those dedicated to their careers to cover for them.

You should be aware of this, because although most government employees will be just as diligent as you are, you may be carrying the weight for other, less motivated employees. And because of all the job security that led you to the government in the first place, you may be stuck with these employees for the duration.

IT MAY BE DIFFICULT TO LEAVE A DEPARTMENT ONCE YOU'RE IN

It may come to pass during your employment that you would like to transfer into another position, or even another agency. Be forewarned, however, that receiving a transfer within the federal government can be just as cumbersome as getting hired was. Every personnel-related action involves large amounts of paperwork and will probably take months to process. Few bosses are likely to volunteer eagerly to get involved in instigating these paper-shuffling procedures. You may get lucky and have your transfer approved right away. Or, you may have to wait until so-and-so in the department you want finally decides to retire and frees up a vacancy.

GOVERNMENT AGENCIES ARE SUBJECT TO INTENSE POLITICAL PRESSURES

Because government agencies have so many constituencies and audiences to please, decisions can be difficult to make. The pressures governing a given situation, combined with political and/ or media pressure, often cloud facts and logic—and even the purpose for which an agency exists. The bottom line is always changing and, in many cases, doesn't make sense.

A GOVERNMENT POSITION ON THE FEDERAL LEVEL MAY REQUIRE YOU TO TRAVEL AS PART OF YOUR WORK

Federal agencies and departments administer programs throughout the United States and, in many cases, overseas. Agencies need many people to ensure that these programs are operating properly and that field offices are doing what they have been asked to do.

If travel or relocation is required, this will usually be stated under "Conditions of employment" on the vacancy announcement. Sometimes a particular job title position is available in a variety of locations. Applicants are asked to indicate their geographic preferences on the application. The vacancy may even state that "failure to specify a geographic preference on your application will result in a rating of ineligible."

YOU MAY HAVE TO WORK HARDER FOR LESS THAN YOU EXPECT

Many people have the mistaken idea that government work is easy. Their perception may be that there is very little to do, ample opportunity for paid vacation and holidays, and unbelievable benefits. This perception is a myth—and the truth can come as quite a shock.

Government employees, for the most part, work *very* hard. And while their salaries and benefits are very good, they are not fantastic. If you're motivated by money alone and want to reach incredible professional heights very quickly, government work is not for you.

COMPARING PUBLIC- AND PRIVATE-SECTOR EMPLOYMENT

The pros and cons considered in the previous section address government work in and of itself. However, a career in the public sector is an alternative to a career in the private sector. So, it's useful to also look at how government work—with its advantages and disadvantages—compares to private-sector work.

GOVERNMENT JOBS ARE MORE SECURE

Government work has always been secure. In the last decade, however, security has become a rare commodity in the private sector. As a result, job security must be considered when comparing public- and private-sector employment.

Do you wake up every morning worrying whether you still have a job? Do you anxiously listen to news reports and rumors about corporate takeovers? Most of the traditionally accepted ideas about job security have been destroyed. Even the terminology has changed: "Laying off" has become "downsizing," which has become "rightsizing"—as if changing the language could disguise the nightmare of losing your job. In the private sector, job security no longer exists. Period. Even a *Fortune 500* company can be acquired by another company. It can always suffer huge profit downturns. And cutting payroll is one of the easiest methods for companies to show a temporary economic gain.

On the other hand, the government doesn't have to show a profit to stockholders every three months. And no one is trying to buy out the Department of Agriculture.

Because of this, security is one of the largest advantages of government work. With government work, you no longer have to worry about basic economic survival. You can finally have peace of mind.

GOVERNMENT PAY AND BENEFITS ARE COMPARABLE TO MOST PRIVATE-SECTOR PAY AND BENEFITS

Government salaries, at least on the federal level, are legally required to be comparable to their private-sector counterparts. Government pay is determined by surveying the salaries in the private sector. In addition, the government has a locality-pay differential for areas of the country that have a higher cost of living, as well as a night differential for night shifts.

In addition, government health-care benefits are strong and consistent across all agencies and departments. This may not be the case with many private-sector jobs. Benefits in the private sector are subject to more frequent change than in civil service—or they may not exist at all.

In addition, civil service retirement plans are very good—and they're guaranteed. Private-sector plans, on the other hand, often become uncertain when it's time to actually pay out. The private sector favors executives in both salaries and benefits, while the government offers the same benefits package to all.

As a quick example of these differences, take a look at something relatively simple: the number of paid holidays a company might offer. Let's begin with paid holidays offered to federal employees:

FEDERAL HOLIDAYS

New Year's Day	Labor Day
Martin Luther King, Jr.'s Birthday	Columbus Day
Washington's Birthday	Veterans Day
Memorial Day	Thanksgiving Day
Independence Day	Christmas Day

How does the private sector compare? There are wide differences. As an example, one *Fortune 500* company gives employees 12 paid holidays. Six are called national holidays (New Year's Day, Memorial Day, Independence Day, Labor Day, Thanksgiving, and Christmas Day). In addition to these, three more paid holidays are decided upon by the employee's local branch, depending on what other companies in the area give. And still another three days are given as personal holidays, chosen by the employee, for a total of twelve. By contrast, a large national retail store has only six paid holidays—the same six listed above. And, being a retailer, this organization is open for two of those six days—Memorial Day and Labor Day. So even though an employee will be paid for the holiday, he or she may also have to work on it.

THE GOVERNMENT HAS LESS DISCRIMINATION THAN THE PRIVATE SECTOR

No one likes to talk openly about discrimination, such as sexism or racism, in the workplace. It exists in both the private and public sectors. However, because the process of hiring and promotion of government employees is ruled by precedent and regulations and is less vulnerable to individual likes and dislikes, there is less discrimination.

This is particularly true with regards to age. In the private sector, youth is prized because of its energy and enthusiasm, its up-to-date knowledge straight from college or grad school, and its lower pay ranges. Someone in his or her 50s may find it difficult to find a new position in the private sector.

In government, however, positions are graded in terms of their salaries—not in terms of age (unless a job has physical requirements). Thus, a federal agency may have a GS-13 position to fill for an accountant. Anyone with the requisite experience is eligible to apply. If you're 37, you won't be paid any more or any less than someone who is 53, as long as you both qualify for the job.

As a result of this leniency toward age, many older workers who are coming from ten or twenty years in the private sector can begin a full second career in government. In addition, veterans who have completed a full twenty-year career in the military can begin a second career as civilian employees of the government. That's much harder to do in the private sector.

GOVERNMENT WORK ALLOWS MORE FLEXIBLE JOB QUALIFICATIONS

How many times have you seen a job advertisement ask for X years of experience or a specific type of college degree? Such qualifications are standard for most private-sector jobs.

In the government, however, the process of qualifying for jobs is much more flexible. Often, a vacancy announcement will indicate that X years of experience can be substituted for X years of college education, or even for a college degree. Because it is a public-sector employer paying salaries with public funds, the government has made a point—supported by laws and legislation—to protect the rights and career aspirations of all Americans. As a result, very few government positions require a specific type of college degree. Not even senior-level positions require a specific degree, and in many cases, they require no degree at all. In practice, this means that a person with no degree can become a top-level manager overseeing the work of those with Ph.Ds.

As long as you present your qualifications effectively on the application forms that you submit, you can qualify for many government jobs that might be out of reach in the private sector. The key, of course, is presenting your qualifications effectively. You'll learn that in the following chapters.

THE PRIVATE SECTOR VALUES "SUPERSTAR" EMPLOYEES, MORE SO THAN THE PUBLIC SECTOR

Working in a government bureaucracy is not about acting alone. Nor is it about taking chances based on sudden hunches, in hopes of taking center stage and getting applauded for your intuition and initiative. Unlike private companies, there are very few "superstars" in the federal government. Instead, there are endless committee meetings to keep people in the loop. Government work is not about being an all-star or a lone wolf. It's more about building a set of working relationships with professionals throughout government service and using these contacts to advance your organization's agenda.

If you are someone who needs attention and recognition, you may well be better off in the private sector. If you don't mind working behind the scenes and don't care who gets the credit as long as the job gets done, you may do very well in a government career.

THE PRIVATE SECTOR OFFERS FASTER, GREATER REWARDS TO ITS EXECUTIVE WORKERS THAN THE PUBLIC SECTOR

Do you want to make a lot of money—and make it quickly? Depending on how important this is to you, the private sector may be the better place.

Top executives in the private sector make as much as five times more than public-sector executives who are managing programs of comparable size. Commissions, stock options, golden parachutes—none of these are available to civil service workers.

DECIDING ON THE BEST JOB FOR YOU

There is no easy formula for comparing civil service jobs to those in the private sector. There are no numbers that result in a right or wrong answer to the question of where you should work. There are only advantages and disadvantages to consider, each of which has its own importance to your particular situation. Many of the advantages are practical: salary, health care, vacation, and pension benefits. Conversely, many of the disadvantages are more a matter of atmosphere, context, and your own personality.

The smart way to make the decision is to be absolutely honest about your needs, your family's needs, what motivates you, and even what drives you crazy. Ask yourself these tough questions:

- How much money is "enough"?

- How much job risk is tolerable?

- How much money does your family need?

- How much risk can your family tolerate?

- What are the health-benefit needs of you and your family?

- How well do you handle change?

- Do you require constant change?

- What type of work environment do you prefer? (slow-paced versus fast-paced, and so on)

- How well do you work with other people?

- Can you be a team player, or must you be the star?

- How much frustration can you tolerate, in exchange for how much security?

You will have to choose which factors make the most sense for you and your personal situation. You'll also have to rely on a certain level of instinct and decide which feels right to you—or at least feels better.

CHAPTER 2

LAUNCHING YOUR FEDERAL GOVERNMENT JOB SEARCH

The federal government is so huge and complicated that it may be difficult to envision yourself as a federal employee. You're familiar with civil service on the local level: You know your town or city's police and fire personnel, at least by sight. You may even be somewhat familiar with civil service on the county level; perhaps you've had jury duty and have toured the county's court and jail system. But, the *federal* government? Since we seldom think of Frank, our letter carrier, as a federal employee, trying to "break into Washington" may summon up the picture of ourselves knocking on the door of the White House.

The federal government has innumerable offices throughout the country. Look in your county phone book for the government listings. The Veterans Administration, Social Security Administration, various divisions of the Armed Forces, Justice Department, Internal Revenue Service, Small Business Department, Department of Transportation, and others all likely have offices surprisingly close to where you live. And everyone in those offices is a Federal employee. You could be too.

BEFORE YOU BEGIN YOUR JOB SEARCH

Before you begin looking for a job within the federal government, you should get familiar with how this whole system works. For example, you may not know that there are two classes of jobs in the federal government—those in the competitive service and those in the excepted service. Those in the competitive service are under the jurisdiction of the U.S. Office of Personnel Management (OPM), and hiring for those jobs must adhere to the civil service laws passed by Congress. These laws ensure fair and equal treatment to job candidates in the hiring process. In other words, one can't hire her cousin unless that cousin is the best candidate for the job. Excepted service agencies are not subject to these civil service laws. In some cases, specific jobs may be excepted from civil service procedures. They are, however, subject to veterans' preference, which will be discussed later.

An agency can choose from among three groups of candidates when filling a position that falls within the competitive service. Primarily, candidates come from a list of eligibles administered by the OPM or by an agency under the OPM's direction. Those on this list have responded to a vacancy announcement and have met the requirements specified in this announcement. Agencies may also hire from a list of candidates who are eligible for noncompetitive movement within the competitive service because they are or were serving under career-type appointments in the competitive service. The third group of eligibles are those that qualify for special noncompetitive appointing authorities including the following:

■ **A VRA or Veterans' Readjustment Appointment eligible**. This is someone who served in the military for a period of more than 180 days active duty, all or part of which occurred after August 4, 1964, and was discharged under other than dishonorable conditions.

■ **Veterans** who are 30% or more disabled.

■ **Peace Corps or VISTA volunteers** who left the service within the last year.

■ **Certain present and former Foreign Service employees** who were appointed under the authority of the Foreign Service Act of 1946.

■ **Certain former overseas federal employees** and/or their family members who seek appointment within three years of their return to U.S.

■ **Certain National Guard Technicians** involuntarily separated within the last year.

■ **Persons with disabilities** who are severely physically disabled or mentally impaired.

■ **Veterans eligible for Veterans' Preference**.

■ **Veterans** who have been separated from the armed forces under honorable conditions after 3 years or more of continuous service.

■ **Certain employees displaced from the District of Columbia, Department of Corrections**.

GENERAL JOB CATEGORIES AND PROGRAMS AVAILABLE AT THE FEDERAL LEVEL

As we said in the last chapter, the federal government is the country's largest employer. That means it has room for almost every imaginable occupation. It also has an enormous variety of special programs to encompass many different hiring situations. Here's a look at some of the occupations:

■ **Professional occupations** require knowledge of a field that is usually gained through education or training equivalent to a bachelor's degree or higher, with major study in or pertinent to the specialized field—for example, engineer, accountant, biologist, or chemist.

■ **Administrative occupations** usually require progressively responsible experience. More than a college education is required, although professional training and study may be involved—for example, personnel specialist or administrative officer.

■ **Technical occupations** involve training and experience—for example, computer programmer, telecommunications specialist, or electronics technician.

■ **Clerical occupations** generally involve structured work in support of office, business, or fiscal operations—for example, clerk-typist, mail clerk, or file clerk.

■ **Skilled trades** involve manual work that usually requires a "journeyman" status in fields such as plumbing, HVAC technician, electricians, carpenters, and machinists.

PART-TIME PROGRAMS AND OTHER NONTRADITIONAL ARRANGEMENTS

Part-time positions—that is, 16 to 32 hours per week—are available in agencies throughout the federal government. Flex time, job sharing, telework, and nontraditional workday and workweek scheduling is also available in some positions. Inquire at personnel offices in agencies where you feel you may want to apply.

STUDENT PROGRAMS

The federal government has a number of programs in place specifically designed to provide employment for students. These programs include the following:

- **The Summer Employment Program** provides training and jobs for those who can only work during the summer months. These positions may also be open to individuals who aren't students. Applications are accepted for summer employment from December through April 15, and the jobs usually run from mid-May through September 30. Hiring is done by individual agencies. Some restrictions limit summer employment in the same agency where the applicant's parent also may be employed.

- **The Student Career Experience Program** is a work/study option for high school, college, graduate and professional school, and vocational and technical school students who are enrolled in school at least half-time. This program offers employment in positions directly related to the student's course of study. Positions in this program can lead to permanent employment upon a student's graduation. Students interested in this option should contact their high school counselors, college employment coordinators, or the agencies where they would like to work.

- **The Student Temporary Educational Program (STEP)** offers temporary employment opportunities for students. These jobs can last for as long as you are a student and do not need to be related to your academic field.

- **Federal Internships** provide professional experience to those who have completed their formal education. The purpose of these programs is to increase the pool of qualified candidates in a particular occupational area. Examples of internship programs are the Hispanic Association of Colleges and Universities' National Internship Program (HNIP) and the Presidential Management Intern Program (PMIP).

- **Volunteer Programs** are unpaid work opportunities that allow students and others to explore various occupations and gain valuable experience.

VETERAN PROGRAMS

U.S. military veterans are entitled to special consideration in federal hiring. In some cases, veterans are entitled to positions that are not open to the general public. In other cases, extra points are added to their exam scores, giving them a competitive advantage. The Veterans' Employment Coordinator at the agency where you want to apply can give you additional information.

PROGRAMS FOR PERSONS WITH DISABILITIES

Persons with disabilities should contact the Selective Placement Coordinator at the agency of interest to explore special placement assistance that is available to candidates with physical, cognitive, or emotional disabilities. By law, the federal government—just as the private sector—will make "reasonable workplace accommodations" for persons with disabilities; this means that the employer may adjust the duties of the job, the location where it's performed, or the methods by which it's performed.

PROGRAMS FOR RESIDENTS OUTSIDE THE CONTINENTAL U.S.

Alaska, Guam, Hawaii, Puerto Rico, and the Virgin Islands offer very limited federal employment possibilities. Local residents will receive first consideration for employment in these areas. Other candidates will be considered only when there are no qualified residents available.

HOW TO FIND FEDERAL JOBS THAT ARE RIGHT FOR YOU

Matching your experience and background to a federal job is perhaps one of the most difficult aspects of getting federal work. Part of this difficulty results from the fact that you have to find the vacancies yourself. You can't simply send in a resume or application and say, "Hey, Washington—here's what I can do. Who wants to hire me?"

There's no centralized personnel department for the federal government. Years ago, the Office of Personnel Management (OPM) used to serve that function. However, with so many agencies and so many applicants, OPM would take months to identify candidates and send their applications to the agency with the opening. Agencies complained that it was almost impossible for them to hire the people they needed *when* they needed them. Finally, the OPM gave up its authority in this area and now each federal agency does its own hiring. The result, however, doesn't make it easier for applicants, for a number of reasons, many of which are discussed below.

YOU MUST LOOK BEYOND THE TITLE

Say you want to become a federal employee. You're open to a number of position types, but because of your background you look for jobs with titles similar to your current title. If you limit yourself to that, you might miss other openings for which you qualify. Instead of looking at a title and thinking, "I don't have the experience to do that," pick titles that make you think, "Gee, that sounds interesting." Then read the qualifications. You just might be eligible.

Also, some titles can be very deceptive. When looking for a federal position, for example, an administrative assistant rightfully may think the position of "secretary" could be appropriate, then discover that it's for a high-ranking executive (think "Secretary of State"). Or, a recent graduate might see impressive-sounding titles such as "Agriculture Science Research Technician" or "Airway Transportation Systems Specialist" and immediately assume these are higher-ranked jobs for people with years of experience. A look at the salary, however, shows that these jobs start at under $22,000—obviously positions for the newer employee. A few extra seconds of investigation can help you decipher the title to get a closer look at the job.

In addition, don't dismiss federal work in general because you think the government wouldn't hire "someone like you." The government needs more than just accountants, soldiers, mechanics, clerks, nuclear scientists, and so on. Recently, there were openings for a graphic illustrator, a sports specialist, an archaeologist, a horticulturist, a manager for a community club, an outdoor-recreation planner, a leisure-travel arranger, and a religious education specialist. What's even more surprising than the variety is that all these jobs were for the same agency—the U.S. Army!

KEEP CHECKING THE ANNOUNCEMENTS

You must apply for a particular position in a particular agency because you're really applying for a specific vacancy, not just a job title. Most agencies don't refer to past applications. They don't "keep your resume on file," which many private-sector companies do. Think of it like this: You're not just applying for, say, an accounting position. When accountant Pat Smith retires, it's Pat Smith's vacancy you're applying for. What this means in terms of legwork is a constant monitoring of openings.

For every opening, agencies must publish an announcement of the vacancy, if they're going to fill it. This means you must constantly watch the job vacancy announcements for the agency you're interested in—or keep track of vacancies for several agencies if you're focused more on the kind of job rather than the agency where you perform it.

APPLY SEPARATELY FOR EACH VACANCY

Each time you spot an appropriate vacancy, you usually have to fill out an application form. You can't ask Agency X to refer to the application you sent in last month to Agency Y—even though that application might have taken days to fill out and was two dozen pages long. Except for a few closely related jobs that might be open within the same agency, each position requires its own application.

TAILOR YOUR APPLICATION OR RESUME TO THE JOB

So you can't use the same application to apply for multiple positions? Big deal. All you need to do is copy your information from one application to another, right? Wrong. Each application or resume needs to be tailored to the position for which you're applying. Use the vacancy announcement as a guide. The language you use on your application should mirror that used on the announcement. Then you must provide details that prove you have the knowledge, skills, and abilities (abbreviated KSAs) required for that job. More information about KSAs will be given later in this chapter. Does this all sound way too difficult? Don't give up yet. USAJOBS, the Federal Government's Employment Information System, has a tool that can help you put together a resume specifically tailored to each job for which you want to apply. It's called the Online Resume Builder, and you can find it on the USAJOBS Web site at www.usajobs.opm.gov. You can print out your resume, save and edit it, and in some cases, submit it electronically to hiring agencies.

WATCH OUT FOR CIVIL SERVICE JOB-HELP SCAMS

About now you may be asking yourself, "Can't anyone help me? Aren't there federal employment agencies?" And the answer is—beware! The government does not sign itself up with employment agencies the way a private-sector company might, so avoid any "employment agency" that promises that the government or a particular agency is its client and that it can help you—for a hefty fee—get the job you want.

Everything you need to get federal work can be had directly from the government, and it's readily available if you're willing to spend the time and do the legwork to find it. All the information is free, the forms and directions are free, and the process of applying is free. A person or agency that suggests otherwise is stealing from you as directly as a pickpocket. Also, beware of a person or agency that guarantees you a job, guarantees you a higher score, or says that there are "hidden" vacancies not listed in the announcements that only *they* can reveal to you.

REMEMBER—YOU CAN DO IT YOURSELF

What's *legitimate* help? Your *Federal Civil Service Jobs* book and other guides on the topic are not only legitimate, they're often your best buy—giving you "the most bang for your buck." These guides can help you save time and effort plus give you valuable proven tips you might not have discovered otherwise. There are also personal coaches who will hold your hand step by step through the search-and-application process. They, too, are legitimate but sometimes provide simply the same information that's in a guide like this, only at higher cost because of the personalized, one-on-one nature of their service.

MAKING CONTACT: HOW AND WHERE TO TRACK DOWN ACTUAL JOB VACANCIES

Although the difficulty involved may convince you otherwise, the federal government *wants* you to work for it and, therefore, has many ways you can find out what openings are available in what agencies. The following sections discuss the many sources for federal employment information and job bank listings.

DIRECT CONTACT

If you know which agency or agencies you want to work for, you may contact them directly to learn what vacancies exist and how to apply for them. At some agencies, you may be able to prepare an application that will be kept on file for future vacancies. Other agencies accept applications only for current or projected openings. Ask, so you'll know whether the agency's openings need constant monitoring.

If a federal agency has an office in your area, you may find its telephone number under "U.S. Government" in the blue pages of the phone book. If the agency has no office in your area, place a call to Information in the District of Columbia, (202) 555-1212, and ask for the telephone number of the personnel office or employment office of the agency you want to reach. Calls to government offices must be made during business hours, so prepare your questions ahead of time to hold down your phone bill.

To get you started, Appendix A, "Important Civil Service Employment Contacts," lists phone numbers, addresses, and Web sites for the major federal agencies.

USAJOBS: THE FEDERAL EMPLOYMENT INFORMATION SYSTEM

USAJOBS is the place to go for Federal employment information. As a matter of fact, hiring agencies are required to post job openings with the OPM, and USAJOBS is where the OPM makes those listings available to citizens. This automated system was developed and is maintained by the U.S. Office of Personnel Management to provide assistance to those seeking employment within the Federal Government. It consists of two components: the Internet and an automated telephone system. Both are available 24 hours a day, seven days a week and provide access to job listings, official forms, and helpful information about applying for employment.

THE INTERNET

You can access the USAJOBS Web site by going to www.usajobs.opm.gov. Once there, you can take a look at the current job vacancy listings, employment information fact sheets, applications, and other forms. Do you see a job that interests you? You can retrieve the complete vacancy announcement, and in some cases, apply for the job on line. As previously mentioned, you can utilize the Online Resume Builder and put together a resume that you can use to apply for federal jobs. **USAJOBS by E-mail** allows you to create and save a profile on line. When job openings that fit your profile come up, you will be notified by e-mail.

AUTOMATED TELEPHONE SYSTEM

You can reach the interactive voice response telephone system by dialing (478)757-3000 (or TDD (478)744-2299). It provides almost all the information available on the USAJOBS Web site, but it is a little more cumbersome to use since it functions like other voice response telephone systems, i.e. Press 1 for…, Press 2 for…, and so on, as you go from menu to menu. It is also more costly, since it's a long distance phone call unless you live in Macon, Georgia. If you have Internet access, or if you can find it somewhere, use it. If the telephone is your only option, it will have to do. You should find what you need there; it just may take you longer to find it.

STATE EMPLOYMENT SERVICE OFFICES

In addition to listing job vacancies with the OPM, hiring agencies are required to post vacancies with State Employment Service Offices. These offices are located throughout each state. Call your local office to find out how you can access these listings. It should be listed in the blue government pages of your local phone book.

THE ANATOMY OF A FEDERAL JOB ANNOUNCEMENT: WHAT TO LOOK FOR AND HOW TO USE IT

When you're looking for a job in the private sector and combing through the classifieds section of the newspaper or looking through job listings posted on an online job board, you will likely encounter small ads that briefly describe the job in question. You will see the job title, a few words about the position, maybe a salary range, and some contact information. Not much to go on, when you think about it. Sometimes you have to be a bit of a mindreader to figure out what the employer is looking for.

At the other extreme is the Federal Job Announcement. Usually, Federal Job Announcements are between four and eight pages long, single-spaced! What could they possibly have to say that fills four to eight pages? Let's take a look at a job vacancy announcement and see. This is only an example of a typical vacancy announcement. While all contain similar information, formats may differ.

VACANCY ANNOUNCEMENT

DEPARTMENT OF THE INTERIOR

BUREAU OF LAND MANAGEMENT

Vacancy Announcement Number: BLM/ID-02-145

Opening Date: 05/07/2002

Closing Date: 06/04/2002

Position: CONTACT REPRESENTATIVE

GS-0962-05/06

Salary: $24,701 – $27,534 per year

Duty Location: 1 vacancy at Boise, ID

VACANCY ANNOUNCEMENT

DEPARTMENT OF THE INTERIOR

BUREAU OF LAND MANAGEMENT

Vacancy Announcement Number: BLM/ID-02-145

Opening Date: 05/07/02

Closing Date: 06/04/02

Position: Contact Representative, GS-962-05/06

Salary: GS-05: $24,701 per year

GS-06: $27,534 per year

Duty Location: Boise, ID

Applications will be accepted from: All qualified persons.

This announcement is open concurrently with BLM/ID-02-146, which is open to any current or former federal employee in the local commuting area who has competitive civil service status or reinstatement eligibility. You must apply to each announcement separately if you wish to be considered under both recruitment methods.

Major Duties:

The incumbent is the primary contact responsible for the dissemination of information to the public. Serves as the public contact function for the Boise Front Unit of the Mountain Home Ranger District, U.S. Forest Service (located within same building). Provides technical expertise on payroll support and serves as the District's lead for payroll, PAYCHECK, and the Bureau Collections and Billing System (CBS). Furnishes general answers to inquiries from members of the public, governmental, and industry representatives. Information includes a general knowledge of public land laws, regulations, policies, land status, scheduled or pending sales, and application procedures for acquisition and use of federal lands and resources. Responds to the other agency programs including information regarding mining claims, surface management of operations, mineral material disposals, rockhounding, fossil collecting, casual use, firewood permits, Christmas tree permits, the Adopt-a-Horse program, and recreation use permits on public land. Prepares replies to written inquiries in a clear and concise manner and provides copies of appropriate regulations and procedural guidance. Explains and interprets land status records, master title plats, sketches, surface management maps, quadrangle maps, and wilderness maps. Stays abreast of changes in laws and regulations affecting public land and is responsible to explain changes to members of the public. Serves as the Primary District Cashier and Collections Officer. Processes biweekly District Time and Attendance reports via PAYCHECK. Acts as the District's primary telephone operator.

Basic Requirements:

To qualify at the GS-5 level, at least one year of specialized experience equivalent to the GS-4 is required. To qualify at the GS-6 level, at least one year of specialized experience equivalent to the GS-5 level is required. Specialized experience is experience with public land records available for public use, explaining the meaning and use of each.

Substitution of Education:

For GS-5: successful completion of a full 4-year course (120 semester hours) leading to a bachelor's degree.

For GS-6: one half year (9 semester hours) of graduate level education, if directly related.

A COPY OF YOUR COLLEGE TRANSCRIPTS ARE REQUIRED IF YOU ARE QUALIFYING ON EDUCATION.

You must meet all qualification requirements by the closing date of this announcement.

For each period of your employment in which you performed a mixture of duties, please indicate the approximate percent of time you spent performing each different type of work.

You will be considered on the basis of your education, experience, training and awards, and the Knowledge, Skills, and Abilities for this position.

Knowledge, Skills, and Abilities:

You should submit a narrative statement on a separate page(s) with specific responses to the knowledges, skills, and abilities (KSAs) in this announcement. Failure to submit your narrative response to the KSAs may negatively affect your eligibility and/or rating for this position.

1. Ability to communicate, both in person and in writing.

2. Skill in using computers and related software to input and compile data. (List software programs you use.)

3. Knowledge of general administrative office procedures (i.e., freedom of information, privacy act, customer service, public relations, time and attendance, telephone etiquette, screening of inquiries—written and in person).

4. Ability to work well under pressure, adapt to frequent changes in workload and priorities, and work in a team environment.

5. Knowledge of accounting principles, policies, and procedures (including any related training, education, and experience in processing financial documents).

Basis of Rating:

If you meet all the basic eligibility requirements for this position, you will be rated and/or ranked on the KSAs required to perform the duties of the position. Please review the KSAs carefully. You will be evaluated based on the quality and extent to which your experience and education show possession of the qualifications required. Credit will be given for the percentage of time that you have spent on those specialized duties listed. Please provide those percentages if your position involved mixed duties; i.e., where only a portion of your work experience would be creditable for this position.

Evaluation will be based upon information submitted in your application.

If you have special priority selection rights under the DOI Career Transition Assistance Program (CTAP) or the Interagency Career Transition Assistance Program (ICTAP) you must be well-qualified for the position to receive consideration for special priority selection. CTAP and ICTAP eligibles will be considered well-qualified if they meet the acceptable level on all ranking elements. Please see more detailed information on the CTAP and ICTAP at the end of this announcement.

Pay, Benefits, and Work Schedule:

This is a permanent full-time position.

You will be eligible for Federal Employee's Health Benefits, Federal Employee's Group Life Insurance, and FICA/Civil Service Retirement benefits.

If this position is filled below the full performance level, you may subsequently be promoted to the full performance level without further competition, provided performance is satisfactory, and time-in-grade and qualification requirements have been met.

Conditions of Employment:

Work is normally conducted in an office setting that has a public contact counter and various machines used in reading or reproduction of records. There is some bending, stooping, and stretching to retrieve various records and informational materials. Time spent in the field will be subject to various terrain and weather conditions.

If appointed to this position, while a BLM employee, you cannot hold an active real estate license, and you cannot have an interest in federal lands, or hold stocks in firms that have interest in federal lands.

Under Executive Order 11935, only United States citizens and nationals (residents of American Samoa and Swains Island) may compete for civil service jobs. Agencies are permitted to hire noncitizens only in very limited circumstances where there are no qualified citizens available for the position.

If you are selected for this position, you will be subject to completion of a favorable background investigation.

Other Information:

This agency provides reasonable accommodation to applicants with disabilities. If you need a reasonable accommodation for any part of the application and hiring process, please notify the agency. The decision on granting reasonable accommodation will be on a case-by-case basis.

PRIVACY ACT REQUIREMENTS (PL 93-579): The application forms prescribed are used to determine qualifications for employment or promotion and are authorized under Title 5, United States Code, Section 3302 and 3361.

If you make a false statement in any part of your application, you may not be hired; you may be fired after you begin work; or you may be fined or jailed.

MOVING EXPENSES ARE NOT AUTHORIZED. Travel, transportation, and relocation expenses will not be paid by the Department. Any travel, transportation, and relocation expenses associated with reporting for duty in this position will be your responsibility.

Only materials submitted with the application package for this vacancy will be used in the evaluation process. All application materials submitted in response to this vacancy announcement will be retained as part of the recruitment file and cannot be returned to you.

If you are applying for Veterans' Preference, you MUST submit evidence of eligibility, such as: DD-214, Certificate of Release or Discharge from Active Duty, or Standard Form 15, Application for 10-Point Veterans' Preference, and the proof requested on the form. You must clearly identify your claim for veterans' preference on your application. You will not be given Veterans' Preference credit if you fail to provide this information with your application. Please see more information on Veterans' Preference at the end of this announcement.

How to Apply

Please submit the following documents to:

USDI—Bureau of Land Management

Idaho State Office

HRM, ID-953

1387 South Vinnell Way

Boise, Idaho 83709-1657

Submit a resume, Optional Application for Federal Employment (OF-612), or other written application format of your choice. Whichever format you choose to use in applying, be sure you provide all of the information requested below:

Job Information:

- Announcement Number, title, and grade(s) for which you are applying

Personal Information:

- Full name, mailing address (with zip code), and day/evening telephone numbers (with area code)
- Country of Citizenship
- If ever employed by the federal government, please show the highest federal Civilian grade held, job series, and dates of employment in grade

Education:

- High School name, city, state and zip code, date of diploma or GED
- Colleges and/or Universities attended, city, state, and zip code
- Major field(s) of study
- Type and year of degree(s) received. If no degree received, show total credit hours received in semester or quarter hours

Work Experience:

- Job title

- Duties and accomplishments

- Number of hours per week

- Employer's name and address

- Supervisor's name and phone number

- Starting and ending dates of employment (month and year)

- Salary

- Indicate if your current supervisor may be contacted

Other Qualifications:

- Job-related training courses (title and year)

- Job-related skills (e.g., other languages, computer software/hardware, tools, machinery, typing speed, etc.)

- Job-related certificates and licenses

- Job-related honors, awards, and special accomplishments (e.g., publications, memberships in professional or honor societies, leadership activities, public speaking, performance awards, etc.). Do not send copies of documents unless specifically requested.

- If you are or have been a federal employee, please submit a copy of your last Notification of Personnel Action, Form SF-50.

If you do not submit the required items, you will not be considered. It is your responsibility to provide documentation/proof of claimed qualifications, education, veterans' preference, status (SF-50) and/or verification of eligibility for non-competitive appointment (and eligibility for Indian Preference for Employment, where applicable). You will not be contacted for additional information if your application is incomplete or inadequate.

The following documents are optional:

- DI-1935, Applicant Background Survey Form. (To be used for statistical purposes only and is not used in the evaluation process or shared with the Selecting Official.)

- OF-306, Declaration for Federal Employment

- A college transcript is recommended if your current job series is not in the same job series as the position being advertised.

- A supplemental statement in narrative format (not exceeding one page per KSA) that describes how the applicant's education, experience, and training relate to the KSAs.

Applications mailed using government postage and/or internal federal government mail system are in violation of agency and postal regulations and will not be accepted.

Your application must be postmarked by the closing date and received within five working days of the closing date to be considered.

Your application materials should not be submitted in notebooks or binders and should not contain extraneous materials such as training certificates or position descriptions.

For additional information about this vacancy announcement, please contact: HRM Staff at (208) 373-3921.

THE DEPARTMENT OF THE INTERIOR IS AN EQUAL OPPORTUNITY EMPLOYER:

Selection for this position will be made solely on the basis of merit, fitness, and qualifications. All applicants will receive consideration without regard to race, color, age, sex, sexual orientation, marital status, religion, national origin, political affiliation, handicap, or other non-merit factors.

Additional information on Veterans' Preference

5-point Preference.

A 5-point preference is granted to veterans who entered the military service prior to October 15, 1976, or who served in a military action for which they received a Campaign Badge or Expeditionary Medal, including the award of the Armed Forces Expeditionary Medal for service in Bosnia during Operation Joint Endeavor, November 20, 1995–December 20, 1996, and Operation Joint Guard, December 20, 1996–to be determined.

5-point Preference.

A 5-point preference is granted to veterans who served during a war; or during the period April 28, 1952 through July 1, 1955; or for more than 180 consecutive days, other than for training, any part of which occurred after January 31, 1955, and before October 15, 1976; or During the Gulf War from August 2, 1990, through January 2, 1992; or in a campaign or expedition for which a campaign medal has been authorized. Any Armed Forces. Expeditionary medal or campaign badge, including El Salvador, Lebanon, Grenada, Panama, Southwest Asia, Somalia, and Haiti, qualify for preference.

A campaign medal holder or Gulf War veteran who originally enlisted after September 7, 1980, (or began active duty on or after October 14, 1982, and has not previously completed 24 months of continuous active duty) must have served continuously for 24 months or the full period called to ordered active duty.

If you are claiming a 5-point veterans' preference, you MUST provide a DD-214, Certificate of Release or Discharge from Active Duty, or other proof of entitlement.

10-point Preference.

You may be entitled to a 10-point veterans' preference if you are a disabled veteran; you have received the Purple Heart; you are the spouse or mother of a 100% disabled veteran; or, you are the widow, widower, or mother of a deceased veteran. If you are claiming 10-point veterans' preference, you will need to submit form SF-15, Application for 10-point Veterans' Preference, plus the proof required by that form.

Additional information on CTAP

A. CTAP (for Non-DoD Agencies Only)

If you are currently an employee of the hiring agency who has received a Reduction in Force (RIF) separation notice, a Certificate of Expected Separation (CES), or notice of proposed separation for declining a direct reassignment or transfer of function outside of the local commuting area, you may be entitled to special selection priority under the Career Transition Assistance Plan (CTAP). To receive this priority consideration you must:

1. Be a current career or career-conditional (Tenure group 1 or 2) competitive service employee who has received a RIF separation notice, a Certificate of Expected Separation (CES), or notice of proposed separation for declining a directed reassignment or transfer of function outside of the local commuting area, AND you are still on the rolls of the agency. You MUST submit a copy of the RIF notice, CES, or notice of proposed separation with your application.

2. Be applying for a position that is at or below the grade level of the position from which you are being separated. The position must not have a greater promotion potential than the position from which you are being separated.

3. Have a current (or last) performance rating of record of at least fully successful or equivalent. This MUST be submitted with your application package.

4. Be currently employed by the hiring agency in the same commuting area of the position for which you are requesting selection priority.

5. Be rated well-qualified for the position. To be rated 'well-qualified,' CTAP applicants must attain an eligibility rating as described in 'Basis for Rating' or higher, not including points for veterans' preference.

Additional information on ICTAP

B. ICTAP (for all Federal Agencies)

If you are a displaced federal employee, you may be entitled to receive special selection priority under the Interagency Career Transition Assistance Plan (ICTAP). To receive this priority you must:

1. Be a displaced federal employee. You MUST submit with your application a copy of the appropriate documentation, such as a RIF separation notice, a Standard Form 50 reflecting your RIF separation, or a notice of proposed removal for declining a directed reassignment or transfer of function to another commuting area. The following categories of persons are considered displaced employees:

    a. Current or former career or career-conditional (tenure group l or 2) competitive service employees who:

        1) Received a specific RIF separation notice; or

        2) Separated because of a compensable injury or illness, whose compensation has been terminated, and whose former agency certifies that it is unable to place; or

        3) Retired with a disability and whose disability annuity has been, or is being, terminated; or

        4) Upon receipt of a RIF separation notice, retired on the effective date of the RIF and submits a Standard Form 50 that indicates 'Retirement in lieu of RIF,' or retired under the discontinued service retirement option; or

        5) Received a notice of proposed removal for declining a directed reassignment or a transfer of function or directed reassignment to another commuting area.

    OR

    b. Former Military Reserve or National Guard Technicians who are receiving a special OPM disability retirement annuity under Section 8337(h) or 8456 of Title 5 United States Code.

2. Be applying for a position at or below the grade level of the position from which you have been separated. The position must not have a greater promotion potential than the position from which you were separated.

3. Have a current (or last) performance rating of record of at least fully successful or the equivalent. You MUST submit a copy of this performance rating with your application package. (This requirement does not apply to candidates who are eligible due to compensable injury or disability retirement.)

4. Occupy or be displaced from a position in the same local commuting area of the position for which you are requesting selection priority.

5. Be rated well-qualified for the position. To be rated 'well-qualified,' ICTAP applicants must attain an eligibility rating as indicated in the 'Basis of Rating' section of this announcement, not including points for veterans' preference.

KEY ELEMENTS OF VACANCY ANNOUNCEMENTS

It's important that you read the job vacancy announcement very carefully and keep it by your side as you complete your application. You will need to refer to it often. Now let's take a look at its key elements and how you should use the information provided by the hiring agency when completing your application.

Hiring Agency: At the top of the announcement, you will find the name of the agency and the name of the bureau within the agency. In this case, the hiring agency is the Department of the Interior, and the specific bureau is the Bureau of Land Management.

Vacancy Announcement Number: Next you'll find this number, which is specific to the particular job opening. It is the number you will refer to in your application and in any correspondence you have about your application.

Opening Date/Closing Date: These dates specify the time period during which applications will be accepted.

Position: In this section, you'll first see the job title for which you are applying. These job titles are very specific to federal jobs. While a job title may be the same as one found in the private sector, its definition may not be. That's why it is imperative that you continue to read through the announcement. Beneath the job title you'll see a combination of letters and numbers. The two letters at the beginning, GS in this example, refer to the salary schedule this position falls under. White collar jobs fall under the General Schedule, or GS. The number that follows it immediately, in this case 0962, refers to the job classification series. The final digits, 05/06 in this announcement, refer to the grade-level. The grade-level is defined by law according to work difficulty, responsibility, and the qualifications required for performance. See the section on salary for more information on grade levels.

Salary: When there are two acceptable grade-levels, you will find a salary range. In this example, someone hired at the GS-05 level will receive an annual starting salary of $24,701 and someone hired at GS-07 will receive a starting salary of $27,534.

Duty Location: Federal jobs are located throughout the country, and abroad. This will tell you where you will be working if you're hired for this job.

Application Will Be Accepted From (or Who May Apply): This tells you if the job is open to everyone or if only current or former federal employees may apply. In some instances, applicants must be displaced from other federal jobs.

Major Duties: Here's the part you've been waiting for. This is where you will find out what you will be doing if you get the job. Read this carefully to determine if the job duties, as described, are what you want to be doing seven days a week, eight hours a day.

Basic Requirements: This section tells you what the requirements are for employment at each grade-level.

Substitution of Education: Education may be substituted for experience at each grade-level.

Knowledges, Skills, and Abilities (KSAs): KSAs are the attributes required to perform a job. They are generally demonstrated through qualifying experience, education, or training. Vacancy announcements generally ask that you submit a narrative on a separate sheet of paper with specific responses to these KSAs. This means you must address each KSA listed.

Basis of Rating: This tells you how applications will be looked at and evaluated against one another.

Pay, Benefits, and Work Schedule: This section will tell you whether the job is permanent or temporary, full-time or part-time. It will also tell you which benefits hirees are eligible for.

How to Apply: This particular announcement tells you where to mail your application and which format to use. Other announcements may tell you how to apply on line. Next, you'll find a list of items you need to submit. Use this as a checklist, checking off or crossing out each item as you complete your application. Nothing should be omitted. Remember—all your information and documentation must be submitted by the closing date.

ADDITIONAL TIPS

Once you read the Job Vacancy Announcement, you will know what the hiring agency expects to see on your application. Here are some other things you should consider:

- **Language that mirrors the job announcement's language.** The federal announcements are lengthy and detailed. Agencies know what they're looking for. Your application should echo the job announcement's language to show the agency that *you* are *exactly* what it seeks. Obviously, this doesn't mean you quote directly from the announcement or falsify your background, experience, or abilities—but do keep the announcement at hand when crafting your application or resume. Focus on what's important to the hiring agency.

- **KSAs or "ranking factors."** Occasionally a vacancy announcement does not state that an applicant is required to include a description of his or her KSAs on the application or resume. Here's one place where you shouldn't follow directions precisely. Go ahead and include those descriptions. If more than one applicant passes the initial screening, the KSAs are used to rank the qualified applicants. An application with no or inadequate KSAs will drop to the bottom of the list.

MAKING YOUR WAY THROUGH THE APPLICATION MAZE

You may apply for most federal jobs using the **Optional Application for Federal Employment (OF-612),** a resume, or any other written format you choose. If you are using the USAJOBS Web site, you can create and store a resume using the Resume Builder. We encourage you to take advantage of this free service. It serves as a guide through what can be a confusing process.

The difficult thing about putting together a federal job application, for many people, is the length of this document. When preparing a standard resume, you've probably been told over and over to stick to one page. This is not the case with a federal job application. Experts feel that you should describe each KSA using at least a half a page. This can seem like an impossible task for those who have difficulty expressing themselves in writing. However, if you want a federal job, you have to overcome this obstacle. You have several options.

The most obvious option is to hire a federal resume writer—someone who is an expert in preparing such documents. This is the most expensive route, and you may want to try your hand at preparing your application or resume yourself before you go this way. However, if you do choose to hire someone, get recommendations. If a federal resume writer hasn't come recommended, make sure you ask that person for references.

If hiring someone isn't a viable option for you, here's some advice to help you through this process:

- **Decide which format to use.** First determine which format to use. Read the vacancy announcement carefully to find out if the hiring agency specifies a preference for one format over another. In some instances, you may be able to apply on line. In either case, your choice is made for you—you use the specified format. If not, you must choose between a resume and Form OF-612, also known as the Optional Application for Federal Employment. If you have Internet access, you can take a look at and even print out this form. Just go to the USAJOBS Web site (www.usajobs.opm.gov) and look for a link to "Employment Forms." You can also order the form from the USAJOBS Automated Phone System discussed earlier. If, after perusing the OF-612, you decide not to use it, remember that your resume must include all the information that is asked for on that form. Personally, we would use the OF-612 because it clearly asks for all the information you need to supply. There's no guesswork involved and no chance of forgetting to include something. However, it's your application, so choose the format with which you're most comfortable.

- **Filling out the form is half the battle.** If you apply for the job, you run the risk of getting rejected. You also may get accepted. If you don't apply for the job, the outcome is clear. So our advice is this: Print out the OF-612 (or order it from the USAJOBS Automated Phone System) and fill it out. See how it looks. Get someone else's opinion. If you aren't happy with the application, keep trying until you are satisfied. Send it in and forget about it. You've given it your best shot.

- **Follow the application instructions.** We can't stress this strongly enough or too many times. Read the vacancy announcement carefully, and then do what it tells you to. Take note of whether they want you to use a particular format to apply. If they prefer you apply on line, you should make every effort to do so. Remember that many public libraries make computers available to their patrons. Many copy shops also have public computers but charge a fee for this service. You may also be required to submit specialized forms. If so, your application can't be processed without these forms. Make sure you submit your application and additional materials to the address indicated in the vacancy announcement.

- **Use Chapter 3 of this book for line-by-line help filling out the form.** Your fastest guide to getting help with your application is right in your hands—in the next chapter.

And remember that when you're gathering information from the vacancy announcement and adding all the necessary detail to your application, you must be familiar with the government's hiring terminology. Appendix D, "Glossary of Civil Service Hiring Terminology," has a complete listing of the most common terms you'll encounter and how the government agencies use those terms.

EXAMINATIONS FOR FEDERAL CIVIL SERVICE JOBS

In the past, most Federal Civil Service Jobs were filled from large registers of applicants maintained by the Office of Personnel Management. To earn a place on this list, applicants had to take a standardized written test. An applicant's test score determined his or her place on the list. Today, most nonclerical positions do not require written standardized tests, while clerical positions do require standardized tests.

Written tests, and sometimes performance tests, are still mandatory for certain competitive and outside-the-register appointments. Occasionally, written exams are required for inservice placement. Those who suffer from test anxiety shouldn't despair. In many cases, you won't be required to take a formal exam, or at least the kind of exam with which you are most familiar. In other words, you won't be put into a room with a bunch of other applicants and asked to use your number two pencil to fill in a bunch of circles. Many of these tests can be taken at home, often on line, and consist of a series of questions about your qualifications for the job. Your answers to these questions determine your ranking among other job candidates. What follows is a list of positions for which the OPM requires applicants to be tested. These are written tests unless otherwise indicated. This list does not take into account special examining provisions, such as "outstanding scholar" direct-hire appointments, waivers based on shortage labor market conditions, or other special circumstances that permit applicants to be exempted from written test requirements.

Series/Title/Position(s)	Grade(s)	Series/Title/Position(s)	Grade(s)
019 Safety Technician	2/3	029 Environmental Protection Assistant	2/3/4
072 Fingerprint Identification	2/3/4	082 United States Marshal	5/7
083 Police	2	083 Park Police	5
083a Police (Secret Service)	4/5	085 Security Guard	2
086 Security Clerical & Assistance	2/3/4	134 Intelligence Aid & Clerk	2/3/4
181 Psychology Aid & Technician	2/3	186 Social Services Aid & Assistant	2/3
189 Recreation Aid & Assistant	2/3	302 Messenger	2/3/4
303 Misc. Clerk & Assistant	2/3/4	304 Information Receptionist	2/3/4
305 Mail & File	2/3/4	309 Correspondence Clerk	2/3/4
312 Clerk-Stenographer (written and performance tests)	3/4/5	312 Reporting Stenographer (performance test only; mandatory for competitive appt. and inservice placement)	5/6
312 Shorthand Reporter (performance test only; mandatory for competitive appt. and inservice placement)	6/7/8/9	318 Secretary	3/4
319 Closed Microphone Reporting (performance test only; mandatory for competitive appt. and inservice placement)	6/7/8/9	322 Clerk-Typist (written and performance tests)	2/3/4
326 Office Automation Clerical and Assistance (written and performance tests)	2/3/4	332 Computer Operation	2/3/4
335 Computer Clerk & Assistant	2/3/4	344 Management and Program Clerical & Assistance	2/3/4
350 Equipment Operator	2/3/4	351 Printing Clerical	2/3/4
356 Data Transcriber (written and performance tests)	2/3/4	357 Coding	2/3/4
359 Electric Accounting Machine Operation	2/3/4	382 Telephone Operating	2/3/4
390 Telecommunications Processing	2/3/4	392 General Telecommunications	2/3/4

Series/Title/Position(s)	Grade(s)	Series/Title/Position(s)	Grade(s)
394 Communications Clerical	2/3/4	404 Biological Science Technician	2/3
421 Plant Protection Technician	2/3	455 Range Technician	2/3
458 Soil Conservation Technician	2/3	459 Irrigation System Operation	2/3
462 Forestry Technician	2/3	503 Financial Clerical & Assistance	2/3/4
525 Accounting Technician	2/3/4	530 Cash Processing	2/3/4
540 Voucher Examining	2/3/4	544 Civilian Pay	2/3/4
545 Military Pay	2/3/4	561 Budget Clerical & Assistance	2/3/4
592 Tax Examining	2/3/4	593 Insurance Accounts	2/3/4
621 Nursing Assistant	2/3	636 Rehabilitation Therapy Assistant	2/3
640 Health Aid & Technician	2/3	642 Nuclear Medicine Technician	2/3
645 Medical Technician	2/3	646 Pathology Technician	2/3
647 Diagnostic Radiologic Technologist	2/3	648 Therapeutic Radiologic Technologist	2/3
649 Medical Instrument Technician	2/3	651 Respiratory Therapist	2/3
661 Pharmacy Technician	2/3	667 Orthotist & Prosthetist	3
675 Medical Records Technician	2/3/4	679 Medical Clerk	2/3/4
681 Dental Assistant	2/3	683 Dental Lab Aid & Technician	2/3
698 Environmental Health Technician	2/3	704 Animal Health Technician	2/3
802 Engineering Technician	2/3	809 Construction Control	2/3
817 Surveying Technician	2/3	818 Engineering Drafting	2/3
856 Electronics Technician	2/3	895 Industrial Engineering Technician	2/3
962 Contact Representative	3/4	963 Legal Instruments Examining	2/3/4
986 Legal Clerk & Technician	2/3/4	990 General Claims Examining (One-grade interval)	4
993 Social Insurance Claims Examining	4	998 Claims Clerical	2/3/4
1001 General Arts & Information	2/3/4	1016 Museum Specialist & Technician	2/3
1021 Office Drafting	2/3	1046 Language Clerical	2/3/4
1087 Editorial Assistance	2/3/4	1101 General Business & Industry	2/3/4
1105 Purchasing	2/3/4	1106 Procurement Clerical & Technician	
1107 Property Disposal Clerical & Technician	2/3/4	1140 International Trade Specialist	5/7
1146 Grain Marketing Specialist	5/7	1152 Production Control	2/3/4

Series/Title/Position(s)	Grade(s)	Series/Title/Position(s)	Grade(s)
1311 Physical Science Technician	2/3	1316 Hydrologic Technician	2/3
1341 Meteorological Technician	2/3	1371 Cartographic Technician	2/3
1374 Geodetic Technician	2/3	1411 Library Technician	2/3/4
1421 Archives Technician	2/3/4	1521 Mathematics Technician	2/3
1531 Statistical Assistant	2/3/4	1541 Cryptanalysis	2/3
1702 Education & Training Technician	2/3	1802 Compliance Inspection & Support (except Detention Enforcement Officer Positions)	2/3/4
1811 Treasury Enforcement Agent	5/7	1812 Special Agent (Wildlife)	7
1863 Food Inspection	5/7	1884 Customs Patrol Officer	5/7
1896 Border Patrol Agent (written test & language proficiency)	5/7	1897 Customs Aid	2/3/4
1981 Agricultural Commodity Aid	2/3	2005 Supply Clerical & Technician	2/3/4
2091 Sales Store Clerical	2/3/4	2101 Airway Transportation System Specialist Department of Transportation Federal Aviation Administration	5/7
2102 Transportation Clerk & Assistant	2/3/4	2131 Freight Rate	2/3/4
2135 Transportation Loss & Damage Claims Examining	2/3/4	2151 Dispatching	2/3/4
2152 Air Traffic Control (mandatory for competitive appt. and inservice placement at grade 5/7; optional at grades above 7)	5/7		

If you apply for a job that falls under the Administrative Careers With America (ACWA) program, you may also be required to take a written exam. Administrative Careers With America is a program that offers competitive, entry-level (GS-5 and GS-7 levels) employment. The ACWA program encompasses several general occupational areas: health, safety, and environmental; writing and public information; business, finance, and management; personnel, administration, and computers; benefits review, tax, and legal; law enforcement and investigation. While a few jobs in this category require applicants to take formal written examinations, other jobs require candidates to complete multiple-choice questionnaires as discussed above. The following is a list of positions that are part of the ACWA program. All are at the GS-5 and GS-7 level. The job series is noted in parentheses. A vacancy announcement will tell you whether you will have to take a test or complete a questionnaire.

- Bond Sales Promotion (011)

- Safety & Occupational Health Management (018)

- Outdoor Recreation Planning (023)

- Park Ranger (025)

- Environmental Protection Specialist (028)

- Security Administration (080)

- Social Insurance Administration (105)

- Unemployment Insurance (106)

- Intelligence (132)

- Manpower Development (142)

- Social Services (187)

- Labor Management Relations Examining (244)

- Wage & Hour Compliance (249)

- Misc. Administration & Program (301)

- Computer Specialist [for alternative B only] (334)

- Administrative Officer (341)

- Management & Program Analysis (343)

- Logistics Management (346)

- Telecommunications (391)

- Financial Administration & Program (501)

- Tax Technician (526)

- Budget Analysis (560)

- Financial Institution Examining [except FDIC positions] (570)

- Hospital Housekeeping Management (673)

- Public Health Program Specialist (685)

- Paralegal Specialist (950)

- Pension Law Specialist (958)

- Contact Representative (962)

- Land Law Examining (965)

- Passport & Visa Examining (967)

- Tax Law Specialist (987)

- General Claims Examining [Two-grade interval] (990)

- Railroad Retirement Claims Examining (993)

- Unemployment Comp Claims Examining (994)

- Veterans' Claims Examining (996)

- General Arts & Information [except for fine arts positions] (1001)

- Public Affairs (1035)

- Writing & Editing (1082)

- Technical Writing & Editing (1083)

- General Business & Industry (1101)

- International Trade Analyst (1101)

- Contracting (1102)

- Industrial Property Management (1103)

- Property Disposal (1104)

- Public Utilities Specialist (1130)

- Trade Specialist (1140)

- Agricultural Program Specialist (1145)

- Agricultural Marketing (1146)

- Agricultural Market Reporting (1147)

- Industrial Specialist (1150)

- Financial Analysis (1160)

- Insurance Examining (1163)

Loan Specialist (1165)

Internal Revenue Officer (1169)

Realty (1170)

Appraising & Assessing (1171)

Housing Management (1173)

Building Management (1176)

Technical Information Services (1412)

Archives Specialist (1421)

Vocational Rehabilitation (1715)

Civil Aviation Security Specialist (1801)

Center Adjudications Officer (1801)

District Adjudications Officer (1801)

General Investigating (1810)

Criminal Investigating (1811)

Game Law Enforcement (1812)

Immigration Inspection (1816)

Securities Compliance Examining (1831)

Alcohol, Tobacco, & Firearms Inspection (1854)

Public Health Quarantine Inspection (1864)

Import Specialist (1889)

Customs Inspection (1890)

Quality Assurance (1910)

General Supply (2001)

Supply Program Management (2003)

Inventory Management (2010)

Distribution Facilities & Storage Management (2030)

Packaging (2032)

Supply Cataloging (2050)

Transportation Specialist (2101)

Transportation Industry Analysis (2110)

Highway Safety (2125)

Traffic Management (2130)

Transportation Operations (2150)

CHAPTER 3

PUTTING TOGETHER YOUR FEDERAL JOB APPLICATION

When you are job hunting in the private sector, you usually design one resume and use that one to apply for several jobs. A savvy job hunter will modify his or her resume slightly to accommodate the description of a specific job. However, a help wanted ad for a private sector job is not very descriptive so you will only need to make minor changes to your resume for each job. Federal Job Vacancy Announcements, on the other hand, are rather long and detailed. This is a double-edged sword. Having all that information allows you to put together a resume that clearly shows that you are qualified for the position. You must take all that information and digest it so that you will know how to use it.

Your goal in writing a resume for the private sector is to make it stand out from all the others. Sometimes you accomplish this task by organizing your resume in a certain way, using bullet points to highlight your skills, or printing it out on cream-colored paper. With a federal resume or job application, your goal is different. If you use the Optional Application for Federal Employment (OF-612), your application will look remarkably similar to all the other people who use that form. In no way does that mean that you should not use that form. We think that the OF-612 is the way to go because it clearly shows you what you need to include. If you are asked to use the online application, again your resume will look exactly like many others. But individuality in resume format is not the goal here. You will set yourself apart from the other candidates by clearly and completely demonstrating your qualifications in writing. In other words, it's what you say, not how you say it.

GIVING YOURSELF THE EDGE IN THE FEDERAL HIRING PROCESS

Remember that you can't approach the federal-employment hiring process the same way you would the private sector. To begin with, you have to hustle more in the beginning—to track down job openings, to apply separately for each one, and to tailor your application or resume to the listed requirements. It's not like applying to one employer, but to dozens—as many agencies and departments as you are interested in.

Above all, you must follow procedure—no matter how brilliant or qualified you may be. In other words, even though you haven't yet been hired, it's time to start thinking like a bureaucrat: Fill out the entire application, answer all the questions, recognize that *more* paperwork is *better* paperwork.

If you approach your federal job search the same way you approach the job search in the private sector, you might be hurt on several different points. For example, you might assume—because it's true elsewhere—that brevity is the heart of a good presentation. When searching for a job with the government, however, this is not the case. You might also assume that if anything crucial were missing from your application package, the hiring agency would call and ask for it. That is another wrong assumption. If an agency does not have the required information to process your application, you could be taken out of consideration—without knowing it.

Information is key to your success. Find out as much as you can beforehand about the particular job, the agency, the application process, and so on. Then, give the agency as much information as you can in return. It's really a very influential factor. In your search, patience and persistence are as important as any of the special qualifications you may bring to the job.

Finally, think of the application as an example of the kind of work you normally do, a way to show the screening panel the neatness, accuracy, and thoroughness you normally bring to the job every day. Your application, whichever format you choose, should be neatly typed. You should pay careful attention to grammar and spelling. Make sure your application is free of all typos. Have someone you trust proofread it for you. As mentioned previously, carefully read the vacancy announcement and be sure to include all required information on your application.

FEDERAL APPLICATION FORMS

With your selected job vacancy announcement in hand, you now begin the process of filling out an application form. There are a wide variety of applications you may use to apply for a job with the federal government. So which do you use?

Basically, you only need two forms. First, you will need what is called an *entry document*, which can be an OF-612 or a resume. Second, you will need a set of KSAs. Let's look at each of these in turn.

THE OF-612

The OF-612 was developed in the mid-1990s and for a few years was available along with the SF-171 as a form one could use to apply for a Federal job. The SF-171 was eventually phased out and now the form to use, if one chooses to use a ready-made form, is the OF-612. It is a relatively simple form, as compared to the SF-171. The OF-612 may be downloaded from the USAJOBS Web site or ordered from the Automated Telephone System. If you choose to download it from the Web site, you have three options. You can download the form as a text file (.txt), a Microsoft Word document, or as a graphic version of the form (.pdf). The Microsoft Word file and the graphic version of the form are both "read-only" files. This means you can't type into them and save them on your computer. You must print out the document and then fill it out, either on a typewriter or by hand. We recommend a typewriter since typewritten text is usually more legible then handwritten text. The text file can be opened in a text editor and you can type directly into it. If you choose this file format, you can use Microsoft Word to complete your application. Just remember to save your document as a .txt file. You can also use Notepad or WordPad. Both are free and are usually installed with Microsoft Windows. Start either program by clicking on Start, Programs, and then Accessories. You'll find both programs listed there. If your file becomes large (over 64 KB) you'll need to switch to WordPad. You can also use a freeware program called NoteTab Light available at www.notetab.com. If you do not own a typewriter and can't find one to use, using a text editor is a great way to complete your application.

The most important thing to remember when completing your OF-612 is to include all the information it asks for. In addition to basic information, such as job title and grade, name, Social Security number, and other contact information, you are also asked about work experience. You must include information about all of the jobs you've held. Be sure to give a full description of your duties and accomplishments. If you print out your OF-612 and then fill it in, you may attach additional sheets of paper. You must include your Social Security number on each sheet of paper you send in. If you are filling out your application and then printing it, you should write your Social Security number at the top of each page. That should help if pages become separated.

One final piece of advice: Remember to sign the form. In fact, federal personnel specialists advise that you sign it in *blue* ink, rather than black. On a quick glance, black ink may look like a photocopy. Since your application must contain an *original* signature, it could get thrown out by mistake.

THE SF-171

Although the SF-171 was phased out a few years ago, you'll sometimes see it as one of the application options listed in a job-vacancy announcement. If you already have an SF-171, you may use it to apply for certain jobs. However, it is no longer available from the federal government.

THE FEDERAL RESUME

Yet another alternative way of applying, the federal resume is probably the least understood, because it often gets confused with a private-sector resume. Unlike a private-sector resume, which is usually no more than one or two pages, a federal resume can be as long or as short as you want it to be.

In fact, the only significant difference between this type of resume and an OF-612 is that the federal resume is generated by you and therefore doesn't have the form's printed lines and boxes all over the page. A good federal resume provides as much information about the details of your work history as an OF-612 does. The higher-level the position you are applying for, the more detailed your federal resume should be. Federal resumes that run 6 to 12 pages are acceptable. In the private sector, job candidates would never turn in a 12-page resume unless they were applying for an upper-level academic or research position and had dozens of publications to their credit.

Warning: Don't be misled by the word "resume" on the vacancy announcement. The resume you're being asked to submit is a federal resume.

If the "How to Apply" section of a vacancy announcement states that you can submit "a resume, or OF-612," the kind of resume you should submit is the federal resume. If you read the vacancy announcement carefully, you will often see a list of details that your resume needs to provide: names and phone numbers of your present and past job supervisors, salaries you earned in these positions, and similar information. On a private sector resume, this information is not expected or needed. However, on a federal resume you are usually asked for and expected to provide this information and more.

SUBMITTING YOUR JOB APPLICATION OR RESUME ON LINE

Welcome to the twenty-first century. Increasingly, more and more federal agencies are allowing applicants to submit applications on line. As a matter of fact, many encourage you to do so. The reason is simple. When you submit an application on line, the hiring agency can take your application and process it using automated employment referral system software. This software scans your resume or application for pertinent information that tells the hiring agency if you meet certain criteria that qualifies you for the job. Several federal agencies use software produced by a company called Resumix™. Years ago, when Resumix™ was mentioned in the "How to Apply" section of a federal job vacancy announcement, it meant the job applicant had to write a computer-scannable resume. The agency would then take the hard copy of your resume and scan it into a computer where it would be read by the Resumix™ software. Using an online application or an online resume writer or builder expedites this process. You are asked for the information the automated employment referral system software needs. Yet, most agencies are aware that some people aren't comfortable, or for some reason, can't apply using this option. Therefore, they often give other application options, such as sending your resume by e-mail or regular mail. You are encouraged to submit your application on line (not by e-mail, but by using the online application form or resume builder) if this option is available. The agency generally prefers this method.

You may say to yourself, "I already have a great resume. Why would I want to retype the whole thing into some silly online application form? I'll just send them what I have or attach the file to an e-mail." Stop right there. It's not that simple. You can't use a regular resume when you know it will have to be read by automated employment referral system software. And furthermore, most agencies won't accept your resume as an e-mail attachment. You have to paste it into the body of your e-mail. You have to put together a special resume. Here are some pointers that will help you do that:

- Do not underline for emphasis.

- Do not use bold or italics for emphasis.

- Do not use forward or backward slashes, such as "supervised each employee in drawing up his/her professional goals."

- Do not use fancy or unusual fonts. Simple typefaces are recommended, such as Courier, Arial, or Times New Roman. No part of any letter may touch any part of any other letter.

- Do not use very small or very large type sizes. The standard is 10 pt. or 12 pt.

- As with every computer document, do not bend, fold, staple, tape, or mutilate your resume in any way.

ONLINE RESUME BUILDERS

The USAJOBS Web site has its own Resume Builder that can be used to help you put together a federal resume. You can save your resume, edit it, print it, and, if indicated on a vacancy announcement, use it to apply for a job on line. Several federal agencies have their own online resume builders and submission systems. The Department of Defense, for example, uses online resume builders and submission systems for civilian job applications. Each military branch has a different application system. Let's take a look at those now.

ARMY

If you are applying for a civilian position in the U.S. Army, you will be asked to use the Army's *Resume Builder* (Resumix™) or may be given instructions on how to format your resume from the job vacancy announcement. The Army does not accept the OF-612 or the SF-171. If you are not a federal civilian employee when applying for a new position, you can apply through the Delegated Examining Unit (DEU). The DEU vacancy announcements can be found at www.usajobs.opm.gov. If you are currently a federal employee, you can apply via Resumix™. You can find the Army's *job kit* at cpolrhp.army.mil/ner.

AIR FORCE

The U.S. Air Force clearly states that they do not accept the OF-612 or the SF-171 at all. You must submit a resume by using the *Air Force Resume Writer*, which is preferred, by e-mail, or by mailing a hard copy. The Air force wants something called a "pre-positioned resume." Here's how it works. First you submit your resume and supplemental data. Then you view the vacancy announcements. You see what job or jobs you want to apply for, and then you "self-nominate." By self-nominating, you're basically saying, "I want *this* job. Take a look at the resume I submitted last week." If this all sounds a bit confusing, the Air Force Personnel Center has put together a *job kit* that takes you through the civilian application process. You can find it at: ww2.afpc.randolph.af.mil/resweb/.

DEPARTMENT OF NAVY

The Department of Navy gives you three options for submitting your application. You may use the *Department of Navy Human Resources (DONHR) Resume Builder*, e-mail, or regular mail. Here's the procedure you should follow. First, conduct your job search. Read the vacancy announcement carefully, and then format and submit your resume. Once you've submitted your resume, you don't need to do it again for each job. You can use *Application Express* to apply for other positions.

THE KSAs OR RANKING FACTORS

Almost every federal vacancy lists criteria that the hiring agency feels is essential for strong job performance. These criteria are called different names by different federal agencies. Some agencies call these *ranking factors, selection criteria*, or *rating factors*. Some agencies actually call them "KSAs." As discussed earlier, KSA stands for "Knowledges, Skill, and Ability" because these are the general criteria an agency expects a successful candidate to possess in order to do the job. Some typical KSAs are "ability to communicate orally and in writing," or "knowledge of the federal budgeting system," or "skill in negotiating contracts with vendors and suppliers." Usually there are four to six of these KSA factors for each vacancy announcement. Many KSAs repeat from one vacancy announcement to another. That means if you're applying for eight different positions as, say, an accounting technician, you'll probably find that all eight vacancy announcements are fairly similar and that the KSAs you wrote for the first one can be reused, almost verbatim, for the others.

You must respond in writing separately—apart from your entry document—to these KSAs in order to be selected for an interview. As a rule of thumb, if you are applying for a position at the GS-5 level or below, a half-page response is usually sufficient. But if you are applying at the GS-7 level or above, you should submit a full-page written response to each factor, detailing examples of times when you used the type of knowledge, skill, or ability referred to in the vacancy announcement.

The KSAs are quite important in the final selection process. Don't ignore or neglect them, as they are usually the difference between a decent application and a winning one.

CRAFTING YOUR APPLICATION TO MATCH CAREER AREA AND AGENCY STANDARDS

The federal government uses a two-stage screening process in selecting candidates to be interviewed and, ultimately, hired. The first stage involves the application that has been asked for in the vacancy announcement. These documents are first screened by a federal personnel clerk to weed out those that are unacceptable or incomplete; then they're screened by a panel of federal mid- to senior-level managers to see who is eligible to compete for the vacancy at the level that was announced. For example, your application as a GS-13 budget analyst might be complete in all its parts, but the panel may determine that you have only enough experience for a GS-11 level—which is not the advertised opening. At that point, your application will be out of the running. As discussed previously, this is sometimes an automated process, using software such as Resumix™.

If your application makes it through the first stage, you go on to the second step in the screening process where the panel then compares you directly to all the other applicants that have made it that far. The panel does this by using your KSAs to rank the "survivors." You can see how providing a wealth of detail on your application helps. You don't get a second chance to explain yourself; there is no back-up plan. Both the application and the KSAs must be as complete as possible from the very beginning.

To develop an effective and competitive application for federal employment, you will need to keep the following points in mind:

- **Remember to describe your professional experience, in detail.** You will have to provide more details than any private-sector job application ever requested. Some of the questions may seem obvious or repetitious. Complete them anyway.

- **Do more than give an official job description.** Most official job descriptions don't capture the true complexity of the work that has to be done. Most competent employees do a lot more than their job descriptions. Unfortunately, instead of writing about what they *really* do in their jobs, many people just repeat the official job description.

- **Give yourself credit.** You've earned it with your good work. But you've got to let people know. Federal screening panels are quite literal in the way they review and score your application. They give you points for what is relevant in your paperwork.

And remember—they *don't* give you any points for what is not included. So don't feel bashful! You won't sound conceited if you point out your accomplishments.

■ **Use your application to narrate your professional victories.** One good way to point out your accomplishments is to describe your professional victories. These could be times when you've made solid decisions; times when you've dealt effectively with problems, special projects, or troubleshooting assignments; or times when you've really demonstrated your value to the organizations for which you've worked. Properly described, these stories are like money in the bank. They make you and your abilities come alive to the screening panel and have impact.

■ **Highlight your professional skills by using an action/result presentation.** Show your skills actually being used. Most actions have a result, especially if your actions were effective. Don't shortchange yourself. If things you have done have generated bottom-line results for your employers, then say so. Did your innovative idea save them money? Did your initiative and persistence make them money? Say so—and how much. Describe what happened. There's nothing more convincing to a skeptical screening panel than to see the word "result" appear again and again throughout your application. It lets them know that *you* know where the bottom line is—and how to get there. *That's* what they are looking for in an employee.

■ **Stop scaring yourself.** Putting together an effective application depends on your attitude, more than your writing skills. Filling out these forms may not be fun, but don't let that discourage you. The task is certainly within your abilities. Also, keep in mind that the application is not a test. There are no right or wrong answers. There are only other competitors like yourself, who find the process just as difficult as you do. If you compete with these applicants effectively, you stand a good chance of winning.

Remember: *Someone's* going to be selected for these positions—and it could possibly be *you*.

"BEFORE" AND "AFTER" EXAMPLES TAKEN FROM FEDERAL JOB APPLICATIONS

What does a good federal job application look like? The easiest way to learn how to write a good federal job application is to see the difference between some bad examples from several different fields—contrasted against actual job-winning entries. Note that the bad examples won't really seem dreadful, just rather ordinary when seen next to the good entries.

DESCRIPTIONS OF MAJOR DUTIES

Bad Example:

Coordinated complex civil cases. Developed detailed reviews and analyses. Researched and prepared comprehensive legal memoranda.

Now, see how much detail has been added to the job-winning version:

Good Example:

Coordinated complex civil cases with various departments or divisions within FDIC. Developed detailed reviews and analyses in preparation for counseling client representatives to improve their request for legal services.

Researched and prepared comprehensive legal memoranda for clients, drawing on my extensive knowledge and experience litigating various issues under the FDI Act, FIRREA, the FDIC Improvement Act, commercial law, real estate law, and the Bankruptcy Code.

Here is another example:

Bad Example:

Served as a contracting officer and contract administrator. Performed pre-award, award, and contract administration duties. Headed evaluation teams reviewing potential contractors. Prepared lease agreements.

> *The added details in the following show how the applicant's duties were much more responsible and varied:*

Good Example:

Served as contracting officer and contract administrator for multimillion dollar supplies and services, construction, and architectural and engineering contracts. Possessed a contracting officer's warrant. Performed pre-award, award, and contract administration duties. Prepared *Commerce Business Daily* synopses and advertisements, developed and reviewed technical specifications, and issued solicitations and Requests for Proposals (RFPs). Headed evaluation teams reviewing potential contractors' financial data. Prepared lease agreements for properties where contractors performed construction work.

DESCRIPTIONS OF ADVANCED TRAINING

Bad Example:

FBI/RTC Bank Failure School (December 7–10, 1993); Basic Examination School for Attorneys (January 1998).

Good Example:

FBI/RTC Bank Failure School (December 7–10, 1993). This was a highly intensive course focusing on the aspects of fraud involving financial institutions, covering such topics as Fraud Detection and Investigation, Forensic Accounting Approach, Prosecution of Financial Institution Fraud Cases, and The Importance of CPAs to Bank Examiners and Criminal Investigations.

Basic Examination School for Attorneys (January 1998). This was a week-long concentrated course focusing on fundamentals of bank supervision, basic report analysis, bank accrual accounting, loan classifications, and financial analysis.

DESCRIPTIONS OF KSAS OR RANKING FACTORS (FOR AN UPPER-LEVEL POSITION)

Bad Example:

Knowledge of materiel life-cycle management functions, programs, and systems used to provide logistical support: Gained valuable understanding of military facilities planning while serving as Acting Chief of the Facilities Management Office. Responsible for issuing policy pertaining to the total acquisition life-cycle baseline parameters. Strong working knowledge of PPBES. Broad experience writing, revising, and implementing policy.

> *Obviously the applicant didn't know that, at this job level, he or she should include a full page for each KSA, explaining how and when the knowledge, skills, or ability was demonstrated. The paragraph above works as a bare-bones outline for the detailed job-winning entry below.*

Good Example:

Knowledge of material life-cycle management functions, programs, and systems used to provide logistical support.

My current job includes a very substantial degree of life-cycle management responsibility. For example, I currently run the policy operation of Acquisition Life Cycle management. In this capacity, the information related to guidance addressing Army's Acquisition Program Baselines (APBs) for Army Acquisition Category (ACAT) I, II, and some representative III programs. Examples of my strong working knowledge in this area include the following:

Analyze the content of the APBs and ensure that APBs adequately address program requirements.

Result:

I recently issued APB policy that now requires APBs to address "total life-cycle costs," which by definition includes operating and support (O&S) costs.

Keep Army and OSD leadership informed regarding how the Army executes their cost, schedule, and performance parameters within their respective APBs.

Result:

Maintain close ties and frequent contacts with officials at all levels in the Army and DoD as well as the respective PEOs and PMs and Command Groups. Any known logistical support requirements would also be captured within the respective APBs.

I have gained substantial working knowledge and hands-on experience through interacting with officials in the Comptroller and Acquisition communities related to acquisition life-cycle subject matter contained within APBs, SARs, and DAES reports, as well as through managing these processes.

Result:

My effort to include O&S costs within APBs is unique. To this point, the other military services have not yet followed suit but will likely do so soon, since it is DoD policy to make Program Managers responsible for "total life-cycle management." If and when this happens, these Program Managers would have total "cradle-to-grave" program responsibility—as well as operational control of the budget dollars to make sure that this level of responsibility is discharged fully and effectively.

> *The job-winning applicants might well have phrased their experience, background, and abilities as in the "bad examples." If these had been private-sector resumes, that might have been enough. But the procedure for applying for a federal job is very different.*

SAMPLES OF COMPLETED APPLICATION FORMS

Now, let's see the results when this kind of attention to detail is applied to the entire form. Following are full-length, filled-in samples of actual job-winning application tools: a filled-in OF-612, a federal resume, a Resumix™ or computer-scannable resume, and a KSA list.

A COMPLETED OF-612

OPTIONAL APPLICATION FOR FEDERAL EMPLOYMENT - OF 612

You may apply for jobs with a resume, this form, or any other format. If your resume or application does not provide all the information requested on this form and in the job vacancy announcement, you may lose consideration for a job.

1 Job title in announcement **Computer Specialist, Supervisory**	2 Grade(s) applying for **GS-0334-14/15**	3 Announcement number **99-63-AP**

4 Last name **XXXXXXX**	First and Middle names **XXXXXX**	5 Social Security Number **000-00-0000**

6 Mailing address **000 Stillwater Place**		7 Phone Numbers (include area code)
City **XXXXXXX**	State **MD** ZIP Code **00000**	Daytime (703) 000-0000 Evening (301) 000-0000

WORK EXPERIENCE

8 Describe your paid and nonpaid work experience related to the job for which you are applying. Do **not** attach job descriptions.

1) Job title (if Federal, include series and grade)
COMPUTER SPECIALIST, GS-0334-13

From (MM/YY) **8/96**	To (MM/YY) **present**	Salary **$71,565**	per **year**	Hours per week **40**

Employer's name and address **Defense Information System Agency (DISA)** **00000 XXXXXXX Square; XXXX, VA 00000**	Supervisor's name and phone number **John XXXXX** **703-000-0000**

Describe your duties and accomplishments

OVERVIEW
- **Computer Specialist** in the Defense Message System (DMS) Operations Branch on the staff of the DMS Global Service Manager. DMS is a computer-based (X.400/X.500) worldwide Department of Defense-wide Area Network messaging system that will replace the obsolete Automated Digital Network (AUTODIN) now in place. The mission of the Branch is to exercise day-to-day management control of, and provide staff level operational direction over, deployed elements of the DMS.

- **Personally responsible** for ensuring that reliable, efficient, effective, and economic DMS operations meet the customer's requirements.

KEY ACTIVITIES
Oversee and manage the global system of Regional Operations and Security Centers (ROSC).

    RESULT
- Visited ROSC-C to assist in bringing the center to full operational status prior to the start of IOT&E.

- Coordinated the requirements and assessments of the three ROSC to prepare the final format of the Continuity of Operation Plan for the DMS portion of the ROSCs worldwide structure.

Develop policy and directives that provide a framework for processes and procedures in the execution of system implementation as well as operational tasks.

    RESULT
- Developed, coordinated, and established the ALLDMSSTA general message in order to establish an electronic means of formally disseminating policy and procedure changes.

- Drawing on program management and cryptologic background, assessed (in concert with D4) the requirements for instituting a viable maintenance management program.

SEE ATTACHMENT

50612-101   NSN 7540-01351-9178   Optional Form 612 (September 1994)
 U.S. Office of Personnel Management

ATTACHMENT

XXXXXX XXXXX. — SSN: 000-00-0000

#1, continued, WORK EXPERIENCE

Monitor the implementation of all hardware and software changes/enhancements to the DMS components and infrastructure.

RESULT
- Formally approved all Field Engineering Notes for distribution and implementation during IOT&E using newly established software distribution procedures, a process that proved to be highly organized and successful.

Conduct operational performance evaluations and ensure overall compliance with technical criteria to maintain the DMS performance above management thresholds.

Maintain liaison with representatives of the Joint Staff, military departments, and other government agencies. Represent the Branch at meetings and conferences with higher echelons.

Obtain, direct, and coordinate necessary technical support when problem resolution requires expertise beyond that of onsite personnel.

RESULT
- Worked closely with the DISA PAC and DISA EUR Regional Service Management staff and the WESTHEM Columbus RCC to develop and implement an interim problem reporting mechanism pending arrival of the DMS Contractor products.

Function as the task monitor for cognizant portions of the DMS that are staffed under contract support and ensure contractor personnel and contract deliverables are in full compliance with requirements as detailed in the contract.

Provide operations input to the implementation design validation process.

EVALUATION OF PERFORMANCE:

"A self-starter who uses initiative to research exiting activities associated with system and network management tools and capabilities to ensure DMS will be able to readily migrate to a fully integrated system." (from Evaluation, 1996)

2) Job title (if Federal, include series and grade)
TELECOMMUNICATIONS SPECIALIST, GS-0391-13

From (MM/YY)	To (MM/YY)	Salary	per	Hours per week
5/95	8/96	$63,442	year	40

Employer's name and address
Space and Naval Warfare (SPAWAR) Systems Command
2451 Crystal Drive; Arlington, VA 22245-5200

Supervisor's name and phone number
CDR XXXXXX
703-000-0000

Describe your duties and accomplishments

OVERVIEW
- **Project Manager** for computer/communication systems deployments of the Nova and MMS (Multi-level Mail Server), which were designated as Navy Defense Messaging System transitional components, and provided for the upgrade of automated messaging services while allowing the Naval Telecommunications System to transition from legacy platforms to the Defense Messaging System (DMS) target X.400 and X.500 architecture and components.

Key Activities

Managed and evaluated the execution of contractor performance for acquisition, installation, maintenance, and software support services. Directed and approved contractor efforts in the development of computer integrated logistic support planning (ILSP) and developed and coordinated site survey and system installation schedules.

RESULT
- Mediated and resolved numerous difficulties, discrepancies, and disagreements between and/or among installation support activities (engineering field activities, contractors, and others).

Provided technical information and direction relative to DMS transitional components that interfaced to host computers.

Reviewed and evaluated computer/communications systems architecture and wiring plans and diagrams. As part of the review process, also developed and submitted detail wiring schematics and diagrams that described errors and corrections.

RESULT
- Used knowledge of Naval Telecommunication System architecture, interface techniques, and capabilities to provide input to the formulation of a system architecture and connectivity between Navy, Marine, Coast Guard, and other DoD and civil agency components where the object was to provide a seamless transition to the target X.400/X.500 DMS architecture.

Primary liaison with various organizational DMS coordinators in order to ensure timely update of requirements and fielding priorities. Represented the Division at internal or external committees, working groups, and meetings.

RESULT
- Prepared and presented a variety of well-received point papers and briefings to provide information, recommendations, and defense of program positions or actions to be executed.

- Established working relationships across organizational boundaries that were essential to process improvement in the delivery of quality customer services.

SEE ATTACHMENT

50612-101

NSN 7540-01351-9178

Optional Form 612 (September 1994)
U.S. Office of Personnel Management

ATTACHMENT

XXXXXX XXXXX. — SSN: 000-00-0000

#2, continued, WORK EXPERIENCE

Provided administrative management for project implementation tracking and monitoring.

As a member of the Software Configuration Control Board, evaluated and recommended adoption or disapproval of software changes and proposals that were relevant to the Nova, MMS, and related systems.

RESULT • Made significant contributions to SPAWAR in the economy, efficiency, and service in the implementation of transitional system platforms (Nova, PCMT, GATEGUARD, and MMS).

EVALUATION OF PERFORMANCE:

"….a model employee who has proven during this period his value to the organization. He has taken the changes driven by organizational restructuring and realignment in stride and has actively promoted the goals and objectives of SPAWAR." (from Evaluation, 1996)

9 May we contact your current supervisor

YES [X]   NO [   ]   If we need to contact your current supervisor before making an offer, we will contact you first.

EDUCATION

10 Mark highest level completed   Some HS [   ]   HS/GED [   ]   Associate [   ]   Bachelor [   ]   Master [X]   Doctoral [   ]

11 Last high school (HS) or GED school. Give the school's name, City, State, ZIP Code (if known), and year diploma or GED received.

Eastern High School, Washington DC

12 Colleges and universities attended. Do **not** attach a copy with your transcript unless requested.

Name		Total Credits Earned		Major(s)	Degree - Year
		Semester	Quarter		(if any) Received
University of the District of Columbia				Electronic Technology	A.S., 1979
City Washington	State DC ZIP Code				
Name National-Louis University				Managment	B.S., 1995
City McLean	State VA ZIP Code 22102				
Name Eastern Michigan University				Information Security	M.S., 1997
City Ypsilanti	State MI ZIP Code 48197				

OTHER QUALIFICATIONS

13 **Job-related** training courses (give title and year). Job-related skills (other languages, computer software/hardware, tools, machinery, typing speed, etc.). **Job-related** certificates and licenses (current only). **Job-related** honors, awards, and special accomplishments (publications, memberships in professional/honor societies, leadership activities, public speaking, and performance awards). Give dates, but do **not** send documents unless requested.

PLEASE SEE ATTACHMENT

GENERAL

14 Are you a U.S. citizen?

YES [X]   NO [   ]   Give the country of your citizenship

15 Do you claim veteran's preference?   NO [   ]   YES [X]   Mark your claim of 5 or 10 points below

5 points [X]   Attach your DD214 or other proof.   1   0 points [   ]   Attach an Application for 10-Point Veterans' Preference (SF-15) and proof required.

16 Were you ever a Federal civilian employee?

NO [   ]   YES [X]   For highest civilian grade give:

Series	Grade	From (MM/YY)	To (mm/yy)
0391/0334	13	10/90	present

17 Are you eligible for reinstatement based on career or career-conditional Federal status?

NO [X]   YES [   ]   If requested, attach SF 50 proof.

18 I certify that, to the best of my knowledge and belief, all of the information on and attached to this application is true, correct, complete and made in good faith. **I understand** that false or fraudulent information on or attached to this application may be grounds for not hiring me or for firing me after I begin work, and may be punishable by fine or imprisonment. **I understand** that any information I give may be investigated.

SIGNATURE   DATE SIGNED

ATTACHMENT

XXXXXX XXXXX. — SSN: 000-00-0000

#13 — OTHER QUALIFICATIONS

Successfully completed numerous courses on COMSEC and computer equipment and systems. Classes of COMSEC equipment and systems on which trained include general purpose data, voice, specialized tactical, bulk, and broadcast. Specific details will be provided on request.

1) George Washington University
   Fiber-Optic Technology for Communications, 2.16 CEUs .... 28 Jun 90
   Application of T-Carrier to Private Networking, 3.60 CEUs .... 27 Jul 90
   Data Communication Standards: Interfaces and Protocols for Open Systems
       Network Architectures, 2.16 CEUs .... 14 Sep 90

2) Data-Tech Institute
   Intensive Introduction to T1/T3 Networking, 1.50 CEUs .... 10 Aug 90

3) Naval Electronic Systems Security Engineering Center
   Contracting Officer's Technical Representative (COTR's) Course .... 23 Aug 89

4) Office of Personnel Management
   Instructor Training Workshop .... 14 May 82
   Project Management: Planning, Scheduling, and Control .... 14 Feb 92

5) Human Resources Office, NW NMCNCR
   Supervisory Development I .... 16 May 86
   Supervisory Development II .... 20 Aug 86

6) Management Concepts Incorporated
   Statement of Work/Specification Preparation .... 1 Jul 87

7) Human Resources Office, Washington, NY
   Managing Conflict .... 19 Apr 90
   How to Negotiate .... 11 May 90
   Value Engineering .... 06 Aug 92

8) Naval Computer & Telecommunication Command
   Acquisition Streamlining .... 15 Mar 91
   Total Quality Leadership Awareness .... 15 Apr 92

9) Department of Navy Program Information Center
   Planning, Programming, and Budgeting System (PEBS) Course .... 30 Sep 92

10) National Defense University, Information Resources Management College
    Information Engineering .... 28 May 93

11) Defense Information Systems Agency
    Defense Data Network Seminar .... 26 Aug 93

12) Naval Computer & Telecommunication Command
    X.400/X.500 DMS/MSP Training (J.G. Van Dyke) .... 10 Mar 95

13) National Security Agency
    Information Systems Security Engineering Course .... 12 May 95

SEE NEXT PAGE

ATTACHMENT (*cont.*)

XXXXXX, ALFRED L. — SSN: 000-00-0000

<u>#13, continued — OTHER QUALIFICATIONS</u>

<u>AWARDS:</u>

Graduated with honors, B.S. Management, 1995

Honors Student Award, MLS Information Security, 1997

Letter of Appreciation for Technical Professionalism from Commanding Officer NAS Memphis, 1980

Sustained Superior Performance Awards: 1982, 1983

Outstanding Performance Awards: 1992, 1993, 1994, 1995, 1996

A COMPLETED FEDERAL RESUME

XXXX XXXXXXX
Announcement number:

XXXXX XXXXXXXX

000000 Alex Guerrero Circle

El Paso, Texas 00000

Home/Fax: (000) 000-0000

E-mail: xxxxxx@xxx.com

Office: (000) 000-0000

E-mail: xxxxx@xxx.org

U.S. citizen

Highest security clearance held: TOP SECRET (1985–90)

Highest Federal civilian grade: GG-1102-12

Date of last promotion: December, 1996

GOAL

Announcement Number:

Position title:

PROFILE

Current responsibility:

Contracting Officer

Border Environment Cooperation Commission

Assigned to facility in Juarez, Mexico

Proven experience managing budgets for contracts ranging in value up to $200 million. Experience supervising up to 5 employees.

Primary focal point for the award of several multi-million dollar construction, architectural and engineering, and management services contracts.

Strategic liaison responsibility. Frequently interact with high-ranking city, county, and state officials, as well as consultants and the general public to provide funding and construction of border projects in Mexico and the United States.

Served as Equal Employment Opportunity Counselor. Also served on Qualification Review Boards to rank applicants for Federal positions.

Designed and implemented operating policies and procedures. Automated library operations and recorded retrieval procedures. Participated in establishment of computerized accounting program for non-appropriated funds.

Accomplished communicator. Principal point-of-contact and lead negotiator during contract deliberations.

Strong written communication skills. Developed and wrote agency-wide operating standards.

XXXX XXXXXXX
Announcement number:

CURRENT TITLE: CONTRACTING OFFICER

Border Environment Cooperation Commission (BECC)   Juarez, Mexico 32470

GRADE: N/A   **SALARY:** $57,000   **HOURS:** 40/week

DATE: January 1998–present   **SUPERVISOR:** XXXXXX

Direct, monitor, and personally oversee the award of architectural and engineering and other management services contracts for the BECC, a quasi-government agency.

> RESULT   Responsible for the development of water/waste water and sanitation master plans, cost and price analysis, development of pre-negotiation memorandums and projects' negotiations, and assembling documentation required to certify projects for construction funds. Selected to fill in for the incumbent Technical Assistance Program Manager during her travel or absence.

Serve as lead negotiator and facilitator for the evaluation team. Responsible for coordinating all business development and contract administration activities for the organization. Direct proposal efforts, lead negotiation teams and chair status meetings with all disciplines involved in complex, high-dollar development projects.

> RESULT   Expertly guiding principals through the contracting process, successfully directed contracting efforts (cradle to grave) for multi-year, multi-million dollar projects.

Supervise and coordinate the work of subordinate staff of U.S. and Mexican nationals, managing planning efforts, devising organizational structures to support quality control, task management, technical operations, and administrative functions.

> RESULT   Establish work schedules, assign tasks, advise subordinates on proper techniques and procedures, and prepare annual performance reviews.

Review Mexico's contracting law and procedures and the UN Model Law on Procurement in order to develop agency-specific procurement standards. Because the BECC was created under a North American Free Trade Agreement (NAFTA) side-agreement and is a bi-national agency, funded by both the U. S. and Mexican governments and the U.S. Environmental Protection Agency (USEPA), the BECC is not required to conform to Federal Acquisition Regulations (FAR). As a result, no such procurement regulations were in place.

> RESULT   Developed procurement standards and procedures for this relatively new agency.

> IMPACT   These procedures are written in a clear, concise, and detailed manner and contain information that is vital to the efficient and effective administration of the procurement program. These procedures were instrumental in securing new contracts with the corporate community and launched the procurement program.

Prepare reviews for the agency's Legal Counsel on contract clauses and other legal issues. Review financial feasibility of projects. Examine environmental and sustainability aspects, as well as criteria required to qualify for construction funding. Where possible, work is coordinated with graduate studies in the MPA program at the University of Texas at El Paso (UTEP).

> RESULT   Successfully handled two protests for disqualification of proposals during the evaluation stage.

> IMPACT   This early resolution of the problem prevented a more serious challenge.

Point-of-Contact for management study and internal needs assessment.

> RESULT   Coordinate project tracking systems, electronic and hard copy record keeping, general operating procedures, manual writing, and accounting/budgeting processes.

> IMPACT   Until my intervention there were few standards or operational practices in place. Recipient, "Excellent" job performance rating.

XXXX XXXXXXX
Announcement number:

TITLE: Contract Specialist (Note: hired as GS-1102-7 Intern; promoted to GS-9/11/12)

U.S. Section, International Boundary and Water Commission   El Paso, TX 79902-1441

GRADE: GG-1102-12   **SALARY:** $45,000   **HOURS:** 40/week

DATE: 12/90-1/98   **SUPERVISOR:** XXXXX

Served as contracting officer and contract administrator for multi-million dollar supplies and services, construction, and architectural and engineering contracts. Possessed a contracting officer's warrant. Performed pre-award, award, and contract administration duties.

> RESULT   Prepared *Commerce Business Daily* synopses and advertisements, developed and reviewed technical specifications, and issued solicitations and Requests For Proposals (RFPs). Headed evaluation teams reviewing potential contractors' financial data. Prepared lease agreements for properties where contractors performed construction work.

Performed price and costs analyses, conducted contract negotiations, monitored expenditures, and developed legal interpretations. Presided over bid openings and site visits.

Set priorities and demonstrated effective leadership. Since contracting does not leave much room for variance, it was my responsibility to ensure that rules were strictly adhered to.

> RESULT   Established good working relationships with diverse groups of individuals in order to effectively solicit compliance with regulatory requirements.

> IMPACT   Anticipated questions and provided necessary information and guidance.

Instituted policy and procedures for Acquisition Division in areas of Ethics, Imprest Funds, and Memorandums of Understanding for grants and cooperative agreements with federal agencies.

> RESULT   Developed technical expertise in all phases of the contracting cycle from per-award through negotiations and contract administration.

> IMPACT   Led staff members through the process of changing and updating old habits and implementing required procedures.

Coordinated with technical and engineering staff, end users, and senior executives within the client organizations and federal contract managers to ensure timely compliance with all terms of the contracts and the Federal Acquisition Regulations (FAR).

> RESULT   Worked with diverse individuals to create cohesive plans and strategies, incorporating the often-divergent objectives of many disciplines. Oversaw several projects of national interest.

> IMPACT   In the operation and maintenance of the Nogales International Wastewater Treatment Plant, made the determination that it would be more cost effective to contract the work out to a private firm than to have the government continue its operation of the plant. As a result of contracting out, the government was able to realize a cost savings over a five-year period.

Main point-of-contact, internally and externally, ensuring that client organizations were satisfied and that contractors delivered goods/services in accordance with Statements-of-Work documents.

Served as Equal Employment Opportunity (EEO) Counselor. Provided supervisors and managers with detailed explanations of applicable EEO laws and regulations prohibiting discrimination. Participated in EEO workshops.

> RESULT   Often called upon to provide assistance in matters involving disciplinary actions, grievances, EEO complaints, and illegal separations.

> IMPACT   Used tact to provide practical advisory services in potentially volatile situations.

XXXX XXXXXXX
Announcement number:

Facilitated affirmative action hiring, providing advice and support for the manager involved. Explaining federal regulations to assist them in devising effective job search strategies.

RESULT	Gained the support of management and employees throughout the organization.
IMPACT	As a result, was able to resolve all issues presented to me at the local level without the need for expensive and disruptive litigation. Recipient of several "Excellent" job performance ratings during this period.

TITLE: Records Officer (Mail and File Assistant)

U.S. Section, International Boundary and Water Commission   El Paso, TX 79902-1441

GRADE: GG-307-07   **SALARY:** $25,000   **HOURS:** 40/week

DATE: 6/85–6/90   **SUPERVISOR:** XXXXXX

Chief, Headquarters Communications and Records Branch with TOP SECRET security clearance and purview over 12 field offices throughout the U.S. and Mexico border region.

RESULT	Exercised primary responsibility for the agency's records management, mail management, correspondence management, library (legal and technical) operations, Freedom of Information and Privacy Act programs, and public relations program.

Conducted assistance visits to field offices to conduct operational audits in records management. Wrote reports of my findings and made recommendations. Taught classes in records management, records disposition, correspondence management, mail management, micrographics management, directives management, copier use, and ADP management.

RESULT	Wrote the Agency's Freedom of Information Act regulations, and rewrote the records disposition and correspondence manuals.

Initiated a records control program for Privacy Act records.

RESULT	Established a directives system, and initiated a micrographics program. Computerized the library's operations as well as its records retrieval procedures.
IMPACT	My ideas were adopted, implemented, and maintained. When completed, these new or revised documents and procedures went a long way in reducing turnaround time, enabling our staff members to make renewed progress toward mission goals.

Supervised and directed the activities of subordinate staff.

RESULT	Managed planning and designed organizational structures capable of supporting strong quality control, task management, technical, and administrative functions.
IMPACT	Established work schedules, assigned tasks, advised subordinates on proper techniques and procedures, and prepared annual performance reviews. Recipient, several "Excellent" job performance ratings during this period.

TITLE: Administrative Clerk

Loan Servicing Department, Small Business Administration   El Paso, TX 79935

GRADE: GS-301-4   **SALARY:** $16,800   **HOURS:** 40/week

DATE: 5/84–6/85   **SUPERVISOR:** XXXXXX

Planned, organized, and coordinated administrative activities of the office.

RESULT	Completed special projects that involved contact with administrative and management staff at all levels within the agency.
IMPACT	Given greater responsibilities than the job called for while in this position. Note: Accepted this position in order to return to federal service.

XXXX XXXXXXX
Announcement number:

TITLE: Homemaker

xxxxxx Alex Guerrero Circle xxxxxx, Texas 00000

GRADE: N/A   **SALARY:** N/A   **HOURS:** N/A

DATE: 5/83–5/84   **SUPERVISOR:** N/A

Stayed home to care for newborn child. Responsible for child care, home operations, budgeting, and family support.

TITLE: Administrative Officer

Administration Division, Department of the Army   WSMR, NM 88022

GRADE: GS-341-9   **SALARY:** $21,000   **HOURS:** 40/week

DATE: 9/81–5/83   **SUPERVISOR:** XXXXX

Administrative management for Morale Support Activities Division's budget, procurement of supplies, publicity, personnel and manpower, and property and facilities management.

Monitored expenditures and developed annual budget forecasts. Established five-year budget plans. Funding was provided through either non-appropriated (self-earning) or appropriated means. Served as principal conduit for all information flow to the director.

> RESULT   Applied accounting techniques that determined if activities were profitable, identified ways of improving activities' income, and determined the need for supplemental funding through appropriated means.

> IMPACT   Computerized accounting program for non-appropriated funds resulted in savings to the government.

Recipient, Letter of Appreciation (1982).

Main point-of-contact for all budget issues for the division, providing interpretation of accounting statements to supervisor, activity managers, and the colonel. Worked with both appropriated and non-appropriated funds. Performed audits of private organizations at the missile range to assure their financial soundness and their compliance with regulatory requirements.

> RESULT   Implemented mandated financial data format changes for private organizations.

> IMPACT   Earned the trust and cooperation of all private organizations serviced and brought them into compliance with regulatory requirements.

Recipient, Special Act Award for working with private organization (1982).

Supervised and directed the work of five staff members (3 civilians and 2 military). Managed planning efforts, devised organizational structures to support quality control, task management, technical operations, and administrative functions.

> RESULT   Established work schedules, assigned tasks, advised subordinates on proper techniques and procedures, and prepared annual performance reviews.

XXXX XXXXXXX
Announcement number:

TITLE: Management Assistant

Administration Division, Department of the Army   WSMR, NM 88002

GRADE: GS-344-7   **SALARY:** $16,000   **HOURS:** 40/week

DATE: 8/79–9/81   **SUPERVISOR:** XXXXXX

Assisted in the analysis and assessment of management issues for the Administrative Management Branch.

RESULT   Suggested solutions to administrative and management problems. Collected data, reviewed and analyzed information. Interviewed managers and employees while observing their operations, taking into account the nature of the organization, the relationship it had with other organizations, its internal organization, and culture.

IMPACT   Reported findings and recommendations to client organization, often in writing. In addition, made oral recommendations. Assisted in implementation of suggestions.

Taught classes in records management, records disposition, correspondence management, mail management, micrographics and directives management, copier use, and ADP management.

RESULT   Recipient, Letter of Appreciation for instructing military personnel in records management (1980).

Conducted audits and wrote reports of findings with recommendations. Allocated timeframes to offices to correct deficiencies and did follow-up visits where appropriate. Held secret security clearance. Acted in behalf of supervisor during her absence.

RESULT   Led individuals to change what they were doing incorrectly in order to conform to regulatory requirements.

IMPACT   Facility was upgraded to exceed all records management requirements.

EDUCATION

Bachelor of Business Administration (B.B.A.)

University of Texas at El Paso, 1993

Masters of Public Administration candidate (M.P.A. degree due: May 1999)

University of Texas at El Paso

PROFESSIONAL ORGANIZATIONS

National Institute of Government Purchasing (NIGP)

National and Local Chapters

RELATED SKILLS

Computer literate in Windows, WordPerfect, MS Word and Works, Lotus (Quattro Pro), and database management software, the Internet, intranets, and online services.

LANGUAGE SKILLS

Fluent in spoken and written Spanish

A COMPUTER-SCANNABLE RESUME

XXXXXXXXX
SSN: 000-00-0000

XXXXXX XXXXX

SSN: 000-00-0000

0000 Spain Drive

Stafford, Virginia 00000

Home: (000) 000-0000

Work: (000) 000-0000

DSN: 000-0000

E-mail: xxxx@xxx.xxx

SUMMARY OF SKILLS

Military Satellite Communications

Manager, Defense Satellite Communications System (DSCS)

Proven Staff Leadership

Task Manager

Lead Evaluator

Contractor Supervision

Liaison and representation

Technical Troubleshooting

Spacecraft Reconfiguration

Data Integration

Operating Parameters

Control and Coordination

Operational Assessments

Contingency Planning

Specialized Engineering

Contingency Communications

Earth Terminals Optimization

System Reliability

Maintainability Standards

Control Concepts

System Capabilities

Interface Requirements

Requirements Analysis

Project Coordination

High-level Briefings

Frequency Modulation

Digital Baseband Equipment

Common-user Communications

Modeling and Simulation

Network Management

Information Security

Communications Link Configurations

System Optimization

Detection of Degradations

EXPERIENCE:

January 1991 to present. 40–50 hours/week.

Telecommunications Manager

TOP SECRET/SCI security clearance

Defense Information Systems Agency (DISA)

Supervisor: XXXXXXX

Pay-grade: GS-391-14

Functional leader within DoD for the DSCS Operational Control System. Integrate complex data and conclusions from various functional areas to formulate policy and develop procedures for operating DSCS to serve DoD and other federal agencies. Recruited by DSCS Operations Branch (DOT) at DCA/DISA. Promoted to GS-0391-14 as of 10-19-92 due to "accretion of duties" and assigned as Deputy/Assistant to the Senior Satellite Communications System Manager; served as primary in his absence. Assumed all management duties effective October 1998 during his transition to retirement. Acting in that capacity to date. Supervise management of DSCS and technical direction of DSCS Operations Control Centers. Manage satellite communication payloads and network coordination. Establish parameters of satellite service. Exercise managerial authority regarding access to DSCS. Prepare and issue Telecommunications Service Requests (TSR). Develop implementation directives for the O&M commands.

Coordinate execution of these directives. Develop objectives, policies, and procedures for the Joint Staff concerning current and projected DSCS operations. Provide liaison and representation regarding operational requirements in the planning, development, programming, budgeting, acquisition, and deployment of DSCS space and ground equipment and related operational control systems. Extensive use of DCAD 800-70-1 and 310-65-1 for TSR services, as governed by MOP 37. Evaluate all requests for DSCS access; prepare DISA's recommendations to the Joint Staff for its approval/disapproval and subsequent entry into the Integrated Consolidated SATCOM Data Base (ICDB). Serve as DNSO representative on ICDB-related matters.

Extensive interaction with, and instruction of, DISA and other Defense and Intelligence Community managers, frequently including decision-makers with limited knowledge of satellite technology. Provide recommendations for communications link configurations that optimize the use of DSCS satellite resources. Plan satellite cut-overs and frequency plans to optimize loading of operational satellites.

RESULTS PRODUCED: Key player in ensuring highly efficient utilization of assets. Instrumental in developing and implementing a reconstitution effort during unexpected transponder failures. Planned and implemented error-free satellite Telecommunications Service Requests. Develop and maintain policies, procedures, concepts of operation, parameters, and standards for DSCS, including ECCM and the use of partial satellites. Develop, produce, and publish operational and control concepts for DSCS in DISAC 800-70-1. Develop new and modified concepts and configurations in support of ongoing missions. Extensive troubleshooting in the following areas: limited bandwidth, restricted available power from satellite transponders, antenna patterns, and earth terminal characteristics, shortage of specific filters or multiplexers, front-line coordination with field sites, creating cut-over plans. Provide inputs for updated edition of DCAC 800-70-1. Initiated change of ENR codes for all strategic satellite terminals in use worldwide.

1989–1991. 40–50 hours/week. **MilNet Manager**

Defense Data Network, Operations

Supervisor: XXXXXXXX

Assigned to DDN Operations as DDN MilNetManger. Operational manager of the DoD global MilNet. Provided direction in network design and implementation from user level to nodal points, including fielding of NACs and CISCO routers.

1987–1989. 40 hours/week. **Integrated Test Facility Manager**

Defense Data Network

Supervisor: LTC XXXX

Managed the Defense Data Network (DDN) Integrated Test Facility (ITF) in Reston, VA.

Responsible for baseline development of BLACKER encryption device. Was detailed into position as Branch Chief upon transfer of LTC XXXX.

1985–1987. 50–60 hours/week. **Head, Communications Department**

NAVELEXDETPAX, Patuxent River, MD.

Supervisor: XXXXXXX

Managed four (4) Telecommuncation Facilities (2 Strategic Genser, 1 Tactical, 1 SCIF) providing Air, Land, and Sea Test & Evaluation Platforms. Conducted performance evaluations at all participating test facilities.

SECURITY CLEARANCE:

TOP SECRET/SCI

EDUCATION

Graduate, Southwest XXXX XXXXX Public High School, April 1961

ADVANCED PROFESSIONAL TRAINING

Customer Service Orientation (40-hour course), 1995

DSCS DOSS/DASA Course (80-hour course), 1991

DSCS Network Engineering Course (40-hour course), 1991

Orientation to Contracting (16-hour course), 1987

COTR Training (40-hour course), 1985

Leadership Management Education and Training, 1981

Satellite Controller Course (three-month course), 1978

Radioman "B" School, (six-month course),1971

Teletype Maintenance and Operation, 1966

Radioman "A" School (seven-month course), 1962

AWARDS AND HONORS

Joint Service Commendation Medal

Vietnam Service Medal, with two Bronze Stars

Recipient of continuous "Outstanding" performance appraisals throughout my tenure at DISA.

KSAs OR RANKING FACTORS

XXXXXXX

XXXXX

<u>EVALUATION FACTORS</u>

1. **ABILITY TO SELECT, DEVELOP, AND SUPERVISE A SUBORDINATE STAFF, WHICH INCLUDED THE ABILITY TO ACTIVELY PURSUE MANAGEMENT GOALS AND SUPPORT THE EQUAL OPPORTUNITY PROGRAM.**

I believe my ability to lead and facilitate the work of others has been demonstrably evident throughout my career. For example, on numerous occasions I have interacted with staffs that I have led by (1) providing a clear sense of direction and (2) setting my expected performance levels at a level that is commensurate with these organizations' objectives, thereby (3) motivating my staff toward a higher level of goal accomplishments.

In addition, I have promoted quality performance through effective use of the agency's performance management system and I have established performance standards, appraised subordinate staffs' accomplishments, and acted to reward or counsel them, as their performance indicated was appropriate. I also have made it my practice to assess my employees' developmental needs and provide opportunities to help maximize their skills, capabilities, and ongoing professional development.

I welcome and value cultural diversity and I use these and other differences as one more tool to foster an environment where people can work together cooperatively, while achieving organizational goals. In all of my leadership roles, I have worked to promote commitment, pride, trust, and group identity, and I have sought to prevent situations that could have resulted in unpleasant confrontations.

Examples of my ability in this area include:

Recruited, supervised, and led the activities of subordinate staff in five (5) separate assignments.

RESULT
- Managed planning efforts, devised organizational structures to support quality control, task management, technical, and administrative functions.
- Established work schedules, assigned tasks, advised subordinates on proper techniques and procedures, and prepared annual performance reviews.

Conducted local Title 10 training sessions to familiarize personnel with Army MDAPs and associated reporting requirements and to equip them to recognize potential threshold breaches when they occur.

RESULT
- Sponsored an Army developmental assignment program whereby individuals within Army competed to participate at HQ, DA. Candidates were screened from applications received from HQ, DA and PEO/PM offices. Those participating gained hands-on experience with the various Title 10 reporting requirements associated with the Army's Major Defense Acquisition Programs (MDAPs).

SEE NEXT PAGE

XXXXXXX

XXXXX

EVALUATION FACTORS

1. **ABILITY TO SELECT, DEVELOP, AND SUPERVISE A SUBORDINATE STAFF, WHICH INCLUDED THE ABILITY TO ACTIVELY PURSUE MANAGEMENT GOALS AND SUPPORT THE EQUAL OPPORTUNITY PROGRAM.** (continued)

Served as Team Leader during major financial management exercises, making determinations regarding proper and effective procedures.

RESULT
- Designed studies, coordinated planning, developed strategy, and identified potential sources for reliable and responsive information and assigned tasks. Teamwork included the compilation and review of budget data reflecting existing operations and data from feasibility studies on proposed programs.

Participated in the development and implementation of recruiting programs to meet EEO requirements and Affirmative Action objectives.

RESULT
- Identified appropriate advertising vehicles for minority recruiting.

- Provided assistance and input in matters involving career development, training, disciplinary actions, grievances, EEO complaints, and separations.

Actively recruited, interviewed, and selected individuals from or for the following positions: Computer Programmers, Budget Analysts, Program Analysts, Budget Clerks, Facilities Managers, and Engineering Technicians.

RESULT
- I have maintained more than a 50% ratio of women/minority positions within the organizations affected.

- I have successfully achieved minority representation in key staff positions within both the Program Management Resource Division and in the Directorate for Assessment and Evaluation.

- All offices in which I have worked have met or exceeded workplace diversity goals during my tenure. I believe that having diversity tools available is crucial for managers to help ensure fair and equitable treatment of employees. Also, I believe if done right, culturally diverse offices can be rewarding and conducive to a high-performing, healthy work environment.

Actively recruited and mentored individuals to fill developmental assignments within the division.

RESULT
- Managed the developmental program in such a way that their parent organizations continued to support our developmental program by staffing vacancies. I keep in touch with many of our former developmental employees and monitor their professional development and progress.

XXXXXXX

XXXXX

EVALUATION FACTORS

2. KNOWLEDGE OF MATERIAL LIFE-CYCLE MANAGEMENT FUNCTIONS, PROGRAMS, AND SYSTEMS USED TO PROVIDE LOGISTICAL SUPPORT.

My current job includes a very substantial degree of life-cycle management responsibility.

For example, I currently run the policy operation of Acquisition Life-Cycle management. In this capacity, the information related to guidance addressing Army's Acquisition Program Baselines (APBs) for Army Acquisition Category (ACAT) I, II, and some representative III programs.

Examples of my strong working knowledge in this area include the following:

Analyze the content of the APBs and ensure that APBs adequately address program requirements.

RESULT
  • I recently issued APB policy that now requires APBs to address "total life-cycle costs," which by definition includes operating and support (O&S) costs.

Keep Army and OSD leadership informed regarding how the Army executes their cost, schedule, and performance parameters within their respective APBs.

RESULT
  • Maintain close ties and frequent contacts with officials at all levels in the Army and DoD as well as the respective PEOs and PMs and Command Groups.

  • Any known logistical-support requirements would also be captured within the respective APBs.

I have gained substantial working knowledge and hands-on experience through interacting with officials in the Comptroller and Acquisition communities related to acquisition life-cycle subject matter contained within APBs, SARs, and DAES reports, as well as through managing these processes.

RESULT
  • My effort to include O&S costs within APBs is unique. To this point, the other military services have not yet followed suit but will likely do so soon, since it is DoD policy to make Program Managers responsible for "total life-cycle management."

  • If and when this happens, these Program Managers would have total "cradle-to-grave" program responsibility—as well as operational control of the budget dollars to make sure that this level of responsibility is discharged fully and effectively.

XXXXXXX

XXXXX

EVALUATION FACTORS

3.   KNOWLEDGE OF ADVANCED LIFE-CYCLE MANAGEMENT PLANNING PRINCIPLES AND PRACTICES.

My strong background in the Comptrollership and Acquisition areas has given me an unusually broad set of qualifications in this area.

Examples of my knowledge in this area include the following:

Gained valuable understanding of military facilities planning while serving as Acting Chief of the Facilities Management office.

RESULT
- This experience exposed me to requirements associated with our proposed military construction, Army (MCA) projects, and the MCA processor.

Currently responsible for issuing policy at HQ, DA level, pertaining to the total acquisition life-cycle baseline parameters (cost, schedule, and performance) for the Army's major programs.

RESULT
- In 1996, the Army adopted the idea to include operating and support cost estimates within Acquisition Program Baselines (APBs). I began enforcing the policy in earnest several months later.
- Soon, the Army will have "total life-cycle" cost data captured routinely in the APBs. This is one example of the "high-level" Army policy areas for which I am responsible (APBs, CARS, DAES, UCRs, and SECDEF program certification) and in which I am intimately involved.

Strong working knowledge of PPBES, the DoD planning, programming, budgeting, and execution system.

RESULT
- Oversee the submission of three budget-cycle positions each year (POM, BES, and PB) as they relate to the Army's ACAT I programs.
- Prepared substantial portions of the internal operating budget (IOB) at the installation level.

Broad experience writing, revising, and implementing policy at HQ, DA level, as it relates to legal reporting requirements associated with Title 10, U. S. Code.

RESULT
- Review, update, and issue revised policy and guidance pertaining to the required content of Major Defense Acquisition Programs (MDAPs - Section 2430), Selected Acquisition Reports (SARs – Section 2432), Nunn-McCurdy Unit Cost Reporting (UCRs – Section 2433) and Acquisition Program Baselines (APBs– Section 2435). Since Title 10 is generally DoD-wide in scope, it must not conflict with DoD policy and guidance. I work closely with the other services and DoD to ensure communication is clear.

XXXXXXX

XXXXX

EVALUATION FACTORS

4. ABILITY TO EFFECTIVELY COMMUNICATE BOTH ORALLY AND IN WRITING REGARDING THE DUTIES OF THIS POSITION.

I have had extensive experience communicating, both orally and in writing. For example, I have defended/advocated my organizations' programs to Congress, DoD, DA, and industry. As a steward of government funds, I often have written to determine the disposition of unliquidated obligations to ensure that the government's money was properly accounted for.

Examples of my ability in this critical skill area include the following:

Frequently prepare written correspondence for senior officials of the Army, DoD, and Congress.

RESULT
- Represent the Army in writing—and in person—in a variety of areas. Much of the interaction is in the form of Integrated Product Teams (IPTs) that often includes aspects of Title 10, DoD 5000, and AR 70-1, which requires substantial subject matter expertise that must be communicated either by written policy or correspondence or both. Some of these areas include:
- Major Defense Acquisition Programs (MDAPs) – 10, USC, Section 2430.
- Selected Acquisition Reports (SARs) – 10, USC, Section 2432.
- Nunn-McCurdy Unit Cost Reporting (UCRs) – 10, USC, Section 2433
- Acquisition Program Baselines (APBs) – 10, USC, Section 2435
- Defense Acquisition Executive Summary (DAES – DoD 5000)

Extensive personal liaison with senior Army and other DoD officials.

RESULT
- Selected to brief the Secretary and Under Secretary of the Army regarding our Title 10, U. S. Code reporting requirements.

Issue written guidance and policy related to a broad area of responsibilities under my authority.

RESULT
- Recently issued new Title 10 policy to the Program Executive Offices (PEOs) and their Project Managers (PMs).
- Wrote Congressional Notification Letters to the House and Senate Leaders informing them of the NM unit cost breaches, for which we subsequently sent Congress reports.

Held managerial and staff leadership positions at installation and HQ, DA levels.

RESULT
- At the installation level, was intimately involved with frequent manpower surveys and writing justifications to defend our TDA.

HOW TO GIVE YOURSELF THE EDGE FILLING OUT A FEDERAL JOB APPLICATION

The key to filling out an eye-catching federal job application is attitude. Just keep reminding yourself how capable you are and that what you're being asked to do is no different from what many less-qualified people were able to do. Once you have yourself pumped up with as much enthusiasm as you can get, follow these tips:

- Be sure your application or resume includes all the mandatory information requested in the job vacancy announcement.

- Leave no lines blank. Fill in "N/A" or "not applicable" to show you're responding.

- Write up your application or resume. Then, go back and write it again, using the first as an outline to expand wherever possible.

- Quantify where possible. How much money did you save the company? How many people did you supervise? How many convictions did you get? How many programs did you institute?

- Remember to respond to each KSA, ranking factor, or selection criteria separately. For grade levels at or above GS-7, respond with a full page to each KSA.

- Sign your application in colored ink, not black, and remember to mail the original, not the copy.

PART II

Representative Civil Service Jobs

CHAPTER 4

SAMPLE FEDERAL CIVIL SERVICE JOBS

This chapter contains job descriptions from the OPM and samples of actual job vacancy announcements. Some of the announcements use terminology that may not be familiar to you, so we've provided you with a quick way to interpret these terms in the section entitled, "Get to Know Hiring Terminology." We suggest that you read through these before you get to the actual announcements, and then refer to them as needed. To give you the most realistic experience possible, the job vacancy announcements are replicas of official descriptions and announcements. For more information and examples of sample vacancy announcements, flip back to Chapter 2, "The Anatomy of a Federal Job Announcement: What to Look For and How to Use It."

By the end of this chapter, you'll be able to determine what positions you might be qualified for and how to apply for a job. This is not meant to be an exhaustive list of every job offered by the federal government, but an overview of what you might find in the course of your job search.

OPM JOB SERIES

The Office of Personnel Management (OPM) organizes jobs into 23 different series, including one, catch-all miscellaneous series. These series include the following:

Accounting and Budget
Biological Sciences
Business and Industry
Copyright, Patent, and Trademark
Education
Engineering and Architecture
Equipment, Facilities, and Service
General Administrative, Clerical,
   and Office Services
Human Resources Management Group
Information and Arts
Information Technology Management
Investigation

Legal and Kindred
Library and Archives
Mathematics and Statistics
Medical, Hospital, Dental, and Public Health
Miscellaneous Occupations
Physical Sciences
Quality Assurance, Inspection, and Grading
Social Science, Psychology,
   and Welfare
Supply
Transportation
Veterinary Medical Science

Within each of these categories, there are several job categories, also called series. For example, in the General Administrative, Clerical, and Office Services Series, some of the job series included are: the Messenger Series, the Information Receptionist Series, and the Clerk-Stenographer Series. If you're looking for a job, you'll want to begin by determining the general series that you're interested in, then within that series, choose the specific job you want. All jobs are categorized into one of these series.

DETERMINING IF YOU ARE QUALIFIED

Now that you know what you want to do and what kinds of jobs are available, how do you determine if you're qualified for the job? There are group qualification standards that state what qualifications you must have to be hired for a particular job. These standards are mandated by the OPM. Most of the jobs fall into one of these 5 categories:

- Clerical and Administrative Support Positions

- Technical and Medical Support Positions

- Administrative and Management Positions

- Professional and Scientific Positions

- Competitive Service Student Trainee Positions

Each of these categories houses many, many jobs—the OPM calls this section "Occupational Coverage." In addition to the group standards, some of the jobs also have individual requirements. These are outlined where applicable.

GET TO KNOW HIRING TERMINOLOGY

Here's the list of terms that apply to many positions discussed in this chapter. Read this over before you begin to read the sample vacancy announcements and descriptions that follow this list.

Academic Year: Consists of approximately 36 weeks of full-time study, 30 semester hours, 45 quarter hours, or the equivalent. One academic year equals approximately nine months of experience.

Crediting Education or Training: Study completed in an institution above the high school level is evaluated as evidence of ability in terms of its relatedness to the knowledge, skills, and abilities required to assume the position of interest successfully. Study completed in a business or secretarial school or other comparable institution above the high school level is creditable provided subjects related to the position of interest were studied. Study completed in a junior college, college, or university is creditable, provided such study included a minimum of 6 semester hours, or the equivalent, per year in subjects that equipped the candidate with the knowledge, skills, and abilities required at the level of the position of interest.

Full-Time Study: In the case of business and commercial schools, it is the equivalent of at least 20 classroom hours of instruction per week, plus necessary outside study. Part-time study is prorated on this basis also, but is creditable only in amounts equivalent to one-half academic year or multiples thereof.

Interviews: The purpose of interviews is to observe and evaluate personal characteristics and qualifications that are essential to the successful performance of the duties of the position.

Physical Requirements: Applicants must be physically and mentally able to efficiently perform the essential functions of the position without hazard to themselves or others. Depending on the essential duties of a specific position, usable vision, color vision, hearing, or speech may be required. However, in most cases, a specific physical condition or impairment of a specific function may be compensated for by the satisfactory use of a prosthesis or mechanical aid. Reasonable accommodation may also be considered in determining an applicant's ability to perform the duties of a position. Reasonable accommodation may include, but is not limited to the use of assistive devices, job modification or restructuring, provision of readers and interpreters, or adjusted work schedules. Also, all positions involving federal motor vehicle operation carry the additional medical requirements.

Quality of Experience: For positions at any grade, the required amount of experience will not in itself be accepted as proof of qualifications. The candidate's record of experience and training must show that he/she has the ability to perform the duties of the position.

Quality of Ranking Factors: A quality ranking factor is a knowledge, skill, or ability that could be expected to significantly enhance performance in a position, but could not reasonably be considered necessary for satisfactory performance. Quality-ranking factors may be used to distinguish the better-qualified candidates from those who meet all other requirements, including selective factors.

Selective Factors*: Selective factors must be job related, represent an extension of the basic knowledge and skills required of the position, and be essential to successful performance of the position. Selective factors are knowledge and skills of a kind and level that reasonably could not be acquired on the job without undue interruption of the organization's production. Selective factors for positions at higher grades typically will be more narrowly defined and/or set at a higher level than is necessary at lower grades. What may be appropriate as a quality-ranking factor at a lower grade may have to be a selective factor in a higher-graded position.

*Alternative definition: a knowledge, skill, or ability that is essential for satisfactory performance in a position and represents an addition to the basic minimum requirements in this standard.

FIVE MAIN JOB CATEGORIES

TECHNICAL AND MEDICAL SUPPORT POSITIONS

EXPERIENCE AND EDUCATION REQUIREMENTS

The following table shows the amounts of education and/or experience required to qualify for positions covered by this standard.

| GRADE | EXPERIENCE | | EDUCATION |
	GENERAL	SPECIALIZED	
GS-1	None	None	None
GS-2	3 months	None	High school graduation or equivalent
GS-3	6 months	None	1 year above high school with course(s) related to the occupation, if required
GS-4	6 months	6 months	2 years above high school with courses related to the occupation, if required
GS-5	None	1 year equivalent to at least GS-4	4-year course of study above high school leading to a bachelor's degree with courses related to the occupation
GS-6 and above	None	1 year equivalent to at least next lower-grade level under education	See NOTE*

Equivalent combinations of education and experience are qualifying for all grade levels and positions for which both education and experience are acceptable.

General Experience: (1) Any type of work that demonstrates the applicant's ability to perform the work of the position, or (2) experience that provided a familiarity with the subject matter or processes of the broad subject area of the occupation.

Specialized Experience: Experience that equipped the applicant with the particular knowledges, skills, and abilities (KSAs) to successfully perform the duties of the position, and that is typically in or related to the work of the position to be filled. To be creditable, specialized experience must have been equivalent to at least the next lower-grade level. Applicants who have the first year of appropriate specialized experience, as indicated in the table, are not required by this standard to have general experience, education above the high school level, or any additional specialized experience to meet the minimum qualification requirements.

Education: High school graduation or the equivalent is qualifying for GS-2. Successfully completed post-high school education is qualifying for grades GS-3 through GS-5. This education must have been obtained in an accredited business or technical school, junior college, college or university for which high school graduation or the equivalent is the normal prerequisite. One year of full-time undergraduate study is defined as 30 semester hours, 45 quarter hours, or the equivalent in a college or university or at least 20 hours of classroom instruction per week for approximately 36 weeks in a business or technical school.

For some occupations covered by this standard, 6 semester hours of specific courses are included in the first year of education that meets the GS-3 requirements. The 6 semester hours allow for subjects that are common to a broad range of degree programs, e.g., subjects in the mathematical, physical, or biological sciences. This inclusion corresponds to the second part of the description of general experience, i.e., the subjects provide evidence of a familiarity with the subject matter or processes of the broad subject area of the occupation. At grades GS-4 and above, a portion of the education is usually directly related to the work of the position to be filled. Examples of related courses are provided in the individual occupational requirements where applicable. However, agencies may require other courses if they are considered to be more related to the position to be filled.

*NOTE: Graduate education or an internship meets the specialized experience required above GS-5 *only* in those instances where it is directly related to the work of the position. One full year of graduate education meets the requirements for GS-7. Two full years of graduate education or a master's degree meets the requirements for GS-9. One year of full-time graduate education is considered to be the number of credit hours that the school attended has determined to represent the first year of full-time study. If that information cannot be obtained from the school, 18 semester hours should be considered as satisfying the one year of full-time study requirement. Part-time graduate education is creditable in accordance with its relationship to a year of full-time study at the school attended.

Training: Completion of appropriate training such as inservice training programs, training acquired while serving in the Armed Forces, and government-sponsored developmental training programs will be allowed credit on a month-for-month basis, generally through the GS-5 level. Such training meets general or specialized experience requirements depending upon its applicability.

Completion of an intensive, specialized course of study of less than one year may meet in full the experience requirements for GS-3. Courses of this type normally require completion of up to 40 hours per week of instruction rather than the usual 20 hours per week and are usually of *at least* three months duration. Such courses may have been obtained through a variety of programs such as those offered by technical schools and military training programs. To be creditable, such a course must have been designed specifically as career preparation for the work of the position being filled, and must have provided the applicant with the necessary knowledges, skills, and abilities to do the work.

Combining Experience and Education: Equivalent combinations of successfully completed post-high school education and experience are also qualifying. The combinations described below are those most typical for these positions, i.e., for grades GS-3 through GS-5. If education is used to meet specialized experience requirements, then such education must include courses directly related to the work of the position. (When crediting education, prorate the number of hours of related courses required as a proportion of the total education to be used.)

For GS-3 level positions, determine the applicant's total qualifying experience as a percentage of the six months' experience required for GS-3; then determine the applicant's education as a percentage of the one year of education that meets the requirements for GS-3. Add the two percentages. The total percentage must equal at least 100 percent to qualify an applicant for GS-3.

For GS-4 level positions, determine the applicant's total qualifying experience as a percentage of the one year of experience required for GS-4; then determine the applicant's education as a percentage of the 2 years of education that meets the requirements for GS-4. Add the two percentages. The total percentage must equal at least 100 percent to qualify an applicant for GS-4.

For GS-5 level positions, only education in excess of the first 60 semester hours of a course of study leading to a bachelor's degree is creditable toward meeting the specialized experience requirements. Two full academic years of study, or 60 semester hours, *beyond the second year* is equivalent to one year of specialized experience. Determine the applicant's total qualifying experience as a percentage of the year of specialized experience required at the GS-5 level. Then determine the applicant's education as a percentage of the education that meets the requirements for GS-5. Add the two percentages. The total percentage must equal at least 100 percent to qualify an applicant for GS-5.

The following are examples of how education and experience may be combined. They are examples only, and are not all-inclusive.

- The position to be filled is a Pharmacy Aid, GS-3. An applicant has two months of experience and 20 semester hours of college. The applicant meets 33 percent of the required experience and 67 percent of the required education. The applicant meets 100 percent of the total requirements and is qualified for the position.

- The position to be filled is an Industrial Engineering Technician, GS-4. An applicant has five months of general experience and 36 semester hours of college. The applicant meets 42 percent of the required experience and 60 percent of the required education. The applicant exceeds 100 percent of the total requirements and is qualified for the position. This example assumes that education is being used to meet the specialized experience requirements, and that at least 7 of the 36 semester hours are in courses directly related to the work of the position.

- The position to be filled is a Recreation Assistant, GS-5. An applicant has 8 months of GS-4 level specialized experience and 80 semester hours of college. The applicant meets 67 percent of the required experience and 33 percent of the required education (i.e., 20 semester hours in excess of the first 60 semester hours). The applicant meets 100 percent of the total requirements and is qualified for the position. At least 8 of the 20 semester hours must be directly related to the work of the position.

USING SELECTIVE FACTORS FOR POSITIONS COVERED BY THIS STANDARD

Selective factors must represent knowledges, skills, or abilities that are essential for successful job performance and cannot reasonably be acquired on the job during the period of orientation/training customary for the position being filled. For example, a requirement for knowledge of microbiological laboratory techniques may be needed immediately to perform the duties of a Biological Technician position in a disease research laboratory. If that is the case, such knowledge could be justified as a selective factor in filling the position.

USING INDIVIDUAL OCCUPATIONAL REQUIREMENTS WITH THIS STANDARD

General experience requirements at the GS-2 and GS-3 levels are described in the group coverage standard so that the applicant pool at those "trainee" levels will be as generally inclusive as possible. Thus, examples of qualifying general experience are not included in the "Individual Occupational Requirements" for positions covered by this qualification standard.

Positions at GS-4 and above require specialized experience, education, or training related to the occupation. Examples of qualifying specialized experience are provided for those occupations where such information is currently available. Examples of qualifying post-high school education or training are also provided.

OCCUPATIONAL COVERAGE

A list of the occupational series covered by this qualification standard is provided below. Some of the positions listed here also have individual occupational requirements.

GS-019 Safety Technician

GS-021 Community Planning Technician

GS-090 Guide

GS-102 Social Science Aid and Technician

GS-119 Economics Assistant

GS-181 Psychology Aid and Technician

GS-186 Social Services Aid and Assistant

GS-189 Recreation Aid and Assistant

GS-404 Biological Science Technician

GS-421 Plant Protection Technician

GS-455 Range Technician

GS-458 Soil Conservation Technician

GS-459 Irrigation System Operation

GS-462 Forestry Technician

GS-621 Nursing Assistant

GS-622 Medical Supply Aide and Technician

GS-625 Autopsy Assistant

GS-636 Rehabilitation Therapy Assistant

GS-640 Health Aid and Technician

GS-642 Nuclear Medicine Technician

GS-645 Medical Technician

GS-646 Pathology Technician

GS-647 Diagnostic Radiologic Technologist

GS-648 Therapeutic Radiologic Technologist

GS-649 Medical Instrument Technician

GS-651 Respiratory Therapist

GS-661 Pharmacy Technician

GS-681 Dental Assistant

GS-683 Dental Laboratory Aid and Technician

GS-698 Environmental Health Technician

GS-704 Animal Health Technician

GS-802 Engineering Technician

GS-809 Construction Control

GS-817 Surveying Technician

GS-818 Engineering Drafting

GS-856 Electronics Technician

GS-895 Industrial Engineering Technician

GS-1021 Office Drafting

GS-1202 Patent Technician

GS-1311 Physical Science Technician

GS-1316 Hydrologic Technician

GS-1341 Meteorological Technician

GS-1371 Cartographic Technician

GS-1374 Geodetic Technician

GS-1521 Mathematics Technician

GS-1541 Cryptanalysis

GS-1862 Consumer Safety Inspection

GS-1981 Agricultural Commodity Aid

GS-2144 Cargo Scheduling

SAMPLE VACANCY ANNOUNCEMENTS

TECHNICAL AND MEDICAL SUPPORT POSITIONS

VACANCY ANNOUNCEMENT NUMBER: XXXX-XXXX-XXXX

Opening Date: June 10, 2002

Closing Date: July 08, 2002

(All required information must be received at the address above by the close of business on the closing date; otherwise, the application will not be accepted.)

This agency provides reasonable accommodation to applicants with disabilities. If you need a reasonable accommodation for any part of the application and hiring process, please notify this agency. The decision on granting reasonable accommodation will be on a case-by-case basis.

Position: Consumer Safety Inspector Relief (HACCP Models Project), GS-1862-8, Night Shift

Temporary, not-to-exceed 1 year

Location: USDA, FSIS, FO, D4, Austin, MN

Please Note: This is a temporary position that will be in effect during the HACCP Models Project in the above stated plant.

This position may be extended or made permanent without further competition.

Inspectors at or above GS-8 outside the model plant interested in a detail should submit an application or a written request for consideration. While not required, you are encouraged to address the job elements and submit a current performance appraisal in order to provide the selecting official with full information regarding your knowledge, skills, and abilities as they relate the position. The Voluntary Reassignment System will not be used because the positions are being filled temporarily, within the local commuting area only.

Positions may be filled on multiple shifts. Applicable local practices will govern assignments to shifts and rotations in these situations.

Duties: The incumbent performs food safety inspection duties within an officially inspected slaughter or combination slaughter and processing establishment that operates under a Hazard Analysis and Critical Control Point (HACCP) and process control system plan(s). The incumbent is assigned to one of several inspection roles in the plant and, on a rotational basis over the course of time, performs both oversight and verification inspection activities, collects and analyzes data, and conducts regulatory oversight activities inside the plant in matters relating to food safety and other consumer protection concerns that arise with respect to carcasses and parts as they proceed through the slaughter process.

Distribution: FSIS, FO, DO, Minneapolis, MN; All FI, FSIS, FO, District-wide

PLEASE POST AND/OR CIRCULATE

Eligibility Requirements: All applicants who wish to be considered for this position must satisfy time-in-grade requirements by having held a position at the next lower grade for a minimum of 52 weeks. In addition, applicants must meet the qualification standards requirements as contained in the Qualifications Standards Handbook. For this position, the applicant must have 52 weeks of specialized experience equivalent to the next lower grade level in the federal service, which is in, or directly related to, the position to be filled. Examples of specialized experience include: experience in meat and poultry inspection and processing; collecting and submitting samples of microbes for laboratory testing; identifying processing and trimming defects relating to meat and poultry; and documenting noncompliance with safety requirements.

The preceding are the general requirements. All candidates must fully meet the requirements of the qualification standard for this position within 30 days after the closing date of the announcement to have competitive status.

Job Elements: Respond to all job elements listed in the vacancy announcement. Failure to address these job elements will result in loss of further consideration for this position. If using FSIS Form 4335-1, one continuation page per job element page may be used to expand your responses. If using other application formats, respond to all job elements listed in the vacancy announcement with no more than 2 one-sided pages per element. Excess beyond 2 pages per job element will be disregarded. Use a legible print size. Print smaller than a "10 point" font on a computer printer or 12 characters per inch typewritten or copies that are too light to read may result in loss of further consideration for this position.

A. Knowledge of and ability to observe operations involving the slaughter of food animals to determine compliance with applicable inspection, SSOP, and HACCP regulations.

Definition: Describe the education, training, and experience that demonstrates your knowledge of and/or ability to learn to monitor plant activities, such as the anti-microbial treatment of carcasses, chilling operations, measurement of moisture absorption and retention levels, removal of processing and trimming defects, removal of fecal contamination, and the removal of diseased carcasses or other conditions affecting consumer safety.

B. Ability to review written documents and records to determine non-compliance with applicable SSOP and HACCP plans, regulations, and procedures.

Definition: Describe the education, training, and experience that demonstrates your knowledge of and/or ability to learn to verify the adequacy and effectiveness of the plant's SSOP, review HACCP plans against a plant's actual slaughter process control activities, verify that the plant is maintaining accurate critical control point and other monitoring records, and verify that the plant is consistently meeting its critical limits or recording deviations and corrective actions.

C. Ability to document in writing the results of a review of a plant's SSOP and HACCP plans and records as well as the actual operation.

Definition: Describe the education, training, and experience that demonstrates your knowledge of and/or ability to learn to prepare written documentation when necessary to demonstrate noncompliance with regulatory requirements.

D. Ability to perform inspection procedures, product samplings, and other basic tests to verify compliance with applicable regulations and procedures.

Definition: Describe the education, training, and experience that demonstrates your knowledge of and/or ability to learn to select a random sample and examine passed carcasses and parts to determine compliance with performance standards after appropriate trimming; select samples at designated locations on the slaughter line to determine compliance with regulatory requirements; send appropriate samples to an Agency laboratory after using specified procedures; and, if directed, perform health and safety verification sampling and tests for detection of specific microbes, residues, or contaminants.

E. Skill in oral communication and dealing effectively with plant officials and other inspection personnel about a variety of regulatory concerns.

Definition: Describe the education, training, and experience that demonstrates your ability to discuss various non-compliance issues and other regulatory matters with plant personnel on an ongoing basis, maintain good communication with other Agency inspection personnel to assure awareness of specific conditions or concerns at the plant, and advise the IIC or supervisory personnel of particularly difficult or sensitive issues.

VACANCY ANNOUNCEMENT NUMBER: XX-XX-XX

Opening Date: 06/10/2002

Closing Date: 06/28/2002

Position: HISTOPATHOLOGY TECHNICIAN
GS-0646-08/08

Salary: $33,886 – $44,055 per year
(Salary Includes 8.64% Locality Pay)

Two Vacancies/Permanent/Full-Time Positions

Tour of Duty: Monday – Friday, 8:00 a.m. – 4:30 p.m.

Duty Location: Gainesville Division
Travel to Lake City may be required

Subject to change in shift hours based on workload.

PATHOLOGY AND LABORATORY MEDICINE SERVICE

Duties Include: The incumbent performs as a technical specialist in providing histologic preparations required to discern the nature and extent of disease in surgical and autopsy specimens. Responsibility for proper preparation, handling, and processing of numerous types of clinical and research samples. Assists Pathologists and the Pathology Specialist in testing new procedures. Evaluates and introduces new techniques relevant to a specialized diagnostic laboratory for pathology. Responds to intraoperative consultation requests, performing specialized procedures including frozen tissue sectioning and staining, preparation of cytologic media, and handling of specimens for specialized procedures including flow cytometry, electron microscopy and cytogenetic studies. Responsible for the operation and maintenance of numerous forms of automated and specialized equipment. Keeps detailed logs and flow records of specimens being processed. Instructs new residents and fellows in histologic and immunohistopathologic techniques. Assists the Pathology Specialist in accessioning and identifying gross examination and description of clinical, surgical, autopsy, and research specimens. Assists in the performance of post-mortem examinations.

MOVING/TRAVEL EXPENSES ARE APPROVED

$2,000 RECRUITMENT BONUS IS APPROVED*

Qualifications: Candidates must be citizens of the United States. Applicants must have one year of specialized experience equivalent to the GS-7 level. Specialized experience is experience in anatomical pathology technician work in (a) cutting very thin sections of human tissue specimens for microscopic examination; and/or in (b) testing and examining body fluids, etc. for abnormalities in cell structure, depending upon the requirements of the position to be filled. Equivalent combinations of education and experience may be qualifying for this position. College transcripts must be submitted to make this determination.

Knowledge, Skills, and Abilities to be Addressed:

1.   Knowledge of tissue processing techniques.

2.   Skill in orienting and positioning minute and delicate tissue specimens.

3.   Ability to operate and maintain a microtome, cryostat, and other laboratory equipment.

4.   Knowledge of stain solubilities, aqueous and organic solvent system characteristics, and basic chemical reactions used in staining.

5.   Knowledge and skill in applying special stain techniques.

Position Description No. 471A

*Selected candidates must sign a written agreement to serve in this position for a period of not less than 24 months in the VA in return for payment of the recruitment bonus. Current federal employees or former federal employees who have a break in service of less than 1 year are not eligible for a recruitment bonus.

ALL APPLICANTS PROVIDING DIRECT PATIENT CARE SERVICES ARE REQUIRED TO DEMON-STRATE PROFICIENCY IN SPOKEN AND WRITTEN ENGLISH AS REQUIRED BY VA HANDBOOK 5005.

THE INCUMBENT MUST MEET THE PHYSICAL REQUIREMENTS OF THE POSITION.

THIS AGENCY PROVIDES REASONABLE ACCOMMODATIONS TO APPLICANTS WITH DISABILI-TIES. IF YOU NEED A REASONABLE ACCOMMODATION FOR ANY PART OF THE APPLICATION AND HIRING PROCESS, PLEASE NOTIFY THE AGENCY. THE DECISION ON GRANTING REASON-ABLE ACCOMMODATION WILL BE ON A CASE-BY-CASE BASIS.

AREA OF CONSIDERATION (WHO MAY APPLY): All permanent employees of the North, Florida/South Georgia Veterans Health System, Reinstatement, Career, Career-Conditional, Transfer eligible, Veterans eligible under the Veterans Readjustment Authority (VRA), Veterans who are preference eligible or who have been separated from the armed forces under honorable conditions after substantially 3 years or more continuous active service, qualified handicapped individuals and CTAP/ICTAP eligible.

Vacancy Announcement Number: XXXXXXXXXXX

Opening Date:	05/26/2001
Closing Date:	05/26/2003
Position:	MEDICAL CLERK GS-0679-03/07
Salary:	$19,667 – $39,779 per year
Duty Location:	Many vacancies in U.S. SOUTHWESTERN STATES
Who May Apply:	OPEN TO ALL U.S. CITIZENS. CIVIL SERVICE STATUS IS NOT REQUIRED.

Resumes accepted will receive consideration as vacancies occur within geographical areas identified by applicants. Management will specify the area of consideration for specific vacancies. Area of consideration may be limited to the activity where the vacancy exists or to a subdivision of the organization. Management may opt to consider candidates other than those who specifically applied for the series of a vacancy. Most positions are located in office, laboratory, or warehouse environments on military installations, in military housing projects, or in leased spaces in the southwest. Some are located in foreign areas or may require foreign travel. Not all series and grades are available in all locations.

This is an open continuous vacancy announcement. Resumes submitted for this announcement will be processed into an inventory resume database and will be used to fill current and future vacancies.

This announcement may be used to fill permanent, temporary (NTE 1 year), and TERM (1-4 year) appointments. Resumes are continuously accepted from all U.S. citizens. Applicants eligible for appointment under other legal appointing authorities including, but not limited to, the following categories must be able to provide the appropriate documentation when requested.

- Current or former permanent federal employees eligible for promotion, reassignment, transfer, or reinstatement

- Nonappropriated Fund employees

- Persons with Disabilities Employment Program

- Current students

- Executive Order 12721

- Veterans Readjustment Appointment (VRA)

- Veterans Employment Opportunity Act of 1998 (VEOA)

- 30 percent Disabled Veterans

We also accept resumes from all U.S. citizens for temporary (NTE 1 year) or TERM (1-4 year) positions who are not eligible for appointment under any other appointing authorities.

VACANCY ANNOUNCEMENT NUMBER: XX-XX-XXX

Opening Date: 06/03/2002

Closing Date: 06/17/2002

Position: ANIMAL HEALTH TECHNICIAN
                          GS-0704-07

Salary: $32,453 – $42,191 per year

Promotion Potential: GS-07

Duty Location: 1 vacancy at ROBBINSVILLE, NJ

This is a temporary position not to exceed one year.

Who May Apply: Open to all qualified U.S. citizens.

Major Duties: The incumbent is responsible for technical and specialized work involved in a variety of animal health programs within an assigned geographical area. The incumbent assists Veterinary Medical Officers with inspection and testing of livestock, poultry, and other avian species on ranches, farms, auctions, markets, etc.; makes arrangements with herd and flock owners and independently draws blood samples, conducts serologic tests, tags, brands, appraises reactor animals, and reports findings; supervises cleaning and disinfection of vehicles and premises that are contaminated by disease; inspects premises to insure compliance with regulations; contacts owners of diseased or exposed animals or poultry; inspects livestock moving in interstate commerce for visible evidence of disease and compliance with federal and state regulations; prepares certificates granting approval of movements; maintains contacts with owners or employees of livestock markets, etc., to provide information, promote animal health programs, and insure compliance with laws, regulations, and policies; trains and/or provides technical supervision to lower graded technicians; traces diseased livestock or animals; and inspects import-export facilities for compliance with requirements.

Qualifications Required: To qualify, applicants must meet all qualification requirements and time in grade requirements within thirty days of the closing date of this announcement.

One year of SPECIALIZED experience reflecting the duties outlined under "Description of Duties." Such experience must reflect the knowledge, skills, and abilities outlined under "Evaluation Criteria," and must be equivalent in level of difficulty and responsibility to the next lower level in the federal service.

Examples of qualifying specialized experience include the following work:

- As a laborer, manager, or owner of a livestock ranch or farm involving the following:
    - Direct work with livestock
    - With livestock in a feed lot
    - As a Livestock Market Inspector
    - As an Animal Welfare Inspector
    - As an assistant to a Veterinarian who works with livestock

This specialized experience must be equivalent to the next lower grade level in the federal service.

There is no education substitution at the GS-7 level.

Knowledges, Skills, and Abilities Required: The following five KSAs are needed for you to be successful in the job. You should individually address each one. If the KSAs shown in your application package indicate that you are among the best qualified, your application will be referred to the selecting official. (Please be precise and specific.)

1. Ability to recognize the presence of animal disease or unusual animal health conditions.

2. Ability to understand and apply law, regulations, policies, or procedures.

3. Ability to work with small and large animals.

4. Ability to plan and organize work.

5. Skill in communicating and gaining the cooperation of others.

Basis of Rating: For CTAP and ICTAP, well-qualified means that the applicant is eligible, qualified, and clearly exceeds qualification requirements for the position as demonstrated. This is determined by either: (1) meeting selective and quality ranking factor levels as specified by the agency; or (2) being rated above minimally qualified under the agency's specific rating and ranking process.

Applicants meeting basic eligibility requirements will be rated and ranked on the knowledges, skills, and abilities, and other characteristics (KSAs) required to perform the duties of the position. Please review KSAs carefully. Include in the write-ups such things as experience in and out of federal service that gave you the specific knowledge, skill, or ability; objectives of your work; and evidence of your success (such as accomplishments, awards received, etc.).

Pay, Benefits, and Work Schedule: This is a temporary appointment not-to-exceed one year and does not confer all of the opportunities usually associated with the competitive service such as tenure, transfer privileges, retention rights during reduction-in-force, and health and life insurance benefits. However, the selectee will be entitled to sick and annual leave accrual.

Conditions of Employment:

- Should have knowledge and skill in the swine industry

- Should have ability to work with computer databases

- This position is subject to unscheduled overnight details of undetermined

- Lengths in the event of animal health emergencies or other conditions

- Requiring immediate response, as required by the Agency

- The duties of this position include euthanasia of animals and carcass

- Disposal in controlling animal disease outbreaks

- Travel of 1-5 nights per month possible

Other Information: If claiming 5-point veterans' preference, a DD-214 must be submitted. If claiming 10-point veterans' preference, both a DD-214 and SF-15 must be submitted.

Candidates will be considered without discrimination for any nonmerit reasons such as race, color, national origin, gender, religion, age, disability, political beliefs, sexual orientation, or marital or family status. (Not all prohibited bases apply to all programs.)

Persons with disabilities who require alternative means for communication of program information (braille, large print, audiotape, etc) should contact USDA's TARGET Center at 202-720-2600 (voice and TDD).

To file a complaint of discrimination, write USDA, Director, Office of Civil Rights, Room 326-W, Whitten Building, 14th and Independence Avenue SW, Washington, DC 20250-9410 or call (202) 720-5964 (voice or TDD).

USDA is an equal opportunity provider and employer. This agency provides reasonable accommodation to applicants with disabilities. If you need a reasonable accommodation for any part of the application and hiring process, please notify the agency. The decision on granting reasonable accommodation will be on a case-by-case basis.

Major Duties: This series includes all positions; the primary duties of which are to perform clerical work in support of the care and treatment given to patients in a ward, clinic, or other such unit of a medical facility. This work includes functions such as serving as a receptionist, performing recordkeeping duties, performing clerical duties relating to patient care and treatment, and providing miscellaneous support to the medical staff of the unit. This work requires a practical knowledge of the medical facility's organization and services, the basic rules and regulations governing visitors and patient treatment, and a practical knowledge of the standard procedures, medical records, and medical terminology of the unit supported.

Qualifications Required: All eligibility and qualification requirements must be met by the cut-off date for the position. Positions at grade level GS-3 require six months general experience or high school graduation or equivalent. Positions at grade level GS-4 require one year general experience or two years education above high school. Positions at grade level GS-5 and above require 1 year specialized experience equivalent to the next lower grade level. Education may be substituted. A four-year course of study leading to a degree qualifies at the GS-5 level. At grades GS-5 and above, a portion of the education is usually directly related to the work of the position to be filled.

Substitute Education for Experience: As permitted by OPM Qualifications Standards.

Knowledges, Skills, and Abilities Required: To be determined, well-qualified candidates must possess skills that are directly related to the duties of the job. The following elements should be addressed within your description of duties in your work experience on your resume. Do not use a separate sheet of paper. 1. Knowledge of the subject matter pertinent to the position. 2. Technical skill to perform the duties of the position. 3. Ability to communicate (both orally and in writing) the technical knowledge of the position.

Basis of Rating: No written test is required.

For permanent positions: Resumes are evaluated by an automated system that matches the skills of applicants to the skills for a vacancy.

For temporary and TERM positions: If qualified, ratings will be based on an evaluation of the quality and extent of experience, education, and training in relation to the ranking factors. In your resume, you should address the ranking factors listed in the above section entitled Knowledge, Skills, and Abilities Required. Rating for this position may result in a lower score if the ranking factors are not addressed in the resume.

ICTAP APPLICANTS: If eligible for Interagency Career Transition Assistance Program (ICTAP), you must submit a copy of your agency Reduction In Force notice, a copy of your most recent performance rating, and a copy of your most recent SF-50 noting current position, grade level, and duty location. You must be found well-qualified to receive this special consideration. ICTAP eligibles will be considered well-qualified if they receive a score of 90 or above (excluding veteran's preference points). Please note on your application that you are applying as an ICTAP eligible. Additional information may be found at www.usajobs.opm.gov/ei32.htm.

Mail the required forms to:

Human Resources Service Center, Southwest
525 B Street, Suite 600
Attn: Code 537 - Resume Intake Team
San Diego, CA 92101-4418

Pay, Benefits, and Work Schedule: All federal employees are required by PL 104-134 to have federal payments made by Direct Deposit.

Conditions of Employment: Selectees may be required to obtain a security clearance and meet all certification requirements (depending on the position to be filled) prior to appointment. Some positions may require successful completion of a physical examination, agility test, pre-employment drug test, and/or participation in the Anthrax vaccine immunization program if applying for an emergency essential position. Selectees who are required to meet one or more of these employment conditions before appointment will receive a tentative offer of employment.

An offer of employment may be rescinded if the selectee fails to report to any of the scheduled appointments, fails the medical/agility/drug test, lacks the certification requirements, or is unable to obtain a security clearance. Incumbents of drug testing designated positions will be subject to random testing. Drug test results will be provided to the employing activity/command.

Other Information:

Promotional Potential: Some positions may have promotion potential to a higher grade than the grade at which filled. Positions with known promotion potential do not guarantee promotion, nor is the promise of promotion implied. Supervisory Probationary Period: A one-year probationary period will be required for first-time managers/supervisors.

Temporary Promotions: Competitive Temporary Promotions may be made using rosters established from this flyer and may subsequently be made permanent without further competition.

Priority Placement/Consideration Programs: All positions are subject to mandatory consideration and placement programs. If you are a displaced employee of a non-DOD federal agency, you may be eligible for special priority consideration under the Interagency Career Transition Assistance Program (ICTAP).

Starting Salaries: Visit the Web site www.opm.gov/oca/payrates/index.htm to obtain current salary information for the area(s) where you are interested in working. You may also call HRSC-SW Faxback at 1-800-831-0622 to request a faxed copy of a pay table (press option 7 at the main menu, then option 1, and then option 2 to receive a catalog of documents from which to select the appropriate pay table). Demonstration Project pay tables are not available on the Web site; however, they are available by Faxback. Relocation expenses may or may not be authorized. If you are applying for a geographic location other than your current one, it is suggested that you indicate at the end of your resume whether or not you are willing to relocate at your own expense.

Veterans Preference: A 5-point preference is granted to veterans who served prior to October 14, 1976 or who served in a military action for which they received a Campaign Badge or Expeditionary Medal. All applicants requesting 5-point preference will be required to provide a DD Form 214, Certificate of Release or Discharge from Active Duty, or other proof of eligibility showing active duty time and the nature of discharge.

You may be entitled to 10-point veterans preference if you are a disabled veteran, you have received a Purple Heart, you are the spouse or mother of a 10 percent disabled veteran, or you are the widow, widower, or mother of a deceased veteran. If you are claiming 10-point preference, please send a SF-15, Application for 10-point Veteran Preference, plus the proof required by that form to:

Human Resources Service Center, Southwest
XXX X Street, Suite XXX
Attn: Code XXX - Resume Intake Team
San Diego, CA 92101-4418

Information on veterans preference eligibility may be obtained from OPM's Web site at http://www.opm.gov/veterans/html/vetsinfo.htm. Candidates claiming veterans preference who are still on active duty will be granted 5-points tentative preference if their application shows that they have the required service (i.e., service in a war, campaign, or expedition).

The Department of Navy is an Equal Employment Opportunity Employer. All qualified candidates will receive consideration without regard to race, color, religion, sex, national origin, age, disability, marital status, political affiliation, sexual orientation, or any other non-merit factor.

The Department of the Navy provides reasonable accommodation to applicants with disabilities. Applicants with disabilities who believe they require reasonable accommodation should contact the Equal Employment Opportunity staff at HRSC Southwest (XXX) XXX-XXXX, DSN: XXX-XXXX to ensure that the Department of the Navy can consider such requests. The decision to grant an accommodation will be made on a case-by-case basis.

VACANCY ANNOUNCEMENT NUMBER: XXX-XX-XXX

Opening Date:	01/01/2002
Closing Date:	Open until further notice
Position:	**MEDICAL SUPPLY AID AND TECHNICIAN** GS-0622-02/05
Salary:	$19,033 – $33,907 per year
Duty Location:	1 vacancy at ANN ARBOR, MI

Who May Apply: Open to current federal employees serving under a career or career conditional appointment, former federal employees with reinstatement eligibility, or persons eligible for non-competitive appointment under Special Authorities. VEOA eligibles (i.e., veterans who are preference eligibles or who have been separated from the armed forces under honorable conditions after completing approximately 3 or more years of continuous active service) may apply.

Major Duties: Duties may include, but are not limited to, the following: Identify and receive contaminated instruments OR supplies and other patient care items; select proper methods for cleaning such items; disassemble and inspect items for wear and tear damage and missing components; operate equipment and instruments to ensure proper functioning prior to sterilization or redistribution; assemble instrument sets and other trays; inspect instruments for proper functioning; schedule operation of sterilizers to permit cooling or aeration of sterilized items prior to use by wards, clinics, services, or the operating room; label all sterilized items with a control number and expiration date; review and sign all recording charts to verify the proper sterilization time, temperature, pressure, humidity and sterilant exposure; assemble case carts using what is needed for different surgical procedures; maintain proper work flow for stocking and rotating supplies in SPD and other storage areas.

THERE ARE CURRENTLY NO OPENINGS FOR THIS OPEN AND CONTINUOUS VACANCY AN-
NOUNCEMENT. APPLICATIONS RECEIVED WILL BE MAINTAINED IN OUR STATUS APPLICANT
SUPPLY FILE THROUGH THE END OF THE CALENDAR YEAR. IN THE EVENT A VACANCY OC-
CURS, YOUR STATUS QUALIFYING GROUP/APPLICATION MAY BE REFERRED UPON REQUEST OF
THE SELECTING OFFICIAL.

Qualifications Required: Applicants must have general and/or specialized experience. When specified,
applicants must also meet any Mandatory (Selective Placement) Factors listed. Status applicants must also meet
time-in-grade requirements and time after competitive appointment requirements by the closing date of this
announcement.

Applicant must have one year of specialized experience equivalent to the next lower grade, which has equipped
the applicant with the particular knowledge, skills, and abilities to successfully perform the duties of the
position. Experience is typically in or related to the work of the position described.

FOR GS-2 LEVEL, APPLICANTS MUST HAVE THREE MONTHS OF GENERAL EXPERIENCE OR BE A
HIGH SCHOOL GRADUATE OR EQUIVALENT. FOR GS-3 LEVEL, APPLICANTS MUST HAVE SIX
MONTHS GENERAL EXPERIENCE OR HAVE ONE YEAR OF EDUCATION ABOVE HIGH SCHOOL
WITH COURSE/S RELATED TO THE OCCUPATION. FOR GS-4 LEVEL, APPLICANTS MUST HAVE SIX
MONTHS OF GENERAL EXPERIENCE AND SIX MONTHS OF SPECIALIZED EXPERIENCE OR TWO
YEARS EDUCATION ABOVE HIGH SCHOOL WITH COURSES RELATED TO THE OCCUPATION. FOR
GS-5 LEVEL, APPLICANTS MUST HAVE ONE YEAR SPECIALIZED EXPERIENCE EQUIVALENT TO
AT LEAST THE GS-4 LEVEL OR HAVE A FOUR YEAR COURSE OF STUDY ABOVE HIGH SCHOOL
LEADING TO A BACHELOR'S DEGREE WITH COURSES RELATED TO THE OCCUPATION.

Knowledges, Skills, and Abilities Required: SEE ABOVE QUALIFICATIONS REQUIREMENTS.

Basis of Rating: APPLICATIONS SHOULD BE COMPLETE AND IDENTIFY EMPLOYERS NAME AND
ADDRESS, CURRENT SUPERVISOR AND PHONE NUMBER, AS WELL AS SPECIFIC EXPERIENCE
GAINED RELATING TO THE POSITION THAT YOU ARE APPLYING FOR. INCOMPLETE APPLICA-
TIONS WILL REDUCE YOUR ELIGIBILITY AND/OR RATING FOR THIS POSITION.

Pay, Benefits, and Work Schedule: All federal employees are required by PL 104-134 to have federal payments made by Direct Deposit.

This position will be filled on a full-time permanent basis. Upon completing any required probationary period,
the position will be permanent.

Conditions of Employment: Under Executive Order 11935, only United States citizens and nationals (residents of American Samoa and Swains Island) may compete for civil service jobs. Agencies are permitted to
hire noncitizens only in very limited circumstances where there are no qualified citizens available for the
position.

Government facilities are required to provide a smoke-free environment for their employees. Smoking will be
permitted only in designated areas.

Other Information: Your Social Security number (SSN) is requested under the authority of Executive Order
9397 to uniquely identify your records from those of other applicants' who may have the same name. As
allowed by law or presidential directive, your SSN is used to seek information about you from employers,
schools, banks, and other who may know you. Failure to provide your SSN on your application materials will
result in your application not being processed.

Before being hired, you will be required to sign and certify the accuracy of the information on your application
if you have not done this using an application form such as the OF-612.

VACANCY ANNOUNCEMENT NUMBER: XX-XX-XX-XXX

Opening Date: 01/01/2002

Closing Date: 12/30/2002

Position: NURSING ASSISTANT
                        GS-0622-04/05

Salary: $22,078 – $24,701 per year

Promotion Potential: GS-05

Duty Location: Many vacancies, Phoenix, AZ

ANNOUNCEMENT # XX-XX-XX-XXX   NURSING ASSISTANT, GS-622-4/5

Opening Date: 01-01-2002

Closing Date: 12-30-2002

LOCATION / DUTY STATION: PHOENIX INDIAN MEDICAL CENTER, NURSING DEPARTMENT

Series/Grade/Salaries

> GS-621-4: $22,078 – $28,697 Per Annum
>
> GS-621-5: $24,701 – $32,113 Per Annum

NUMBER / TYPE OF POSITION: VARIOUS POSITIONS—Full-Time, Part-Time,

Intermittent. OR Rotating Shifts AND

- Temporary, Not to Exceed Varies—See conditions of employment

- Temporary employees with a duration of 13 months or longer are entitled to Federal Benefits, i.e., Health or Life Insurance, and Retirement.

Area of Consideration: COMMUTING AREA

Who May Apply: Merit Promotion Plan (MPP) Candidates: Applications will be accepted from status eligibles (e.g., reinstatement eligibles and current permanent employees in the competitive federal service) and from current permanent IHS employees in the Excepted Service who are entitled to Indian Preference and from individuals who are eligible for excepted appointments in IHS under some other authority (e.g., handicapped authority, etc.). Those MPP candidates eligible for Indian Preference, who so desire, may also apply under ESEP provisions by indicating on their application, "Consideration under both MPP and ESEP."

Excepted Service Examining Plan (ESEP) Candidates: Applications will be accepted from individuals entitled to Indian Preference. Current permanent IHS Excepted Service employees and Competitive Service employees or Reinstatement eligible entitled to Indian Preference may also apply under the provision of the Indian Health Service Excepted Service Examining Plan. (If selected under the Excepted Service Examining Plan, individuals may be appointed under Schedule A authority without regard to Time-In-Grade requirements.)

Applications will be accepted from individuals eligible for non-competitive appointment (e.g., applicants eligible for appointment under the Veterans Readjustment Act, the severely handicapped, those with a 30 percent or more compensable service-connected disability). Veterans who are preference eligibles or who have been separated from the armed forces under honorable conditions after 3 years or more of continuous active service may apply. Applications will be accepted from USPHS Commissioned Officers.

Supervisory/Management: NO

Promotional Potential: YES, TO GS-5 GRADE LEVEL

Housing: NO GOVERNMENT HOUSING

Travel Expenses: NO EXPENSES PAID

Brief Description of Duties: Demonstrates the ability to observe basic bodily functions. Demonstrates the ability to contribute to the plan of patient care according to patient needs and established standards and hospital policies and procedures. Demonstrates expertise in basic nursing care. Provides basic instruction to patients, families, and significant others. Promotes orderly functions of the nursing unit. Evaluates patient care given. Communicates effectively with patients and their significant others, co-workers, physicians, and personnel from other departments in the hospital. Participates in the educational development of self and co-workers. Attends and participates in nursing committees to maintain and upgrade skills. Attends and participates in staff meetings when on duty, or reads and initials staff meeting minutes when off duty at the time when staff meetings were held. Receives formal and informal on-the-job training to include classroom instruction and demonstrations of procedures and techniques by professional or licensed nursing personnel. Must maintain current basic CPR certification for continued employment.

Qualification Requirements: The following shows total amount of experience required and allowable substitution of education:

GRADE	GENERAL EXPERIENCE	SPECIALIZED EXPERIENCE
GS-4	6 months	6 months
GS-5	None	1 year equiv. to at least GS-4

or

EDUCATION:

GS-4   2 years above high school with courses related to the occupation, if required.

GS-5   4-year course of study above high school leading to a bachelor's degree with courses related to the occupation.

General Experience: (1) Any type of work that demonstrates the applicant's ability to perform the work of the position, or (2) experience that provided a familiarity with the subject matter or processes of the broad subject area of the occupation.

Specialized Experience: Experience that equipped the applicant with the particular knowledge, skills, and abilities (KSAs) to perform successfully the duties of the position and that is typically in or related to the work of the position to be filled. To be creditable, specialized experience must have been equivalent to at least the next lower grade level.

Qualifying specialized experience includes nonprofessional nursing care work in a hospital, outpatient clinic, nursing home, or other medical, nursing, or patient care facility, or in such work as that of a home health aid performing duties such as:

* Providing personal nursing care such as providing pre- and post-operative care.

* Support duties for diagnostic and technical treatment procedures, such as setting up and operating special medical equipment and apparatus.

- Caring for mentally ill patients, including observing, recording, and reporting changes in their behavior and providing reassurance and encouragement.

- Assisting surgeons and registered nurses in operating room activities, including passing instruments, maintaining sterile conditions, and draping and positioning patients.

Education: Successfully completed post-high school education is qualifying for grades GS-3 through GS-5. This education must have been obtained in an accredited business or technical school, junior college, college or university for which high school graduation or the equivalent is the normal prerequisite. One year of full-time undergraduate study is defined as 30 semester hours, 45 quarter hours, or the equivalent in a college or university or at least 20 hours of classroom instruction per week for approximately 36 weeks in a business or technical school. To receive credit for education you must submit your transcripts.

Training: Completion of appropriate training such as inservice training programs, training acquired while serving in the Armed Forces, and government-sponsored developmental training programs will be allowed credit on a month-for-month basis, generally through the GS-5 level. Such training meets general or specialized experience requirements depending upon its applicability.

Combination of Education and Experience: Equivalent combinations of education and experience are qualifying for which both education and experience are acceptable as stated in the Operating Manual for Qualification Standards for General Schedule positions.

Evaluation Methods: When required by Personnel Regulations, an evaluation will also be made to the extent to which experience, education, training, self-development, outside activities, and/or awards demonstrate the basically qualified applicants possess the Ranking KSAs described below. This will determine the Highly qualified applicants among the basically-qualified eligibles. Measurement of possession of the KSAs will be accomplished through review of the application, performance appraisals, (MPP candidates only), the Narrative Statement related to the KSAs, employment interviews, and reference check results.

Ranking KSAs:

1. Knowledge and skill to use a body of standardized patient care procedures.

2. Knowledge of medical terminology.

3. Ability to communicate orally.

The information you provide is considered to be a part of your application and as such is certified by your signature on the application or equivalent.

Special Application Requirements: In addition to those listed in the "How to Apply" section, candidates must also include:

- Declaration for Federal Employment (OF-306)

- Transcripts to receive credit for education

CLERICAL AND ADMINISTRATIVE SUPPORT POSITIONS

Experience and Education Requirements:

The following table shows the amounts of education and/or experience required to qualify for positions covered by this standard.

GRADE/ POSITIONS	EXPERIENCE		EDUCATION
	GENERAL	SPECIALIZED	
GS-1 All positions	None	None	None
GS-2 All positions	3 months	None	High school graduation or equivalent
GS-3 Clerk-Steno			
All other positions	6 months	None	High school graduation or equivalent
			1 year above high school
GS-4 All positions	1 year	None	2 years above high school
GS-5 Clerk-Steno			
All other positions	2 years	None	4 years above high school
	None	1 year equivalent to at least GS-4	(except Reporting Stenographer)
GS-6 and above All positions	None	1 year equivalent to at least next lower grade level	Generally, not applicable

Equivalent combinations of education and experience are qualifying for all grade levels and positions for which both education and experience are acceptable. Proficiency requirements are described below.

General Experience: (All positions except Reporting Stenographer, Shorthand Reporter, and Closed Microphone Reporter)—Progressively responsible clerical, office, or other work that indicates ability to acquire the particular knowledge and skills needed to perform the duties of the position to be filled.

Specialized Experience: (All positions except Reporting Stenographer, Shorthand Reporter, and Closed Microphone Reporter)—Experience that equipped the applicant with the particular knowledge, skills, and abilities (KSAs) to perform successfully the duties of the position, and that is typically in or related to the position to be filled. To be creditable, specialized experience must have been equivalent to at least the next lower grade level. Applicants who have the one year of appropriate specialized experience, as indicated in the table, are not required by this standard to have general experience, education above the high school level, or any additional specialized experience to meet the minimum qualification requirements.

Experience for Reporting Stenographer, Shorthand Reporter, and Closed Microphone Reporter: One year of experience equivalent to at least the next lower grade level using the skills and equipment appropriate to the position to be filled is required for all positions. Following is a description of qualifying experience for these positions.

- Reporting Stenographer, GS-5: Experience as a clerk-stenographer, secretary, reporting stenographer, or in other positions that included application of stenography and typing skills as a significant part of the work.

- Reporting Stenographer, Shorthand Reporter, and Closed Microphone Reporter, GS-6: Experience as a reporting stenographer, hearing reporter, or in other positions in which the primary duty was to make and transcribe manual or machine-written shorthand records of hearings, interviews, or similar proceedings.

- Shorthand Reporter and Closed Microphone Reporter, GS-7 and above: Experience as a court reporter, or hearing reporter, or in other positions in which the primary duty was to make verbatim records of proceedings.

Education: High school graduation or the equivalent is creditable at the GS-2 level for the occupations listed, except Clerk-Stenographer, where it is creditable at the GS-3 entry level.

Successfully completed education above the high school level in any field for which high school graduation or the equivalent is the normal prerequisite is creditable at grades GS-3 through GS-5 for all positions except Reporting Stenographer, GS-5. This education must have been obtained in an accredited business, secretarial or technical school, junior college, college or university. One year of full-time academic study is defined as 30 semester hours, 45 quarter hours, or the equivalent in a college or university, or at least 20 hours of classroom instruction per week for approximately 36 weeks in a business, secretarial, or technical school.

As a general rule, education is not creditable above GS-5 for most positions covered by this standard; however, graduate education may be credited in those few instances where the graduate education is directly related to the work of the position.

Intensive Short-Term Training: Completion of an intensive, specialized course of study of less than one year may meet in full the experience requirements for GS-3. Courses of this type normally require completion of up to 40 hours per week of instruction rather than the usual 20 hours per week and are usually of *at least* 3 months duration. Such courses may have been obtained through a variety of programs such as those offered by business or technical schools and through military training programs. To be creditable, such a course must have been designed specifically as career preparation for the work of the position being filled and must have provided the applicant with the necessary knowledge, skills, and abilities to do the work.

Combining Education and Experience: Equivalent combinations of successfully completed post-high school education and experience may be used to meet total experience requirements at grades GS-5 and below, except for Reporting Stenographer, GS-5.

For GS-3 and GS-4 level positions, determine the applicant's total qualifying experience as a percentage of the experience required for the grade level; then determine the applicant's education as a percentage of the education required for the grade level; then add the two percentages. The total percentage must equal at least 100 percent to qualify an applicant for that grade level.

For GS-5 level positions (except Clerk-Stenographer, which does not require specialized experience), only education in excess of the first 60 semester hours (i.e., beyond the second year) is creditable toward meeting the specialized experience requirement. One full academic year of study (30 semester hours) *beyond the second year* is equivalent to six months of specialized experience.

The following are examples of how education and experience may be combined. They are examples only, and are not all inclusive:

The position to be filled is a Payroll Clerk, GS-4. An applicant has eight months of qualifying experience and 20 semester hours of college. The applicant meets 67 percent of the required experience and 33 percent of the required education. The applicant meets 100 percent of the total requirements and is qualified for the position.

The position to be filled is a Clerk-Typist, GS-4. The applicant has 4 months of qualifying experience and one year of business school. The applicant meets 33 percent of the required experience and 50 percent of the required education. The applicant meets 83 percent of the total requirements and is not qualified for the position.

The position to be filled is a Clerk-Stenographer, GS-5. An applicant has one year of qualifying experience and 90 semester hours of college. The applicant meets 50 percent of the required experience and 75 percent of the required education. The applicant exceeds 100 percent of the total requirements and is qualified for the position.

The position to be filled is an Editorial Assistant, GS-5. The applicant has 9 months of specialized experience and 75 semester hours of college (15 semester hours beyond the second year and the equivalent of 3 months of specialized experience). The applicant meets 75 percent of the required experience and 25 percent of the required education. The applicant meets 100 percent of the requirement for one year of specialized experience and is qualified for the position.

Proficiency Requirements

Clerk-Typist, Office Automation Clerk/Assistant, Clerk-Stenographer, Data Transcriber, and Positions with Parenthetical Titles of (Typing), (Office Automation), (Stenography), or (Data Transcription)

In addition to meeting experience or education requirements, applicants for these positions must show possession of the following skills, as appropriate. Applicants may meet these requirements by passing the appropriate performance test, presenting a certificate of proficiency from a school or other organization authorized to issue such certificates by the Office of Personnel Management local office, or by self-certifying their proficiency. Performance test results and certificates of proficiency are acceptable for 3 years. Agencies may verify proficiency skills of self-certified applicants by administering the appropriate performance test.

Clerk-Typist, GS-2/4; Office Automation Clerk/ Assistant (any grade); (Typing) (any grade); and (Office Automation) (any grade):

- 40 words per minute typing speed

- Data Transcriber, GS-2/4; and (Data Transcription) (any grade):

- skill in operating an alphanumeric data transcribing machine,

- *or* 20 words per minute typing speed for GS-2 transcription duties

- *or* 25 words per minute typing speed for GS-3 and GS-4 transcription duties

Clerk-Stenographer, GS-3/4:

- 40 words per minute typing speed *and*

- 80 words per minute dictation speed

Clerk-Stenographer, GS-5:

- 40 words per minute typing speed *and*

- 120 words per minute dictation speed

- (Stenography) (any grade):

- 40 words per minute typing speed *and either*

- 80 words per minute dictation speed for GS-3 and GS-4 stenographic duties

- *or* 120 words per minute dictation speed for GS-5 stenographic duties

NOTE: The level of proficiency for stenographic and data transcribing duties required by positions with parenthetical titles is based on the grade level of those duties and not necessarily on the overall grade of the position. For example, a position classified as Secretary (Stenography), GS-318-5, may require either 80 or 120 words per minute dictation speed depending upon the level of difficulty of the stenographic duties. A position classified as Payroll Clerk (Data Transcription), GS-544-4, may require either 20 or 25 words per minute typing speed depending upon the level of difficulty of the transcribing duties. Therefore, before filling positions of this type, first determine the grade level of the duties that require the additional skill, and then determine the skill level required.

Reporting Stenographer, Shorthand Reporter, and Closed Microphone Reporter

In addition to meeting the experience requirements, applicants for these positions must show possession of the following skills with equipment appropriate to the specific position.

Reporting Stenographer, GS-5/6:

- 120 words per minute dictation speed

Shorthand Reporter and Closed Microphone Reporter, GS-6:

- 160 words per minute dictation speed

Shorthand Reporter and Closed Microphone Reporter, GS-7 and above:

- 175 words per minute dictation speed

Applicants must also be able to produce accurate typewritten transcripts of recorded proceedings. Applicants for competitive appointment and inservice applicants for initial assignment to these three positions at all grade levels must demonstrate the specific skill and level of proficiency required by the position to be filled. Also, inservice applicants for promotion to positions that have a higher proficiency requirement than the position previously held must demonstrate the higher level of proficiency. Applicants may demonstrate that proficiency by either passing a dictation test at the required speed or presenting a certificate of proficiency showing speed and accuracy equivalent to those used in the Office of Personnel Management performance tests for these positions. The certificate must show that the candidate demonstrated the required proficiency, i.e., dictation speed and accuracy, to a teacher of stenography, shorthand reporting, or closed microphone reporting, within the past year. Applicants for these positions may not self-certify dictation proficiency.

Using Selective Factors for Positions Covered by This Standard

Selective factors must represent knowledge, skills, or abilities that are essential for successful job performance and cannot reasonably be acquired on the job during the period of orientation/training customary for the position being filled. It is unlikely, for example, that a requirement for experience with a particular brand of word processing software could be justified as a selective factor for an Office Automation Clerk position. Since knowledge of that software may be desirable, such knowledge could be appropriately used as a quality-ranking factor. On the other hand, proficiency in the correct use of medical terminology may be needed immediately to perform the duties of a Medical Records Technician position to provide continuity in an agency's medical records program. If that is the case, knowledge of medical terminology could be used as a selective factor in filling the position.

Requirements include:

1. Words per minute are based on a 5 minute sample with three or fewer errors.

2. The maximum number of errors allowed in a dictation sample equals 10 percent of the required dictation speed (80 words per minute or 120 words per minute) multiplied by the number of minutes in the sample.

3. The maximum number of errors allowed in a dictation sample for these three positions equals 5 percent of the required dictation speed multiplied by the number of minutes in the sample.

Occupational Coverage

A list of the occupational series covered by this qualification standard is provided below. Some of the positions listed below may also have individual qualification standards.

GS-029	Environmental Protection Assistant	GS-544	Civilian Pay
GS-072	Fingerprint Identification	GS-545	Military Pay
GS-086	Security Clerical and Assistance	GS-561	Budget Clerical and Technician
GS-134	Intelligence Aid and Clerk	GS-592	Tax Examining
GS-203	Human Resources Assistance	GS-593	Insurance Accounts
GS-302	Messenger	GS-675	Medical Records Technician
GS-303	Miscellaneous Clerk and Assistant	GS-679	Medical Support Assistance
GS-304	Information Receptionist	GS-962	Contact Representative
GS-305	Mail and File	GS-963	Legal Instruments Examining
GS-309	Correspondence Clerk	GS-986	Legal Assistance
GS-312	Clerk-Stenographer and Reporter	GS-998	Claims Assistance and Examining
GS-318	Secretary	GS-1001	General Arts and Information
GS-319	Closed Microphone Reporting	GS-1046	Language Clerical
GS-322	Clerk-Typist	GS-1087	Editorial Assistance
GS-326	Office Automation Clerical and Assistance	GS-1101	General Business and Industry
GS-332	Computer Operation	GS-1105	Purchasing
GS-335	Computer Clerk and Assistant	GS-1106	Procurement Clerical and Technician
GS-344	Management and Program Clerical and Assistance	GS-1107	Property Disposal Clerical and Technician
GS-350	Equipment Operator	GS-1152	Production Control
GS-351	Printing Clerical	GS-1411	Library Technician
GS-356	Data Transcriber	GS-1421	Archives Technician
GS-357	Coding	GS-1531	Statistical Assistant
GS-359	Electric Accounting Machine Operation	GS-1702	Education and Training Technician
GS-361	Equal Opportunity Assistance	GS-1802	Compliance Inspection and Support
GS-382	Telephone Operating	GS-1897	Customs Aid
GS-390	Telecommunications Processing	GS-2005	Supply Clerical and Technician
GS-392	General Telecommunications	GS-2091	Sales Store Clerical
GS-394	Communications Clerical	GS-2102	Transportation Clerk and Assistant
GS-503	Financial Clerical and Assistance	GS-2131	Freight Rate
GS-525	Accounting Technician	GS-2135	Transportation Loss and Damage Claims Examining
GS-530	Cash Processing		
GS-540	Voucher Examining	GS-2151	Dispatching

Vacancy Identification Number: XXXXXXX

Opening Date:	MARCH 25, 2002
Cut-Off Dates:	APRIL 15, 2002, MAY 6, 2002
	MAY 28, 2002, JUNE 17, 2002,
	JULY 8, 2002, JULY 29, 2002,
	AUGUST 19, 2002, SEPTEMBER 9, 2002
	SEPTEMBER 30, 2002
Closing Date:	INDEFINITE
Salary:	GS-3 (6772) $8.67 – $11.27 PER HOUR (**$9.67 – $12.57 PER HOUR**)*
	GS-4 (6773) $9.74 – $12.66 PER HOUR (**$10.86 – $14.11 PER HOUR**)*

*Salary reflects locality pay. Night differential of an additional 10 percent is given for all regularly scheduled evening work, 6:00 p.m. until closing.

Promotional Potential: GS-5

Note: APPLICANTS THAT APPLIED UNDER VACANCY ANNOUNCEMENT XXXXXX MUST REAPPLY

Position: LIBRARY TECHNICIAN (DECK ATTENDANT TRAINEE), GS-1411-3

LIBRARY TECHNICIAN (DECK ATTENDANT), GS-1411-4

THESE ARE EXCEPTED SERVICE APPOINTMENTS

Location: WASHINGTON, D.C. - 20 VACANCIES

Employing Agency: BOOK SERVICE SECTION, COLLECTION ACCESS LOAN AND MANAGEMENT DIVISION, LIBRARY SERVICES, PUBLIC SERVICE COLLECTIONS, LIBRARY OF CONGRESS, JOHN ADAMS BUILDING, AND THOMAS JEFFERSON BUILDING

TYPE OF APPOINTMENT: PERMANENT, NON-SUPERVISORY, BARGAINING UNIT POSITION

TOUR OF DUTY: PART-TIME—20 HOURS PER WEEK. MAY BE REQUESTED TO WORK MORE HOURS ON AN AS NEEDED BASIS. SOME EVENINGS, WEEKENDS, AND/OR HOLIDAY DUTY AS REQUIRED. INCUMBENTS SELECTED FOR THESE POSITIONS MAY BE CONVERTED TO A FULL-TIME TOUR OF DUTY WITHOUT FURTHER COMPETITION.

AVAILABLE SCHEDULES

Day Schedules:

1. 8:30 a.m. - 12:30 p.m., 3 weekdays and all day Saturday; **or**

2. 12:30 p.m. - 4:30 p.m., 3 weekdays and all day Saturday.

NOTE: IN ADDITION TO NOTING YOUR WORK SCHEDULE SELECTIONS ON THE OPM FORM 1203-FX (FORM C), APPLICANTS MUST ALSO INDICATE ON THEIR APPLICATION, IN PRIORITY ORDER, THE SCHEDULE(S) FOR WHICH THEY WOULD LIKE TO BE CONSIDERED. FAILURE TO SELECT A SCHEDULE MAY DELAY THE PROCESSING OF YOUR APPLICATION FOR THESE POSITIONS.

Major Duties: Incumbents will work under the supervision of a team leader and will be responsible for the maintenance, servicing, and shelving of a given segment of the library's general collection. Specific responsibilities will include:

- Retrieving materials from a broad base of requesters, often requiring verification of incomplete or inaccurate information.

- Substituting editions and searching for material not readily available.

- Shelving and maintaining the collection, including minor shifting, identification of cataloging and/or labeling errors, and shelf-reading.

- Producing large quantities of accurate work on a continuing rapid basis in pressure situations.

Qualification Requirements:

FOR GS-3 LEVEL:

A. Have at least six months of general clerical, library, or other work that demonstrates experience in filing books, correspondence or other documents; or following guidelines or procedures; and/or working with others.

OR

B. Have completed at least one full year of education above high school. This education included at least 30 semester hours of coursework in a college or university or at least 20 hours of classroom instruction per week for approximately 36 weeks in a business or technical school.

OR

C. Have a combination of education and experience that is qualifying for the GS-3 level. (Applicants applying at the GS-3 level may combine education and experience to achieve the required six months of experience. Five semester hours of education above high school is equivalent to one month of experience. For example, four months of experience and 10 hours of post-high school education would equal six months of experience.

FOR GS-4 LEVEL:

A. Have at least six months of related clerical, office, or library experience at the GS-3 level in the federal service or at a comparable level of difficulty outside the Federal service performing duties directly related to the duties of these positions.

OR

B. Have completed at least two years of education above high school. This education included at least 60 semester hours or 90 quarter hours of coursework in a college or university.

OR

C. Have a combination of education and experience that is qualifying for the GS-4 level. (Applicants applying at the GS-4 level may combine education and experience to achieve the required six months of experience. Ten semester hours of education above high school is equivalent to one month of GS-3 experience. For example, four months of GS-3 level experience and 20 hours of post-high school education would equal six months of GS-3 level experience.)

Physical Requirements: The incumbent may perform strenuous physical work requiring standing for extended periods of time, walking, kneeling, stooping, bending, pushing and pulling carts, reaching, and lifting. After an offer of employment has been made and before commencement of the duties the selectee must be physically qualified by the Library's Health Services Office.

Other Information: To be eligible for federal employment, male applicants born after December 31, 1959, must certify at the time of appointment that they have registered with the Selective Service System or are exempt from having to do so under Selective Service law.

Basis for Rating: Ratings will be based on responses to the occupational questions in this document. Please follow all instructions carefully. Errors or omissions may affect your score.

Please note: If a determination is made that you have rated yourself higher than is supported by your description of experience and/or education OR that your application is incomplete, the following process will take place.

After a review of all the experience and training, a single best level reflecting the KSAs of the rating schedule (70, 80, or 90) will be assigned for your total experience including education and/or training.

Vacancy Announcement Number: XXX-XX-XXXX

Opening Date: 04/15/2002

Closing Date: 09/30/2004

Position: EMERGENCY EQUIPMENT DISPATCHER
                   GS-2151-04

Salary: $23,285 – $30,266 per year

Duty Location: Many vacancies, GREAT LAKES, IL

Areas of Consideration: The Human Resources Service Center - Northeast (HRSC-NE) is soliciting resumes to fill current and/or future vacancies in this occupational series. Resumes accepted will receive consideration as vacancies occur within geographical areas identified by applicants on the Additional Data Sheet (ADS) form available on the Resume Builder. Management will specify the area of consideration for specific vacancies. Area of consideration may be limited to the activity where the vacancy exists or to a subdivision of the organization. Management may elect to consider candidates other than those who specifically applied under this announcement.

Who May Apply: Current federal employees serving under a career or career-conditional appointment in the competitive service; former federal employees with reinstatement eligibility; Interagency Career Transition Assistance Plan (ICTAP) eligibles; persons eligible for non-competitive appointment under special authorities; or preference eligibles or veterans who have been honorably separated from the Armed Forces after substantially completing an initial 3-year term of active service. Selecting Official may choose to limit consideration to subgroups of those who apply. Candidates whose current or previous permanent position is at the same grade level, or at a higher grade level, than the announced position (or its target), and who meet the qualification requirements will be referred to the Selecting Official as noncompetitive candidates.

Major Duties: Answers calls and requests for emergency services and information received by telephone, computer, alarm equipment, radio, or walk-in complaints. Questions the caller to obtain essential facts and dispatches the appropriate response units. Operates and monitors multi-line telephone system and alarm panels. Coordinates the communications of emergency response personnel with other organizations during routine and emergency operations. Required to monitor radio traffic from the surrounding areas as part of Mutual Aid Agreement. Obtains requested information without delay concerning files, records, license plate registration, base decals, drivers license, and any other information the patrol officers may request. Maintains necessary logs and journals. Prepares reports for all Fire/Ambulance incidents, which occur on his or her assigned shift. Responsible for the issuance of building key to authorized personnel and ensuring that these persons are authorized to possess the keys by verifying that authorization by identification cards and photograph comparisons. Qualified to be armed with a .12 gauge shotgun for the security and protection of the weapons in the police department armory, which is physically located within the Emergency Communications Center and must be observed 24 hours a day. Performs all other duties as required, i.e., keeps office area neat and clean to maintain a professional appearance. Provides basic first aid and CPR emergency instructions to callers until arrival of emergency crews. Must successfully complete a basic telecommunication course within one year of employment. Works extended periods without rest breaks and eats meals as the work situation permits. Must be able to work rotating shifts and irregular work schedules. Occasionally required to work overtime hours. This position requires a character investigation.

Qualifications Required: All eligibility and qualification requirements must be met by the referral date. Applicants must meet time in grade requirements as described by 5 CFR 300 Subpart F. Positions in this series may include individual occupational requirements or positive educational requirements. Please refer to OPM Qualification Standards Operating Manual for General Schedule positions Part III Index at www.opm.gov/qualifications/index.htm.

Substitution of Education for Experience: Please refer to the following Web site for education that may be substituted for experience: www.opm.gov/qualifications/index.htm (Part III Index).

Basis of Rating: Resumes are evaluated by an automated system (RESUMIX) that matches the skills extracted from the candidate's resume to the skills identified for the position. In addition, other requirements (i.e. time-in-grade, education, area of consideration, specialized experience, etc.) must be met to determine the qualified candidates referred to the Selecting Official for consideration.

Pay, Benefits, and Work Schedule: Salaries—Visit the Web site at www.opm.gov/oca/payrates/index.htm to obtain current salary information for the area(s) where you are interested in working.

Conditions of Employment: Preemployment Requirements—Selectees may be required to successfully complete a probationary period, obtain a security clearance, and meet all certification requirements (depending on the position to be filled) prior to appointment. Some positions may require successful completion of a physical examination, agility test, preemployment drug test, and/or participation in the Anthrax vaccine immunization program if applying for an emergency essential position. Selectees required to meet one or more of these employment conditions before appointment will receive a tentative offer of employment.

A tentative offer of employment will be rescinded if the selectee fails to report to any of the scheduled appointments, fails the medical/agility/drug test, lacks the certification requirements, or is unable to obtain a security clearance. Incumbents of drug testing designated positions will be subject to random testing. Drug test results will be provided to the employing activity/command.

Special Requirements: U.S. citizenship required. All federal employees are required by PL 104-134 to be paid through Direct Deposit/Electronic Funds Transfer; The Defense Authorization Act of 1986 requires that male applicants 18-26 years of age, be registered with the Selective Service to be eligible for appointment. To obtain information on your registration status, you may write to: Selective Service System, Registration Information Office, P.O. Box 94638, Palatine, IL; vacancies filled from announcements covering multiple grade levels may be filled at any grade level and may have promotion potential; positions filled through this announcement may be part-time, intermittent, seasonal, temporary, term, or permanent. If filled on a temporary or TERM basis, the action may be terminated any time prior to the established not-to-exceed date. If filled on a temporary basis, may be extended or become permanent without further competition.

Faxed applications will NOT be accepted. Applications mailed in government postage paid envelopes will NOT be accepted. Use of postage paid official envelopes is a violation of OPM & Postal regulations. Once submitted, applications become the property of the Department of the Navy and will NOT be returned or copied. All extraneous documents not specifically requested will NOT be used.

Other Information: This position is subject to mandatory consideration and placement programs (PPP&RPL). Individuals who have special priority selection rights under the Interagency Career Transition Assistance Program (ICTAP) must be well-qualified for the position to receive consideration for special priority selection. ICTAP eligibles will be considered well qualified if they meet the basic qualification requirements, demonstrate above average proficiency in performing the duties of the position in which they are applying, and meet any required skills identified by management. Federal employees seeking ICTAP eligibility MUST submit proof that they meet the requirements of 5 CFR 330.704. This includes a copy of the agency notice, a copy of their most recent Performance Rating and a copy of their most recent SF-50 noting current position, grade level, and duty location. Please annotate your ICTAP eligibility clearly on responses to the Additional Data questions.

Vacancy Announcement Number: XXX-XXXX-XX/XXXXX

Opening Date: 04/20/2002

Closing Date: 06/28/2002

Position: DATA TRANSCRIBER
GS-0356-04/04

Salary: $23,707.00 – $30,000.00 per year

Promotion Potential: GS-04

Duty Location: 3 vacancies at BOSTON METRO AREA, MA

Who May Apply: Open to all qualified persons.

Major Duties: Transcribes and/or key verifies a wide variety of taxpayer prepared tax returns, related schedules, and/or documents.

Identifies missing, incorrect, and unrecognizable data and takes appropriate course of action to resolve errors, or refers to others for correction. Performs other duties as assigned.

Qualifications Required: One year of progressively responsible clerical, office, or other work that indicates ability to acquire the particular knowledge and skills needed to perform the duties of this position.

OR

Two years of education above the high school level in any field of study in an accredited business, secretarial or technical school, junior college or university.

OR

An equivalent combination of successfully completed education and experience. Data skills of 4,000 keystrokes per minute and a 90 percent accuracy rate are required.

Basis of Rating: Ratings will be based on the numerical score you received on your Notice of Results issued by the U.S. Office of Personnel Management.

Passing a written test is required. Self-certification of 4000 keystrokes/hr with a 90% accuracy rate is also required.

Pay, Benefits, and Work Schedule: This is a permanent, career-conditional appointment. Selectee will be eligible for health and life insurance, annual (vacation) and sick leave, and will be covered under the Federal Employees Retirement System.

This position will be filled on a full-time permanent basis. Upon completing any required probationary period, the position will be permanent.

Conditions of Employment: Under Executive Order 11935, only United States citizens and nationals (residents of American Samoa and Swains Island) may compete for civil service jobs. Agencies are permitted to hire noncitizens only in very limited circumstances where there are no qualified citizens available for the position.

As a condition of employment, male applicants born after December 31, 1959, must certify that they have registered with the Selective Service System or are exempt from having to do so under the Selective Service Law.

A background security investigation will be required for all new hires. Appointment will be subject to the applicant's successful completion of a background security investigation and favorable adjudication. Failure to successfully meet these requirements will be grounds for termination.

Selectee must undergo appropriate tax checks prior to appointment. This position requires completion of a one year probationary period.

Conditions of Employment: Fingerprints will be required as part of the preemployment process.

Other Information: First consideration will be given to CTAP and ICTAP eligibles. You must clearly identify your claim for veterans preference on your application.

5-POINT PREFERENCE. A 5-point preference is granted to veterans who served prior to 1976 and served at least six months on active duty. Those who served after 1980 and 1982 must have served at least two years on active duty.

A 5-point preference is also granted to veterans who served on active duty during the Gulf War from August 2, 1990 through January 2, 1992. The law grants preference to anyone who is otherwise eligible and who served on active duty during this period regardless of where the person served or for how long. "Otherwise eligible" means that the person must have been released from the service under honorable conditions and must have served a minimum of two years on active duty, or if a Reservist, must have served the full period for which called to active duty.

If you are claiming a 5-point veteran preference, please provide a DD-214, Certificate of Release or Discharge from Active Duty, or other proof of entitlement. Tentative preference will be granted in the absence of paperwork.

10-POINT PREFERENCE. You may be entitled to a 10-point veteran preference if you are a disabled veteran; you have received the Purple Heart; you are the spouse or mother of a 100 percent disabled veteran; or, you are the widow, widower, or mother of a deceased veteran. If you are claiming 10-point veteran preference, you will need to submit an SF-15, Application for 10-point Veteran Preference, plus the proof required by that form.

If you make a false statement in any part of your application, you may not be hired; you may be fired after you begin work; or you may be subject to fine, imprisonment, or other disciplinary action.

This agency provides reasonable accommodations to applicants with disabilities. If you need a reasonable accommodation for any part of the application and hiring process, please notify the agency. The decision on granting reasonable accommodation will be on a case-by-case basis.

THE IRS IS COMMITTED TO ENSURING THAT ALL EMPLOYEES PERFORM IN A MANNER WARRANTING THE HIGHEST DEGREE OF PUBLIC CONFIDENCE AND DEMONSTRATE THE HIGHEST LEVEL OF ETHICS AND INTEGRITY.

VACANCY ANNOUNCEMENT NO: XXXXXXXXXXXXX

Opening Date: June 06, 2002

Closing Date: June 21, 2002

Position Title (Pay Plan-Series): Administrative Support Assistant (-0303)

Grade: 07

Comments: TYPE OF POSITION: Full-Time

Salary: $30,887

Region: South Central

Organization: US Army Engineer District, Mobile Construction Division
Mobile, AL 36628-0001

Special Notes: Permanent Change of Station (PCS) expenses will NOT be paid. Department of the Army Relocation Services for Employees (DARSE) will NOT be paid.

Priority Consideration: Employees entitled to priority consideration have already been given consideration for this position. To be further considered, apply under this announcement and compete with other candidates. Selection is subject to restriction resulting from DoD Priority Placement Program. There is only one vacancy to be filled by this announcement.

Duty Station: Redstone Arsenal, AL

Area of Consideration: Army employees with competitive status; and eligible Army CIPMS employees. Department of Defense employees serving on a Career or Career-Conditional Appointment.

Interagency Career Transition Assistance Plan (ICTAP) eligibles: Current or former employees displaced from non-DOD agencies. Individuals seeking ICTAP eligibility must submit a copy of their Reduction in Force (RIF) separation notice (Notification Letter of SF 50) and a copy of their most recent performance rating.

Duties: Performs work related to the practical and technical aspects of office administration including issues related to budgeting, supply management and purchasing, personnel administration, time keeping, data processing, project tracking, and files management. Collects data for the office operating budget; sets up controls to monitor expenses during the year; and recommends budget adjustments including restructuring budget allocations to deal with changing situations such as varying costs for equipment or services and changes in the availability of funds. The employee makes purchases through open market purchase by blanket agreement, cash order or similar methods; processes and tracks purchase documents. Completes requests for personnel actions and writes position descriptions; serves as training coordinator for the office/group. Collects data for several office operations, analyzes the data, sets up controls to monitor them and independently troubleshoots as needed. Contract Administration: Prepares and reviews contract modification packages to ensure completeness. Coordinates with contractors, Area Office, and Mobile District personnel to ensure all required actions are complete. Inputs all required contract actions, i.e., payment estimates, changes orders, fund commitments and obligations, contract modifications, etc. in RMS contract administration database and in CEFMS. Responsible for checking funding allocation for all contractor payment estimates and change orders. Compiles data for and assists in the preparation of reports originating in the Area Office for transmittal of information on contract operations to the Area Office, District Office, and Using Agencies. These include reports on construction operations, project status, and other engineering information. Responsible for compilation and computation of monthly estimates of the contractor's earnings, from which payment vouchers to the contractors are prepared. These estimates are compiled from percentages of work in place of measurements furnished.

Qualification Requirements: The Qualification Standard Handbook is summarized; due to the length of the standard, it cannot be printed in its entirety. Applicants may review the Operating Manual of Qualification Standards for General Schedule positions in its entirety by visiting their local Civilian Personnel Advisory Center (CPAC). Applicants must have at least 52 weeks of specialized experience to the GS-06 grade level. Specialized experience is experience that provided the knowledge and abilities to successfully perform the duties of the position, and that is typically in or related to the position being filled.

Time In Grade Requirements: Generally, an employee may be advanced to this position if he/she served for at least 52 weeks in a position at or above the GS-06 level. Non-appropriated fund service, non-general schedule service, or combinations of certain other creditable service may be used to satisfy time-in-grade requirements when appropriate. Each case will be judged on its own merit. Candidates are eligible for referral if they meet time-in-grade requirements not later than 30 days after the closing date of the RESUMIX vacancy announcement.

Selective Placement Factors/Knowledge, Skills, and Abilities (KSAs):

Standard/Other Requirements:

1. Failure to provide all of the required information as stated in the announcement may result in an ineligible rating or may affect the overall rating.

2. Permanent change of station (PCS) funds will not be authorized.

3. Direct Deposit is REQUIRED: As a condition of employment, candidates appointed, competitively promoted or reassigned are required to enroll and participate in Direct Deposit/Electronic Funds Transfer within 60 days following the effective date of that action.

4. Application/Resume deadline: Application/Resume must be received by the Closing Date of the Vacancy Announcement.

5. Male applicants born after December 31, 1959 are required to complete a Pre-Employment Certification Statement for Selective Service registration prior to appointment. Failure to comply may be grounds for withdrawal of an offer of employment, or dismissal after appointment.

6. Candidates must meet time-in-grade requirements (if applicable).

7. Where to Apply: Applicants must have both a resume and a self-nomination on file with the SE Resumix database. Resumes and self-nominations must be received in the SE Resumix database by the closing date of the announcement.

If you have a resume on file with the SE Resumix database, you need only self-nominate in order to be considered. You do not need to resubmit your pre-positioned resume unless you have significant changes or skills to add. If you do not have a resume on file with the SE Resumix database region, you must submit a resume in one of the following ways:

a. Army's Resume Builder (preferred method)

cpol.army.mil/rb/rb_entry.cgi is an online process for you to complete a resume, any necessary supplemental information, and then forward electronically to the recruiting CPOC. Once you have built your resume, you must click the South Central button that will send your resume to be processed into the SE Resumix database. The button on the Builder for SouthEast has been removed.

b. Resumes may be emailed to the South Central CPOC for inclusion in the SE Resumix database. Format and information required to submit an email resume can be found online in our Job Kits available via CPOL (www.cpol.army.mil). Once at CPOL, click on Regional Home Page, South Central Region, Employment Information, then Job Kits. Your local Army CPAC also has resume/application information. Some restrictions on e-mail resumes:

   (1) E-mail: se.resume@cpocscr.army.mil

   (2) The subject of the e-mail is Resume

   (3) The resume must be in the body of the email; attachments will not be reviewed due to virus precautions.

c. Resumes may be mailed to the South Central CPOC for inclusion in the SE Resumix database format and information required to submit a mail resume can be found online in our Job Kits available via CPOL (www.cpol.army.mil). Once at CPOL, click on Regional Home Page, South Central Region, Employment Information, then Job Kits. Your local Army CPAC also has resume/application information.

Some restrictions on mailing resumes:

   (1) Mailing Address: South Central Civilian Personnel Operations Center Sparkman Complex, Bldg 5304, Room 4156, Customer Focus Division B

   (2) ATTN: SAMR-CP-SC-B-R Resumix Team, Redstone Arsenal, Alabama 35898

   (3) Faxed resumes are NOT accepted.

   (4) Resumes/self-nominations received in government postage paid envelopes will not be accepted.

Self-nominations

In addition to having a resume on file, you must submit a self-nomination. You may self-nominate by:

a. Using the self-nomination button found at the bottom of this announcement (Preferred Method). Completion of the form and clicking the Submit button will create and send a self-nomination.

b. E-mail a self-nomination.

  (1) E-mail address is selfnom@cpocscr.army.mil

  (2) Subject is selfnom (immediately followed by the announcement number)

c. Mail or fax a self-nomination:

  (1) Fax number is XXX-XXX-XXXX/DSN: XXX-XXXX

  (2) Mailing address is: South Central Civilian Personnel Operations Center, Sparkman Complex, Bldg 5304, Room 4156, Customer Focus Division B, ATTN: SAMR-CP-SC-B-R Resumix Team, Redstone Arsenal, Alabama 35898

A self-nomination form may be obtained from your local Army CPAC or on-line in our Job Kits located via the Army Civilian Personnel Online (CPOL) home page (www.cpol.army.mil). Once at CPOL, click on Regional Pages, South Central Region, Employment Information, then "Job Kits." You may self-nominate by also submitting the following information: Name, Address, Social Security Number, Current Pay Plan, Series and Grade, Source Code, Announcement Number, Pay Plan, Series and Grade of Vacancy, Duty Location of the Vacancy, Closing Date of the Announcement, Lowest Acceptable Grade Level, and your Work Phone Number.

THE DEPARTMENT OF THE ARMY IS AN EQUAL OPPORTUNITY EMPLOYER.

All qualified applicants will receive appropriate consideration without regard to non-merit factors such as race, color, religion, sex, national origin, marital status except where specifically authorized by law, age, politics, disability, or sexual orientation which do not relate to successful performance of the duties of this position. Reasonable accommodation to individuals with disabilities will be provided upon request.

SELECTION FOR THIS POSITION IS SUBJECT TO RESTRICTIONS RESULTING FROM DEPARTMENT OF DEFENSE REFERRAL SYSTEM FOR DISPLACED EMPLOYEES.

Army Civilian Personnel Online (CPOL)

Vacancy Announcement Number: XX-XXXXX-XXX

Opening Date: 06/03/2002

Closing Date: 06/24/2002

Position: ADMINISTRATIVE CLERK
AD-0303-00/00

Salary: $22,655 – $41,876 per year

Promotion Potential: AD-00

Duty Location: 1 vacancy at WASHINGTON, DC

Who May Apply: Open to all qualified persons.

Duties and Responsibilities: The District Court Administration Division (DCAD) is responsible for overseeing the formulation and execution of district court budgets, analyzing their use of resources, developing and monitoring the implementation of effective management procedures, and communicating with the district court clerks. The incumbent of this position will be responsible for the following duties:

1.   Collecting and compiling data submitted from district courts and inputting into specialized databases and spreadsheets.

2.   Compiling data into nationwide reports and providing it to program managers for analysis and program management.

3.   Drafting travel authorizations and compiling reports on the travel of division staff members and managers.

4.   Developing division calendars to track division staff activities.

5.   Monitoring the receipt of court information to ensure courts have filed required reports, and contacting courts by telephone to request submission of required reports.

Qualifications Required: Applicant must have one year of specialized experience equivalent to the next lower grade, which has equipped the applicant with the particular knowledge, skills, and abilities to successfully perform the duties of the position. Experience is typically in or related to the work of the position described.

Knowledges, Skills, and Abilities Required: Candidates should submit a narrative statement on a separate page(s) with specific responses to the knowledge, skills, and abilities (KSAs) in this announcement. Failure to submit your narrative response to the KSAs for this job may negatively affect your eligibility and/or rating for this position.

Supplemental Factors: The following factors are expected to enhance performance significantly in this position. Applicants must submit a narrative statement addressing each factor listed below. Each factor should be addressed separately and include a description of the demonstrated experience that is directly related to the duties, responsibilities, and supplemental factors for this position. Submission of a separate narrative statement for each factor is a MANDATORY requirement.

1.   Ability to use various software applications in the Windows environment (e.g., WordPerfect, Excel, database software).

2.   Ability to organize and structure work assignments to meet deadlines and to effectively utilize work hours.

3.   Ability to deal effectively, in person or by telephone, with senior managers and court staff on a wide variety of nontechnical matters handled by the office.

4.   Ability to review and check work product for accuracy before final preparation of reports.

Basis of Rating: Applicants' experience and education will be rated against the job elements listed. Numerical ratings will be assigned to eligible applicants. Best-qualified applicants will be referred to the selecting official in score order.

Pay, Benefits, and Work Schedule: All federal employees are required by PL 104-134 to have federal payments made by Direct Deposit.

This is a permanent, career-conditional appointment. Selectee will be eligible for health and life insurance, annual (vacation) and sick leave, and will be covered under the Federal Employees Retirement System.

This position will be filled on a full-time permanent basis. Upon completing any required probationary period, the position will be permanent.

Condition of Employment: Under Executive Order 11935, only United States citizens and nationals (residents of American Samoa and Swains Island) may compete for civil service jobs. Agencies are permitted to hire noncitizens only in very limited circumstances where there are no qualified citizens available for the position.

Other Information: This position is in the excepted service. It is excluded from provisions of the career transition assistance program.

VACANCY ANNOUNCEMENT NO.: XX-XX-XX

Position: Clerk-Typist (OFFICE AUTOMATION)

Pay Plan, Series, and Grade: GS-0322-05

Starting Salary: $26,200 PER ANNUM

Opening Date: June 19, 2002

Closing Date: July 10, 2002

No. of Positions: 1

Promotion Potential: NONE

Location: VA CONNECTICUT HEALTH-CARE SYSTEM, WEST HAVEN CAMPUS

Hours Per Week: 40

Contact for Position Information: XXXXX XXXXX AT (XXX) XXX-XXXX Ext. XXXX

Relocation Expenses Paid: NO

OPEN TO ALL U.S. CITIZENS

EQUAL EMPLOYMENT OPPORTUNITY

Actions to fill this position will not be based on discriminatory factors that are prohibited by law.

This announcement is for a permanent, career or career-conditional, appointment.

Descriptions and Duties: Incumbent reads, classifies, and marks material for indexing and cross-referencing in decimal and alphanumeric systems that may be extensively cross-referenced or when subject matter of materials is overlapping or difficult to discern. Creates, copies, edits, calculates, revises, retrieves, stores, and prints a wide range of documents in final form from handwritten drafts such as correspondence, mailing labels, reports, graphs, indices, statistics, calendar, table of contents, etc. involving highly technical and specialized terminology. Receives and answers routine telephone inquiries or refers to appropriate staff member; maintains office files in subject and chronological order. Other duties as assigned.

Qualifications: You must be able to type at least 40 words per minute and you must state your typing speed in your application package. One year of specialized experience, equivalent to the next lower grade level. Specialized experience is that which has equipped the applicant with the particular knowledge, skills, and abilities to perform successfully the duties of the position, and that is typically in or related to the position to be filled.

Applicants must state the hours per week worked and starting and ending date (month and year) for all qualifying experience.

You must demonstrate that you have the qualifications for the position by describing the duties you have regularly performed and the degree of independence you had while performing them.

If your qualifying experience is only part of your job, you must show the actual time, such as number of hours a week or percent of the position, that you spent in doing the qualifying activities in order to receive proper credit. Credit will be given for appropriate unpaid experience or volunteer work. Part-time experience will be prorated in calculating the amount of qualifying experience.

The required amount of experience will not in itself be accepted as proof of qualification for this position. Your application must clearly describe and demonstrate that you have the ability to perform the duties of the position. The primary consideration is the scope, depth, and responsibility level of experience.

Substitution of Education: NONE

Medical/Physical Requirements: The candidate must be able to do the work of the position without harm to self or others.

English Language Proficiency: If you are appointed to a direct patient-care position, you must be proficient in spoken and written English as required by 38 USC 4104(c).

Veterans Preference: A 5-pt. preference is granted to veterans who entered the military service prior to October 14, 1976 or who served between August 2, 1990 through January 2, 1992 or who have served in a military action for which they received a Campaign Badge or Expeditionary Medal. However, you may be entitled to a 10-pt veteran's preference if you are a disabled veteran or Purple Heart recipient; you are the widow, widower, or mother of a deceased veteran. You will need to submit a Standard Form (SF) 15 and proof of your claim.

Basis of Rating: The information you provide on your application/resume determines if you meet the minimum qualifications for this position. The experience on your application/resume, and/or educational documentation, should support the qualifying requirements of the position. If basically qualified, you will be rated and ranked based on your answers to the questions in the Supplemental Questionnaire. It is important that your application or resume contains sufficient information to support the experience and education that you claim in the questionnaire. If you do not provide sufficient information you will be rated ineligible.

Rating Factors: Qualified candidates experience, education, training, and other characteristics will be evaluated based upon the degree they possess the following knowledge, skills, and abilities (KSA). Applicants should submit concise narrative statements on a separate page(s) with specific responses to the following rating factors. Failure to submit your narrative responses to the KSAs may negatively affect your rating for this position.

1. Demonstrate your skill in operating an electronic typewriter, word processor, and related software equipment.

2. Demonstrate your knowledge of processing procedures and functions for several varieties of software and/or advanced software functions to produce a wide range of documents.

3. Demonstrate your knowledge of database software.

4. Demonstrate your knowledge of organization in order to replenish office supplies, set up controls and suspense dates, and respond to requests.

Who May Apply: Applications will be accepted from:

1. Current permanent federal employees who are eligible for transfer.

2. Former permanent federal employees who are eligible for reinstatement.

3. Individuals eligible for appointments based on severe disabilities and 30 percent compensable disabled veterans.

4. Veterans who are eligible for a Veterans Readjustment Appointment (VRA).

    a) Compensably disabled Vietnam Era Veterans or Post Vietnam with disability ratings of 30 percent or greater.

    b) Vietnam Era Veterans who are not disabled or who have a disability rating of less than 30 percent have a period of 10 years from the date of their last discharge from active duty.

    c) Post Vietnam Era Veterans who are not disabled or who have a disability rating of less than 30 percent have a period of eligibility of 10 years from the date of their last discharge from active duty.

5.   Veterans who are preference eligible or who have been separated from the armed forces under honorable conditions after three years or more of continuous active service may apply.

All eligible veterans applying for this position must provide the member with four copies of their DD-214 military discharge papers.

Reinstatement & Transfer Eligible: Reinstatement eligible must submit a copy of their last Notification of Personnel Action (SF-50). Transfer eligible must include a copy of their latest Notification of Personnel Action (SF-50) as well as last performance appraisal.

VACANCY ANNOUNCEMENT NUMBER: XXX-XXXX-XX/XXXXX

Opening Date: 04/20/2002

Closing Date: 06/28/2002

Position: **TAX EXAMINING CLERK**
                           GS-0592-05/05

Salary: $25,822.00 – $33,570.00 per year

Promotion Potential: GS-07

Duty Location: 7 vacancies at Boston Metro area, MA

Who May Apply: Open to all qualified persons.

Major Duties: Provides technical information to taxpayers on a wide range of individual, employment, and excise tax issues including all filing, depositing, and payment requirements. Provides limited assistance in other tax areas. Assists taxpayers in preparation of a variety of tax returns. Resolves refund inquiries and responds orally or in writing to taxpayer inquiries.

Qualifications Required: One year of specialized experience such as accounting, bookkeeping, etc. that indicates ability to acquire the particular knowledge and skills needed to perform the duties of this position.

OR

Four years of education above the high school level.

OR

An equivalent combination of successfully completed education and experience.

Basis of Rating: Ratings will be based on the numerical score you received on your Notice of Results issued by the U.S. Office of Personnel Management.

A written test is required.

Pay, Benefits, and Work Schedule: This is a permanent, career-conditional appointment. Selectee will be eligible for health and life insurance, annual (vacation) and sick leave, and will be covered under the Federal Employees Retirement System.

This position will be filled on a full-time permanent basis. Upon completing any required probationary period, the position will be permanent.

Conditions of Employment: Under Executive Order 11935, only U.S. citizens and nationals (residents of American Samoa and Swains Island) may compete for civil service jobs. Agencies are permitted to hire noncitizens only in very limited circumstances where there are no qualified citizens available for the position.

As a condition of employment, male applicants born after December 31, 1959, must certify that they have registered with the Selective Service System, or are exempt from having to do so under the Selective Service Law.

A background security investigation will be required for all new hires. Appointment will be subject to the applicant's successful completion of a background security investigation and favorable adjudication. Failure to successfully meet these requirements will be grounds for termination.

Selectee must undergo appropriate tax checks prior to appointment. This position requires completion of a one year probationary period.

Fingerprints will be required as part of the preemployment process.

Other Information: First consideration will be given to CTAP and ICTAP eligibles.

Veterans—Long. You must clearly identify your claim for veterans preference on your application.

5-POINT PREFERENCE. A 5-point preference is granted to veterans who served prior to 1976 and served at least six months on active duty. Those who served after 1980 and 1982 must have served at least two years on active duty.

A 5-point preference is also granted to veterans who served on active duty during the Gulf War from August 2, 1990 through January 2, 1992. The law grants preference to anyone who is otherwise eligible and who served on active duty during this period regardless of where the person served or for how long. "Otherwise eligible" means that the person must have been released from the service under honorable conditions and must have served a minimum of two years on active duty, or if a reservist, must have served the full period for which called to active duty.

If you are claiming a 5-point veteran preference, please provide a DD-214, Certificate of Release or Discharge from Active Duty, or other proof of entitlement. Tentative preference will be granted in the absence of paperwork.

10-POINT PREFERENCE. You may be entitled to a 10-point veteran preference if you are a disabled veteran; you have received the Purple Heart; you are the spouse or mother of a 100 percent disabled veteran; or, you are the widow, widower, or mother of a deceased veteran. If you are claiming 10-point veteran preference, you will need to submit an SF-15, Application for 10-point Veteran Preference, plus the proof required by that form.

If you make a false statement in any part of your application, you may not be hired; you may be fired after you begin work; or you may be subject to fine, imprisonment, or other disciplinary action.

This agency provides reasonable accommodations to applicants with disabilities. If you need a reasonable accommodation for any part of the application and hiring process, please notify the agency. The decision on granting reasonable accommodation will be on a case-by-case basis.

THE IRS IS COMMITTED TO ENSURING THAT ALL EMPLOYEES PERFORM IN A MANNER WARRANTING THE HIGHEST DEGREE OF PUBLIC CONFIDENCE AND DEMONSTRATE THE HIGHEST LEVEL OF ETHICS AND INTEGRITY.

VACANCY ANNOUNCEMENT NUMBER: XXX-XXXX

Opening Date:	06/14/2002
Closing Date:	06/28/2002
Position:	**EXECUTIVE ASSISTANT** FP-0318-07/05
Salary:	$31,716–$58,280 per year
Duty Location:	1 vacancy at Washington Metro Area, DC

All applications must be postmarked by the closing date and received within 5 working days after that date.

Location:	Inter-America and Pacific Region (IAP)
Area of Consideration:	Washington, DC ALL SOURCES

Salary Range: FP-7 $31,716–$46,576   **SUPERVISORY:** No
FP-6 $35,479–$52,101
FP-5 $39,686–$58,280

Duties: This position is located in the immediate office of the Regional Director for the Inter-America and Pacific (IAP) region. The incumbent serves as an executive assistant responsible for collecting, researching, and summarizing information related to any of the program areas falling under the Regional Director (RD) and for performing administrative duties in support of the RD. Prepares regular and special summary records and reports; makes necessary arrangements for meetings and conferences; assembles background materials for the RD and prepares reports of conference proceedings; makes all necessary travel arrangements for the RD and completes travel vouchers.

Career Ladder: FP-5 is the full performance level for this position. If selected from this vacancy announcement at a lower level, the employee may be considered for promotion without further competition.

Mandatory Qualifications: In order to be selected for this position, applicants must be U.S. citizens, must not have been employed in intelligence-related activities, and must submit applications that clearly documents how they meet each of the following mandatory requirements.

Applicants must have at least one year of specialized experience equivalent to the next lower grade in the Federal Service. The one year of specialized experience must have included managing and coordinating the functions of an office to include (1) reviewing, researching, analyzing, and interpreting data; and (2) drafting letters and reports. All requirements must be met by July 28, 2002.

Desired Qualifications: The following qualifications are not mandatory for selection to this position. However, highly-competitive applicants will have most of the following: (1) experience in reviewing and controlling correspondence and other documents; (2) experience in administrative work such as making arrangements for meetings, conferences, and travel; (3) experience in meeting and dealing with people at all levels inside and outside an organization including the public; and (4) experience in using computers and word processing software, preferably Macintosh and Microsoft Word. To receive maximum consideration, it is essential that applicants specifically address how they meet the Mandatory and Desired Qualifications.

Competitive Service Student Trainee Positions: This standard describes the qualification requirements for student trainee positions made under career-conditional or career appointments in the competitive service. This standard is not applicable to students who are temporarily employed during summer vacations and who have not been appointed to a student trainee program in the competitive service as described above.

A student may be appointed to any position that leads to qualification in a two-grade interval professional, administrative, or technical occupational series and that provides an opportunity for the student's growth and development toward the target position.

A list of the occupational series covered by this standard is provided below.

REQUIREMENTS FOR INITIAL APPOINTMENT

Student trainees qualify as described below.

GRADE	LEVEL OF EDUCATION
GS-2	High school diploma or equivalent
GS-3	Completion of 1 academic year of post-high school study
GS-4	Completion of 2 academic years of post-high school study or associate's degree

The required education must lead to a bachelor's degree with specialization in or directly related to the field in which the student trainees will receive training on the job. The degree of specialization in this field must satisfy on graduation the specific educational requirements in the qualification standard for the corresponding two-grade interval positions.

Promotion Requirements: Student trainees may be promoted to higher-graded trainee positions based on completion of portions of the education and student trainee work experience.

To GS-3: Completion of one full semester or the equivalent of post-high school study and one period of student trainee work experience.

To GS-4: (a) Completion of one academic year of study and two periods of student trainee work experience; or (b) completion of $1\frac{1}{2}$ academic years of study and one period of student trainee work experience.

Upon completion of all the requirements for a bachelor's degree in an appropriate field, student trainees may be reassigned or promoted in the appropriate target series to GS-5 or GS-7 if they meet the qualification requirements of the target occupation, including minimum educational requirements, if any.

Explanation of Terms: An academic year of undergraduate education is defined as 30 semester hours, 45 quarter hours, or the equivalent in an accredited college or university.

For purposes of this standard, a period of student trainee work experience is the equivalent of two months (320 hours) of full-time work experience.

Test Requirements: A written test is not required for these positions.

OCCUPATIONAL COVERAGE

A list of the occupational series covered by this qualification standard is provided below.

GS-099 General Student Trainee

GS-199 Social Science Student Trainee

GS-299 Personnel Management Student Trainee

GS-399 Administration and Office Support Student Trainee

GS-499 Biological Science Student Trainee

GS-599 Financial Management Student Trainee

GS-699 Medical and Health Student Trainee

GS-799 Veterinary Student Trainee

GS-899 Engineering and Architecture Student Trainee

GS-999 Legal Occupations Student Trainee

GS-1099 Information and Arts Student Trainee

GS-1199 Business and Industry Student Trainee

GS-1299 Copyright and Patent Student Trainee

GS-1399 Physical Science Student Trainee

GS-1499 Library and Archives Student Trainee

GS-1599 Mathematics and Statistics Student Trainee

GS-1699 Equipment and Facilities Management Student Trainee

GS-1799 Education Student Trainee

GS-1899 Investigation Student Trainee

GS-1999 Quality Inspection Student Trainee

GS-2099 Supply Student Trainee

GS-2199 Transportation Student Trainee

VACANCY ANNOUNCEMENT NUMBER: XXXX-XX-XX

Opening Date:	06/07/2002
Closing Date:	06/20/2002
Position:	ANIMAL PACKER WG-5001-07/07
Salary:	$14.14/hour
Duty Location:	Many vacancies at YOSEMITE NAT'L PARK, CA

This is a re-advertisement of these vacancies. Previous applicants need not reapply to be considered.

These positions are located in the Maintenance Division, Roads and Trail Branch, and the Utilities Branch, Backcountry Utilities, at various park locations. Multiple vacancies may be filled through this announcement. Positions listed are projected vacancies. Total work under these temporary/seasonal positions is expected to last from 3 to 6 months (not to exceed 1,039 hours in a service year) beginning March – September 2002. Positions may be terminated or extended at any time prior to the end of the projected season. Tour of duty will normally be 40 hours per week and may include periods of overtime work, holiday work, night shifts, and weekend work. This announcement will be used to fill vacancies that occur through September 30, 2002. Positions may also be filled on a part-time or intermittent basis at management's discretion.

Area Information: Positions are at various locations within Yosemite National Park. Yosemite Valley is located 208 miles from San Francisco, 81 miles from Merced, and 94 miles from Fresno. Shopping, dental, medical, postal, and laundry services are available in the park. Some positions are located in isolated, backcountry wilderness settings. Elevation at the Valley floor is approximately 4,000 feet. The park is open year-round with the majority of activities occurring during the busy season from March through October.

Housing Information: Government housing (some with accommodations for the disabled) within the park MAY be available on a limited basis and assigned based on management's needs. Nongovernment housing may be available in the local communities of Groveland, Mariposa, Midpines, Bootjack, Catheys Valley, and Oakhurst.

Who May Apply: Applications will be accepted from: Open to the Public. Applicants must be U.S. citizens at least 18 years of age or 16 years of age and a high school graduate.

This is a mandatory drug and alcohol testing designated position under Department of Transportation and REQUIRES a valid Class A license and a current first aid certification.

Major Duties: Incumbent will pack supplies, materials, and equipment for loading onto pack mules. Will lead mules and transport supplies to backcountry trail crew camps throughout the park. Is responsible for making minor repairs to pack equipment and tack. Is responsible for shoeing saddle horses and pack mules in remote backcountry locations. Selectee must possess a California Class A Commercial Drivers License with correct endorsements. Please indicate this information on your application.

Qualifications Required: Selective factor—You must have a current valid California Class A Commercial Drivers License or equivalent from another state and must state this in your application to qualify. Your application must demonstrate that you have the ability to perform the duties of these positions without more than normal supervision. The following Supplemental Experience Statement must accompany your application to ensure you receive full credit for your experience and training.

Knowledge, Skills, and Abilities Required:

1. Ability to perform various skills of packer and animal caretaker occupations without more than normal supervision (SCREEN-OUT)—SUPPLEMENTAL EXPERIENCE STATEMENT REQUIRED—See section on "Other Information."

2. Ability to use and maintain applicable equipment and hand tools.

3. Ability to perform strenuous physical labor.

4. Ability to work safely.

YOU MUST SUBMIT SUPPLEMENTAL EXPERIENCE STATEMENTS IDENTIFIED BELOW WITH YOUR APPLICATION.

A SUPPLEMENTAL EXPERIENCE STATEMENT/MOTOR VEHICLE OPERATOR QUALIFICATIONS STATEMENT IS REQUIRED. This is a mandatory drug and alcohol testing designated position under the Department of Transportation regulations. Please provide your license number, class, and expiration date on your application. Failure to provide this information on your application may result in you not receiving further consideration.

Basis of Rating: For CTAP and ICTAP, well-qualified means that the applicant meets the qualification standard and eligibility requirements for the position, meets minimum educational and experience requirements, meets all selective factors where applicable, and is able to satisfactorily perform the duties of the position upon entry.

Ratings will be based on an evaluation of your experience as it relates to the qualification requirements and on the knowledge, skills, and abilities (KSAs) listed. You should provide detailed evidence of the KSAs in your application in the form of clear, concise examples showing level of accomplishment and degree of responsibility. Applicants who meet the minimum qualifications will be listed alphabetically and considered for appointment in Priority Group Order:

Group I: Qualified applicants entitled to 10-point preference who have a compensable service connected disability of 10 percent or more;

Group II: All other qualified applicants entitled to 10-point preference and 5-point preference;

Group III: All other qualified applicants.

Pay, Benefits, and Work Schedule: This is a temporary appointment not to exceed 1,039 hours. May work various shifts, weekends, and holidays.

All federal employees are required by PL 104-134 to have federal payments made by direct deposit.

Conditions of Employment: This is an alcohol and drug testing designated position (DOT/CDL). Under Executive Order 11935, only U.S. citizens and nationals (residents of American Samoa and Swains Island) may compete for civil service jobs. Agencies are permitted to hire noncitizens only in very limited circumstances where there are no qualified citizens available for the position.

As a condition of employment, male applicants born after December 31, 1959 must certify that they have registered with the Selective Service System, or are exempt from having to do so under the Selective Service Law.

A background security investigation will be required for all new hires. Appointment will be subject to the applicant's successful completion of a background security investigation and favorable adjudication. Failure to successfully meet these requirements will be grounds for termination.

Other Information: If claiming 5-point veterans' preference, a DD-214 must be submitted. If claiming 10-point veterans' preference, both a DD-214 and SF-15 must be submitted.

Your Social Security number is requested under the authority of Executive Order 9397 to uniquely identify your records from those of other applicants' who may have the same name. As allowed by law or presidential directive, your SSN is used to seek information about you from employers, schools, banks, and other who may know you. Failure to provide your SSN on your application materials will result in your application not being processed.

Before being hired, you will be required to sign and certify the accuracy of the information in your application if you have not done this using an application form such as the OF-612.

If you make a false statement in any part of your application, you may not be hired; you may be fired after you begin work; or you may be subject to fine, imprisonment, or other disciplinary action.

Applicants with disabilities will receive consideration for reasonable accommodations in the hiring process for any physical, mental, or emotional impairment. Applicants should submit requests for reasonable accommodation with their job applications and provide supporting medical documentation. The decision on granting reasonable accommodation will be on a case-by-case basis.

For additional information regarding this position and to obtain application materials, contact:

HUMAN RESOURCES
(XXX) XXX-XXXX
TDD Phone number: (XXX) XXX-XXXX

The federal government is an Equal Opportunity Employer. Selection for this position will be made without regard to political, religious, or labor organization affiliation or nonaffiliation, marital status, race, color, sex, national origin, nondisqualifying handicapping condition or age.

Please include the following supplemental experience statement with your application.

SUPPLEMENTAL EXPERIENCE STATEMENT

ANIMAL PACKER, WG-5001-07

ANNOUNCEMENT NUMBER: XXXX-XX-XX

NAME OF APPLICANT:_____

SELECTIVE FACTOR: You must possess a valid Class A California State Drivers License or equivalent. Please provide the following:

Class:_____ CDL Number (or equivalent):_____

Expiration Date:_____

KSA 1. Ability to perform various skills of the packer and animal caretaker occupations without more than normal supervision (SCREEN-OUT)

Tell about your experiences packing and transporting supplies and materials to remote backcountry locations by horse or mule. Did you have a helper or helpers? Was your supervisor always available for assistance with non-routine assignments?

Do you have experience packing and transporting supplies and equipment of unusual size and proportions or weight? Have you ever transported explosives or other dangerous material? Give examples of items packed.

List and describe the types of hitches you have used in transporting materials.

Briefly describe your experience in handling, tending, and hauling horses and mules.

Describe equipment you have used to haul stock.

Describe your background in training and riding horses (trained and untrained).

Describe the extent of your experience in shoeing horses and mules in backcountry locations.

Describe your knowledge of veterinary first aid and horse and mule nutrition.

How many and what types of pack animals have you led on a string? Describe the terrain over which you have had to lead them.

KSA 2. Ability to use and maintain pertinent equipment and handtools

For each of the tools listed below, indicate whether you are U (unskilled), S (skilled), E (expert, journeyman level), or I (capable of instruction):

-saddles

-bridles

-hobbles

-horseshoes

-harnesses

-forges

-anvils

-hoof nippers

-dental floats

-rasps

-hammers

-knives

-punches

-curry combs

-sling and cargo ropes

-cargo boxes

-manties

-others (list)

KSA 3. Ability to perform strenuous physical labor

Tell about your job or home duties that show you can perform strenuous, sustained physical labor.

What athletic sports or hobbies do you participate in that require physical stamina?

KSA 4. Ability to work safely

Have you had any job related accidents within the last five years? If so, indicate the nature of the injury, work days lost, date, and job being done at time of accident.

Have you completed any safety or first aid training within the last three years?

If so, list below:

Type of training   When received   Completed?

List any certificates you have received.

Please complete the following Supplemental Experience Statement and submit with your application:

MOTOR VEHICLE OPERATION SUPPLEMENT EXPERIENCE STATEMENT

1. TRAFFIC VIOLATIONS: Provide the information requested below for each time you were given a ticket or arrested for breaking a driving law during the past five years. Do not include any record where you were found not guilty. Do not include parking tickets. Please provide:

Type of violation

Month/year

City, county, state

Details of action taken (e.g., length of suspension or amount of fine)

While on ice?

License revoked or suspended?

Fined or forfeited collateral?

Sentenced?

2. DRIVERS INFORMATION: Please provide the following:

Permit or license number

State in which issued

Date of expiration

Type/class of license

Restriction

Other states where you obtained a license during the past five years (indicate type of license obtained).

3. ACCIDENT RECORD: Please provide the following information for each accident

you have had during the past five years, whether your fault or not:

Type of accident

Month/year

City, county, state

Amount of damage to your car

Amount of damage to other party's car

Did your insurance company make payment to the other party?

Describe charges placed against you, if any

Details of action taken (sentence, length of suspension, or fine)

While on the job?

Were you judged at fault?

Was anyone killed?

License revoked or suspended?

Fined or forfeited collateral?

Sentenced?

4. EVIDENCE OF SAFE DRIVING:

Have you received a safety award? Date received:

Have you ever received a citation for safe driving or for being a safe worker? Date received:

Have you ever received a discount on your automobile insurance for a good driving record? Date received:

Did you ever successfully complete a course in Driver Education? Date completed:

I certify the above stated levels of experience are true and correct to the best of my knowledge.

_____

Signature of applicant and date

COMPETITIVE STUDENT SERVICE TRAINEE POSITIONS

VACANCY ANNOUNCEMENT NUMBER: XX XX-STUDENT

Opening Date:	08/01/2001
Closing Date:	Open until further notice
Position:	ARCHIVES AID GS-1421-02/03
Salary:	$8.66–$9.45 per hour
Duty Location:	Many vacancies at ST. LOUIS, MO

Location: NARA, National Personnel Records Center, 9700 XXXX Avenue, St. Louis, MO.

Duties: The majority of positions open and sort mail, pull and refile records, arrange and shelve records from other government agencies, and/or relocate records within the center. Some positions serve as a clerk performing various office automation and/or clerical tasks. Office automation positions involve typing form letters, memos, and other routine correspondence or performing data entry.

Work Environment: Work may be performed in a moderately heated and uncooled warehouse setting where there is dust and dirt.

Physical Requirements: For positions involving pulling and refiling records, applicants must be physically able to climb caster-equipped ladders and handle boxes of records weighing up to 50 pounds that are stored up to 14 feet above the floor. Positions involve considerable standing, walking, stooping, bending, and lifting.

Eligibility Requirements: To be eligible for student employment, applicants must be pursuing an educational program, e.g., technical or vocational school, two-year community college, four-year college or university, graduate school, etc. Applicants must be currently enrolled or accepted for enrollment as a degree-seeking student and must carry at least a half-time course load.

Qualifications Required: For the GS-2 level, applicants must have three months of general/clerical experience or be a high school graduate.

For the GS-3 level, applicants must have six months of general/clerical experience or have one year of college (i.e., 30 semester or 45 quarter hours).

For positions requiring typing or office automation skills, applicants must be able to type 40 words per minute.

Other Information: Appointments are generally made for a one-year period, but may be for a shorter period. Appointments may be extended in one-year increments as long as the employee continues to be eligible for a student appointment. Work schedules may be full-time or part-time. Work schedules will be arranged to accommodate school schedules. These appointments will not lead to permanent employment in the competitive federal service. Enrollment in Direct Deposit/Electronic Funds Transfer is mandatory as a condition of employment for all new employees.

VACANCY ANNOUNCEMENT NUMBER: XX-XX-XXX

Opening Date:	06/04/2002
Closing Date:	Open until further notice
Position:	BUSINESS AND INDUSTRY STUDENT TRAINEE GS-1199-04/04
Salary:	$22,759–$29,582 per year
Promotion Potential:	GS-04
Duty Location:	1 vacancy at Sacramento, CA

THIS ANNOUNCEMENT HAS BEEN AMENDED TO CHANGE STATUS TO OPEN UNTIL FILLED AREA OF CONSIDERATION* LIMITED TO LOCAL COMMUTING AREA BECAUSE OF NATURE OF THE POSITION, WHICH REQUIRES STUDENT STATUS AND PART-TIME EMPLOYMENT DURING SCHOOL YEAR.

*This position is part of the Student Career Experience Program. The program requires participants to be enrolled in a four-year college in a field related to the position being filled. In this instance, the participant must be enrolled in a business curriculum. The program also requires that Indian Health Service, the student, and the school sign a written agreement as to the nature of work assignment, schedule of work assignments and class attendance, evaluation procedures, requirements for continuation, and successful completion of the program. Individuals who successfully complete the program and work at least 640 hours prior to receipt of their degree may be converted to a full-time career-conditional position as a contract specialist, GS-1102-5 (target GS-11) within 120 days following graduation without further competition.

Brief Description of Duties: Employee works in the Contracts and Grants Branch, which performs contracting services for the California Area Office. Contracts are for services and supplies that the California Area Office needs to support its own operation and for direct care and Indian contracted health-care services. The employee will assist contract specialists in various pre-award and post-award activities, including assisting in the development of statements of work, data requirements, monitoring, and closing out contracts.

Qualification Requirements: Each applicant must meet the following requirements:

1) Have successfully completed at least two academic years of study beyond the high school level;

2) Be currently enrolled or accepted for enrollment as a degree-seeking student and must be taking at least a half-time academic load in an accredited four-year college or university in a business-related curriculum. The definition of half-time is the definition provided by the school in which the student is enrolled; and

3) Be a U.S. citizen.

Method of Evaluating and Ranking Candidates: Your official transcripts along with a resume will be used to determine if you meet these requirements. Applicants who meet the basic qualification requirements described in this announcement will be further evaluated to determine the extent to which they possess the knowledge (K), skills (S), and abilities (A) described below. All applicants should provide clear, concise examples that show level of accomplishment or degree to which they possess the KSAs as a separate attachment.

1. Ability to analyze financial information

2. Ability to meet tight deadlines and handle multiple tasks

3. Ability to tactfully interact with others

4. Ability to write

VACANCY ANNOUNCEMENT NUMBER: XXXX-CODE XXX-XXX

Opening Date: 10/10/2001

Closing Date: 10/10/2002

Position: CHEMIST (STUDENT TRAINEE)
GS-1399-03/07

Salary: $8.54 per hour–$14.50 per hour

Duty Location: Many vacancies at San Diego, CA

Open to all qualified persons.

Major Duties: This is a trainee position. The trainee assists the Project Manager and staffed Geologists/Engineers/Chemists in preparing permits and reports, performs soil and groundwater samples, takes various site measurements, and serves as a field point of contact. Incumbent receives exposure to standard geological, chemical, and engineering practices, and field equipment used in sampling, air monitoring, excavation, surveying, drilling, and related Site Assessment and Remediation activities. Incumbent is in a training capacity under direct supervision of a Project Manager or staff Geologist/Engineer/Chemist.

Qualifications Required: U.S. citizenship (A noncitizen who is lawfully admitted to the United States as a permanent resident or who is otherwise authorized to be employed may be considered for the SCEP. To be eligible for conversion the student must be a U.S. citizen). Enrolled, or accepted for enrollment, as a degree-seeking (or certificate/diploma) student in an accredited high school, technical, or vocational school, two- or four-year college/university, or graduate or professional school. Enrolled for at least a half-time academic course load, maintain a satisfactory school standing, and a minimum of 2.0 Grade Point Average. Must meet the college/university cooperative education (SCEP) requirements. School curriculum must be related to the SCEP position for which applying.

Basis of Rating: The SCEP program is a planned career development program that integrates classroom theory with related, paid work experience in a Department of the Navy organization. The SCEP is a partnership between the student, the college or training institution, and the Department of the Navy. The program is designed to provide planned progressive student employment opportunities leading to possible permanent federal employment.

Pay, Benefits, and Work Schedule: Supplemental income, paid holidays, vacation and sick leave, salary increases, promotional opportunities, health and life insurance, plus other optional benefits.

Gain on-the-job experience in field of study and realistic exposure to career opportunities.

May work full-time or part-time. Number of hours a student can work per week is flexible, as long as the work schedule does not interfere with academic requirements.

VACANCY ANNOUNCEMENT NUMBER: XXXXXXXXXX

Opening Date: 02/13/2002

Closing Date: 06/28/2002

Position: CLERK
GS-0303-02/02

Salary: $19,255 per year–$24,227 per year

Duty Location: Many vacancies at Santa Barbara county, California, CA

Applications Will Be Accepted From:

Open to the General Public.

Students enrolled or accepted for enrollment as a degree seeking student taking at least a half-time academic, technical, or vocation course load in an accredited high school, technical, vocational, two- or four-year college or university, graduate, or professional school.

Current career or career-conditional permanent non-Air Force federal employees; previous career or career-conditional permanent federal employees with reinstatement eligibility; veterans with a 30 percent or more service-connected disability; veterans eligible for Veterans' Readjustment Appointment (VRA); individuals eligible under Executive Order 12721; permanent Air Force employees in a Leave Without Pay (LWOP) status.

THIS POSITION MAY BE FILLED WITH A: CURRENT CAREER OR CAREER-CONDITIONAL PERMANENT NON-AIR FORCE FEDERAL EMPLOYEES; PREVIOUS CAREER OR CAREER-CONDITIONAL PERMANENT FEDERAL EMPLOYEES WITH REINSTATEMENT ELIGIBILITY; VETERANS WITH A 30 PERCENT OR MORE SERVICE-CONNECTED DISABILITY; VETERANS ELIGIBLE FOR VETERANS READJUSTMENT APPOINTMENT (VRA); INDIVIDUALS ELIGIBLE UNDER EXECUTIVE ORDER 12721; PERMANENT AIR FORCE EMPLOYEES IN A LEAVE WITHOUT PAY (LWOP) STATUS.

LIST ALL ELIGIBILITIES (NONCOMPETITIVE APPOINTMENT, TEMP, STEP, ETC.) THAT YOU ARE ELIGIBLE FOR UNDER QUESTION 2 IN THE SUPPLEMENTAL DATA AREA OF THE RESUME. IF YOU ARE CURRENTLY A STUDENT, YOU MUST LIST ELIGIBILITY "STEP" TO BE CONSIDER UNDER THAT CATEGORY. SEE AIR FORCE JOB KIT AT WWW.AFPC.RANDOLPH.AF.MIL/AFJOBS.HTM FOR MORE INFORMATION REGARDING ELIGIBILITIES.

THIS IS A TEMPORARY SUMMER EMPLOYMENT POSITION LASTING UP TO 120 DAYS. EMPLOYMENT DATES ARE FROM APPROXIMATELY MAY THROUGH SEPTEMBER. ACTUAL LENGTH OF EMPLOYMENT IS CONTINGENT UPON BUDGET, WORKLOAD, AND WEATHER.

SELF-NOMINATION CANDIDATES WILL BE REFERRED EVERY TWO WEEKS BEGINNING IN MARCH ON AN AS NEEDED BASIS UNTIL ALL POSITIONS ARE FILLED.

Major Duties: The primary purpose of this position is to perform a variety of routine, recurring clerical work in office, business, or fiscal operations, requiring training and experience gained from previous work experience and training. Receives telephone calls and visitors. Answers the telephone and refers callers/visitors to appropriate personnel based on specific name or functional area request. Relays routine information when no subject matter knowledge is involved. Takes and delivers messages when staff members are unavailable. Makes and keeps appointment calendar following specific instructions from staff members. Processes incoming mail. Picks up, receives, opens, sorts, and distributes mail to appropriate individuals following specific instructions. Checks accuracy of address indicators that appear wrong. Delivers other correspondence to other offices as directed. Maintains a mail control log. Prepares and maintains office records of various types. Sorts, codes, and files documents in an established alphabetical or simple subject-matter filing system.

Obtains information from files as requested. From detailed instructions, prepares and maintains forms such as time sheets and timecards for personnel within the office. Performs routine, miscellaneous clerical work. Reproduces and assembles copies of a variety of correspondence as instructed. Uses office copying machines. Utilizes FAX machines. Maintains and orders office supplies, as requested by other staff members.

Qualification Requirements: Qualification Standards for General Schedule Clerical and Administrative Support Positions for GS-303 Series, dated 22 Mar 99:

3 Months General Experience

Or

High School Diploma or Equivalent

Recruitment Knowledge, Skills, and Abilities (KSA):

1. Ability to learn general office administrative and clerical procedures to distribute mail, answer telephone, make appointments, and file material.

2. Ability to learn organization and functions sufficient to receive visitors, telephone calls, and distribute mail by specific name/functional area.

3. Ability to read and interpret specific procedural guides such as instructions, manuals, established policies and procedures for assigned tasks such as filing, distributing mail, or ordering supplies, which are directly applicable to the work.

Conditions of Employment: NONE

SELF-NOMINATION MUST BE RECEIVED BY THE CLOSING DATE OF THE ANNOUNCEMENT.

Due to security reasons, the Air Force Personnel Center's (AFPC) civilian employment Web site is currently restricted to .mil (military) domains until further notice.

If you are unable to access our Web at www.afpc.randolph.af.mil/afjobs, you may obtain employment information, job vacancy announcements, and self-nomination (apply) through the AFPC Job Line.

External Applicants: X-XXX-XXX-XXXX

Internal Applicants: X-XXX-XXX-XXXX

Job Conditions: This is a summer job.

Temporary employment not to exceed one year.

Position includes evening and weekend work.

Temporary employment only.

Salary includes locality pay.

Selection of this position is contingent upon proof of U.S. citizenship.

Basis of Rating: Applicants will be rated on an evaluation of the quality and extent of experience, education, and training as described in their resume to the knowledge, skills, and abilities (KSAs) listed in this announcement.

Pay, Benefits, and Work Schedule: The General Schedule (GS) basic pay schedule, which may vary by geographic locality, is based on "comparability with local prevailing rates," which means that your pay is based on what private industry is paying for similar work levels in similar pay areas.

Other Information: This agency provides reasonable accommodations to applicants with disabilities. If you need a reasonable accommodation for any part of the application and hiring process, please notify the agency. The decision on granting reasonable accommodation will be on a case-by-case basis. This position is subject to provisions of the DOD Priority Placement Program and the Interagency Career Transition Assistance Plan Program (ICTAP).

We recommend you visit the following Web sites for bases in which you are interested for information on the local community, cost of living expenses, education, employment, housing availability, relocation, and support services:

Standard Installation Topic Exchange Service: www.dmdc.osd.mil/sites

Official public Air Force sites: www.af.mil/sites

The Department of Air Force will not pay or assume liability for personal travel, moving expenses, or other relocation costs incurred in accepting employment, except under very unusual circumstances.

PROFESSIONAL AND SCIENTIFIC POSITIONS

This qualification standard covers positions in the General Schedule that involve the performance of two-grade interval professional and scientific work. The specific requirements for entry into each occupation covered by this standard may also have individual occupational requirements.

Basic Requirements for All Grades

Applicants who meet the basic requirements described in the individual occupational requirements are fully-qualified for the specified entry grade (generally grade GS-5). Applicants who wish to qualify for positions at higher grade levels (generally grade GS-7 and above) must also meet the requirements shown in the table on page 120, in addition to meeting the basic requirements.

The individual occupational requirements typically provide at least two methods for applicants to meet the basic requirements of the occupations covered by this standard:

(A)   Successful completion of a full four-year course of study in an accredited college or university leading to a bachelor's or higher degree that included a major field of study or specific course requirements, which is described in paragraph A in the individual occupational requirements.

Where specific course requirements are not indicated in paragraph A, the number of semester hours required to constitute a major field of study is the amount specified by the college or university attended. If this number cannot be obtained, 24-semester hours will be considered as equivalent to a major field of study. The nature and quality of this required course work must have been such that it would serve as a prerequisite for more advanced study in the field or subject-matter area. Related course work generally refers to courses that may be accepted as part of the program major.

OR

(B)   Appropriate combination of education and experience that is typically specified in paragraph B of the individual occupational requirements. The "paragraph B" method generally requires that an applicant possess a core of educational credit, such as described in paragraph A above, plus additional education and/or experience. The method of determining the number of semester hours required to constitute a major field of study is the same as described in paragraph A.

The quality of the combination of education and experience must be sufficient to demonstrate that the applicant possesses the knowledge, skills, and abilities required to perform work in the occupation, and is comparable to that normally acquired through the successful completion of a full 4-year course of study with a major in the appropriate field. In addition to courses in the major and related fields, a typical college degree would have included courses that involved analysis, writing, critical thinking, research, etc. These courses provided an applicant with the skills and abilities sufficient to perform progressively more responsible work in the occupation. Therefore, creditable experience should have demonstrated similarly appropriate skills or abilities needed to perform the work of the occupation.

The individual occupational requirements for some series make no provision for combining experience and education. Therefore, they do *not* include paragraph B provisions.

For a small number of occupations or positions covered by this standard, applicants may possess certain kinds of experience *in lieu* of education. In such cases, applicants may meet minimum qualification requirements through experience equivalent to a four-year degree. These situations are generally described in paragraph C of the individual occupational requirements.

Applicants whose experience is used to meet the basic requirements through a paragraph B or C provision may qualify for grades above the entry level if that experience includes one year of specialized experience. In such cases, the specialized experience would have to be evaluated to determine if it is at the appropriate grade level in the normal line of progression.

Additional Experience and Education Requirements for GS-7 and Above

In addition to meeting the basic entry qualification requirements, applicants must have specialized experience and/or directly related education in the amounts shown in the table below.

GRADE/ POSITIONS	EDUCATION	SPECIALIZED EXPERIENCE
GS-7	one year of graduate-level education *or* superior academic achievement	one year equivalent to at least GS-5
GS-9	two years of progressively higher level graduate education leading to a master's degree *or* master's or equivalent graduate degree	one year equivalent to at least GS-7
GS-11	three years of progressively higher level graduate education leading to a Ph.D. degree *or* Ph.D. or equivalent doctoral degree	one year equivalent to at least GS-9
GS-12 and above		one year equivalent to at least next lower grade level
Research Positions		
GS-11 research positions	Master's or equivalent graduate degree	one year equivalent to at least GS-9
GS-12 research positions	Ph.D. or equivalent doctoral degree	one year equivalent to at least GS-11
GS-13 and above research positions		one year equivalent to at least the next lower grade level

Note: Education and experience may be combined for all grade levels for which both education and experience are acceptable.

While the levels of experience shown for most positions covered by this standard follow the grade level progression pattern outlined above, users of the standard should refer to the OPM Web site at: www.opm.gov/qualifications/SEC-II/S2-TOC.HTM for guidance on crediting experience for positions with different lines of progression.

Combining Education and Experience: When combining education with experience, first determine the applicant's total qualifying education as a percentage of the education required for the grade level; then determine the applicant's experience as a percentage of the experience required for the grade level; finally, add the two percentages. The total percentage must equal at least 100 percent to qualify an applicant for that grade level. For example, an applicant for a GS-184, Sociology, position has successfully completed 60 undergraduate semester hours, including 24-semester hours in sociology, and, in addition, has two full-time years of appropriate experience that demonstrates that the applicant possesses the necessary analytical and communication skills. The applicant would qualify for GS-5, since the 60-semester hours (the equivalent of two years of undergraduate education, or 50 percent of the total requirement) were supplemented by two additional years of appropriate experience that provided the remaining 50 percent of the total required education and experience.

Specialized Experience: Experience that equipped the applicant with the particular knowledge, skills, and abilities to perform successfully the duties of the position and that is typically in or related to the work of the position to be filled. To be creditable, specialized experience must have been equivalent to at least the next lower grade level in the normal line of progression for the occupation in the organization.

Superior Academic Achievement: The superior academic achievement provision is applicable to all occupations covered by this standard. See the "General Policies and Instructions" for specific guidance on applying the superior academic achievement provision.

Graduate Education: Completion of graduate-level education in the amounts shown in the table, in addition to meeting the basic requirements, is qualifying for positions at grades GS-7 through GS-11, and GS-12 research positions if it provided the knowledge, skills, and abilities necessary to do the work. One year of full-time graduate education is considered to be the number of credit hours that the school attended has determined to represent one year of full-time study. If that number cannot be obtained from the school, 18-semester hours should be considered an academic year of graduate study. Part-time graduate education is creditable in accordance with its relationship to a year of full-time study at the school attended.

Research Positions: Positions that primarily involve scientific inquiry or investigation, or research-type exploratory development of a creative or advanced scientific nature, where the knowledge required to perform the work successfully is typically and primarily acquired through graduate study (master's or equivalent degree for GS-11, Ph.D. or equivalent for GS-12). The work is such that the academic preparation will equip the applicant to perform the full range of professional work of the position after a short orientation period.

1. Qualification on the basis of education: Applicants for such research positions can be considered qualified for GS-11 if they possess an appropriate master's or equivalent graduate degree and qualified for GS-12 if they possess a Ph.D. or equivalent doctoral degree.

2. Qualification on the basis of experience: Applicants who furnish positive evidence that they have performed highly creative or outstanding research that has led or can lead to major advances in a specific area of research, to a major advance in the discipline or field of science involved, or to major advances in science in general, can be rated under this provision for highly demanding research positions requiring similar abilities. Under these circumstances, applicants can be rated eligible for the next higher grade level above that for which they would normally be rated, provided they have not been rated eligible at this higher grade on the basis of meeting the graduate study requirements described in paragraph 1 above. To receive this rating, the work must have been creative in the sense that it developed a basic principle, product, concept, method, approach, or technique; or it provided a body of basic information that opened the way for a major advance in the discipline or field of science involved, or to advances in science in general, by providing a method of solving other problems, opening areas of research, or providing the means of exploiting the application of science in a major area.

   Applicants cannot receive an "extra" grade for education and an additional "extra" grade for appropriate experience.

Combination of Graduate Education and Professional Experience: Combinations of successfully completed graduate level education and specialized experience may be used to meet total experience requirements. Only graduate level education in excess of the amount required for the next lower grade level may be combined with experience. For example, an applicant with six months of appropriate experience equivalent to GS-7 (50 percent of the experience requirement for GS-9) and 27 semester hours of appropriate graduate education (50 percent of the education requirement for GS-9, in excess of that required for GS-7) would be qualified for a GS-9 position (assuming that there is no evidence that the attended college or university requires more than 18-semester hours as equivalent to a year of graduate study).

Using Selective Factors for Positions Covered by This Standard

There are a variety of situations where agencies would be warranted in limiting consideration to applicants who possess the particular qualifications required to perform the work of positions covered by this standard. For example, an agency may require specific kinds of training appropriate for filling positions concerned with scientific research and development activities, or may require specific educational courses or combinations of courses (where the individual occupational requirements permit applicants to qualify based on several combinations of educational course work) to meet other specialized agency requirements. An agency filling an international economist position may require knowledge of international economics. In this case, since applicants can qualify on the basis of education, the agency may require certain types of educational courses. Similarly, in some cases, consideration may be limited only to those applicants who possess an appropriate license, registration, or certification, if possession of such is determined to be necessary for carrying out the responsibilities of a position and/or required by statute.

Occupational Coverage

A list of the occupational series covered by this qualification standard is provided below. All occupational series covered by this standard have individual occupational requirements.

GS-020 Community Planning

GS-101 Social Science

GS-110 Economist

GS-130 Foreign Affairs

GS-131 International Relations

GS-140 Manpower Research and Analysis

GS-150 Geography

GS-170 History

GS-180 Psychology

GS-184 Sociology

GS-185 Social Work

GS-190 General Anthropology

GS-193 Archeology

GS-401 General Biological Science

GS-403 Microbiology

GS-405 Pharmacology

GS-406 Agricultural Extension

GS-408 Ecology

GS-410 Zoology

GS-413 Physiology

GS-414 Entomology

GS-415 Toxicology

GS-430 Botany

GS-434 Plant Pathology

GS-435 Plant Physiology

GS-436 Plant Protection and Quarantine

GS-437 Horticulture

GS-440 Genetics

GS-454 Rangeland Management

GS-457 Soil Conservation

GS-460 Forestry

GS-470 Soil Science

GS-471 Agronomy

GS-480 General Fish and Wildlife Administration

GS-482 Fishery Biology

GS-485 Wildlife Refuge Management

GS-486 Wildlife Biology

GS-487 Animal Science

GS-493 Home Economics

GS-510 Accounting

GS-511 Auditing

GS-512 Internal Revenue Agent

GS-601 General Health Science

GS-630 Dietitian and Nutritionist

GS-631 Occupational Therapist

GS-633 Physical Therapist

GS-635 Corrective Therapist

GS-637 Manual Arts Therapist

GS-638 Recreation/Creative Arts Therapist

GS-639 Educational Therapist

GS-644 Medical Technologist

GS-665 Speech Pathology and Audiology

GS-690 Industrial Hygiene

GS-696 Consumer Safety

GS-801 General Engineering

GS-803 Safety Engineering

GS-804 Fire Protection Engineering

GS-806 Materials Engineering

GS-807 Landscape Architecture

GS-808 Architecture

GS-810 Civil Engineering

GS-819 Environmental Engineering

GS-830 Mechanical Engineering

GS-840 Nuclear Engineering

GS-850 Electrical Engineering

GS-854 Computer Engineering

GS-855 Electronics Engineering

GS-858 Biomedical Engineering

GS-861 Aerospace Engineering

GS-871 Naval Architecture

GS-880 Mining Engineering

GS-881 Petroleum Engineering

GS-890 Agricultural Engineering

GS-892 Ceramic Engineering

GS-893 Chemical Engineering

GS-894 Welding Engineering

GS-896 Industrial Engineering

GS-1015 Museum Curator

GS-1221 Patent Adviser

GS-1223 Patent Classifying

GS-1224 Patent Examining

GS-1226 Design Patent Examining

GS-1301 General Physical Science

GS-1306 Health Physics

GS-1310 Physics

GS-1313 Geophysics

GS-1315 Hydrology

GS-1320 Chemistry

GS-1321 Metallurgy

GS-1330 Astronomy and Space Science

GS-1340 Meteorology

GS-1350 Geology

GS-1360 Oceanography

GS-1370 Cartography

GS-1372 Geodesy

GS-1373 Land Surveying

GS-1380 Forest Products Technology

GS-1382 Food Technology

GS-1384 Textile Technology

GS-1386 Photographic Technology

GS-1420 Archivist

GS-1510 Actuary

GS-1515 Operations Research

GS-1520 Mathematics

GS-1529 Mathematical Statistician

GS-1530 Statistician

GS-1550 Computer Science

GS-1701 General Education and Training

GS-1710 Education and Vocational Training

GS-1720 Education Program

GS-1725 Public Health Educator

GS-1730 Education Research

GS-1740 Education Services

GS-1750 Instructional Systems

VACANCY ANNOUNCEMENT NUMBER: XXXXXX

Opening Date: 11/08/2001

Closing Date: 09/30/2002

Position: AERONAUTICAL INFORMATION SPECIALIST
NI-1361-01/03

Salary: $30,693–$74,405 per year

Duty Location: Many vacancies at ST. LOUIS, MO

NOTE: Applicants who have previously applied to this announcement do not need to reapply.

NOTE: This announcement will be used to establish a deferred inventory of applicants. Limited opportunities exist. Your resume will be maintained for twelve months. If you wish consideration beyond twelve months, you will need to resubmit an updated resume. Top Secret security clearance and access to Sensitive Compartmented Information (TS/SCI) is required. This process may take up to one year or more to be completed.

Who May Apply: Open to all qualified persons.

Major Duties: Serves as an Aeronautical Analyst that specializes in matters concerning military and civil aeronautical and air facility data. This encompasses knowledge of all phases of flight including planning, enroute, and terminal. The Aeronautical Analyst evaluates information from many sources, analyzes, edits, and converts data to meet specifications, and compiles and publishes all products required for operational flight navigation. Analysts use computer systems and specialized software to maintain an aeronautical database and extract aeronautical information from imagery to support a wide variety of products. Analysts work cooperatively with their counterparts in the U.S. armed services, Federal Aviation Administration (FAA), National Ocean Service (NOS), the U.S. intelligence community, and many foreign aeronautical offices to provide timely, accurate information and products.

Qualifications Required:

1. Experience and Education Combination—Experience that demonstrates a knowledge of the various types of work in the field of aeronautical operations such as:

    (a) Civilian or military operational flight experience as a captain, pilot, copilot, navigator, or navigation instructor that averaged a minimum of 200 hours of flying time per year accumulative to 800 hours of flying time; OR

    (b) Civilian or military air traffic control experience involving the application of procedures and knowledge of such operations, including shift-type or supervisor responsibilities at a high-density station, center, or tower; OR

    (c) Instruction in navigation (including celestial) and techniques at an accredited college or university or U.S. Training School, or other comparable experience; OR

    (d) Civilian or military experience in the aeronautical field, which involved the acquisition, collection, selection, analysis, evaluation, and preparation of reliable aeronautical information on navigation and related operations, including publications related to navigation. The following education requirements are highly desired: Undergraduate and/or graduate education that included 30 semester hours of study at an accredited college or university, 9 semester hours of which must be in mathematics, statistics, physics, navigation, astronomy, geography, meteorology, engineering, cartography, computer/computer science, aeronautical, or other Geographic Information System (GIS) subjects.

OR

2. The following higher education may substitute for the requirements of a combination of experience and education. Undergraduate and/or graduate education from an accredited college or university that includes a minimum of 60-semester hours. Twenty-four of those 60 hours must meet the following criteria:

    (a) Nine of the 60-semester hours must include Private Pilot Ground School (3 hours), Commercial Pilot Ground School (3 hours), and Instrument Pilot Ground School (3 hours).

    (b) Fifteen additional semester hours of the 60 must be in mathematics, statistics, physics, navigation, astronomy, geography, meteorology, engineering, cartography, computer/computer science, aeronautical, or other Geographic Information System (GIS) subjects.

Desired Qualifications but NOT Required: A private pilot license, commercial pilot license, instrument pilot license, air transport pilot, certified flight instructor, certified flight instructor instrument, or control tower operator licenses are not required for the occupation, but they are highly desired. Final salary determinations will be commensurate with the depth and breadth of competencies demonstrated in the resume and transcripts.

NOTE: Application packages will be accepted from students in accredited schools as noted above or who expect to complete all of the scholastic requirements within one year after filing their applications. Completion of academic requirements will be subject to verification at the time of appointment. Submit a legible photocopy of college transcript at the time of application. A second copy of the transcript showing date and type of degree(s) conferred may be submitted once degree requirements are completed.

Physical Requirements: The work is primarily sedentary with occasional walking and carrying of light items required. The majority of work is performed in a normal office environment that is well-lighted, heated, and ventilated. Color Vision is required; the ability to distinguish red and green colors is mandatory.

Basis of Rating: APPLICANT'S EXPERIENCE AND EDUCATION WILL BE RATED AGAINST CRITICAL SKILLS NECESSARY FOR SUCCESSFUL JOB PERFORMANCE.

Pay, Benefits, and Work Schedule: This position requires shift work and may include evening and weekend work.

All federal employees are required by PL 104-134 to have federal payments made by direct deposit.

Conditions of Employment: Under Executive Order 11935, only U.S. citizens and nationals (residents of American Samoa and Swains Island) may compete for civil service jobs. Agencies are permitted to hire noncitizens only in very limited circumstances where there are no qualified citizens available for the position.

In accordance with Executive Order 12564, applicants selected for this position are required to submit to a drug test and receive a negative drug test result prior to appointment. In addition, this position is a drug-testing designated position subject to random testing for illegal drug use.

The individual selected will be subject to random drug testing.

A background security investigation will be required for all new hires. Appointment will be subject to the applicant's successful completion of a background security investigation and favorable adjudication. Failure to successfully meet these requirements will be grounds for termination.

The selectee must be able to obtain and keep a Top Secret security clearance.

Physical Examination (May Be Required).

Color Vision (Required).

Travel Overseas (Required).

Shift Work (May Be Required).

Permanent Change of Station (PCS)—includes travel/transportation expenses (pending available funds).

Other Information:

1. NIMA positions are in the Excepted Service under 10 USC 1601 appointment authority. All candidates must be U.S. citizens and are subject to a thorough background inquiry and medical examination. You and your immediate family members (i.e., mother, father, brothers, sisters, spouse, and children) must be U.S. citizens to obtain the required security clearances, except in rare cases. Some positions may be subject to a polygraph examination. All applicants tentatively selected for this position will be required to submit to urinalysis to screen for illegal drug use prior to appointment. Employees are required to sign an agreement not to disclose, in any fashion, classified information to unauthorized persons. Participation by civilian employees in the DOD Direct Deposit/Electronic Fund Transfer of Pay Program is required.

2. NIMA IS AN EQUAL OPPORTUNITY EMPLOYER. Applicants are assured of equal consideration regardless of race, sex, age, religion, color, national origin, lawful political affiliation, marital status, sexual orientation, membership in an employee organization, or nondisqualifying physical or mental disability.

3. This agency provides reasonable accommodation to applicants with disabilities. If you need a reasonable accommodation for any part of the application and hiring process, please notify Human Resources at (314) 263-4888 or DSN 693-4888, Ext. 138.

4. NIMA has implemented pay banding for all former General Schedule (GS) employees. The NIMA system consists of five pay bands and does not include regularly scheduled within grade increases. Annual performance evaluations determine the amount of increase within a pay band an employee will receive. The annual promotion process determines those employees who move to a higher band. The *basic salary ranges and equivalent GS grade levels for the five pay bands are:

Pay Band 01 $14,757–$38,493 (Equivalent to GS-01 through GS-07)

Pay Band 02 $31,191–$51,854 (Equivalent to GS-08 through GS-10)

Pay Band 03 $41,684–$68,274 (Equivalent to GS-11 through GS-12)

Pay Band 04 $59,409–$95,948 (Equivalent to GS-13 through GS-14)

Pay Band 05 $82,580–$112,863 (Equivalent to GS-15)

* These are the basic pay amounts. The federal government has established numerous pay localities to provide locality pay adjustments that add to total pay according to geographic duty locations.

VACANCY ANNOUNCEMENT NUMBER: XXXXXXX-ROTATOR

Open: 04/24/2002

Close: UNTIL FILLED

Vacancy announcement may close fourteen days from opening date without notice.

The National Science Foundation is seeking qualified candidates for a position to be filled in the Division of Atmospheric Sciences, Directorate for Geosciences. The Division manages and coordinates the foundation-wide atmospheric sciences activities. The selected candidate will be assigned to the Atmospheric Chemistry Program (ATC) within the Division of Atmospheric Sciences (ATM). This position will be filled at the level of Associate Program Director.

We have specific interest in people with expertise in the tropospheric or stratospheric chemistry, biogeochemical cycles, and/or chemistry of atmospheric aerosols.

Position will be filled on a one or two year Visiting Scientist Appointment, Temporary Appointment or under the terms of the Intergovernmental Personnel Act (IPA). Temporary and Visiting Scientist appointments will be made under the Excepted Authority of the NSF Act. For temporary appointments of more than one year, the usual civil service benefits (retirement, health and life insurance) are applicable. For Visiting Scientist appointments, individuals are in a non-pay leave status from the home institution and are appointed to NSF's payroll as a federal employee. NSF withholds Social Security and provides reimbursement for fringe benefits. For IPA assignments, the individual remains on the payroll of his/her institution and the institution continues to administer pay and benefits. NSF reimburses the institution for NSFs negotiated share of the costs. Individuals eligible for an IPA assignment include employees of state and local government agencies, institutions of higher education, Indian tribal governments, federally funded research and development centers, and qualified nonprofit organizations. The individual remains an employee of the home institution.

Duties and Responsibilities: Assists in the implementation, review, funding, post-award management, and evaluation of the program and contributes to the intellectual integration with other programs supported by the Division. Designs and implements the proposal review and evaluation process for relevant proposals. Selects well-qualified individuals to provide objective reviews on proposals either as individuals or as members of a panel. Conducts final review of proposals and evaluations, and recommends acceptance or declination. Manages and monitors on-going grants, contracts, interagency and cooperative agreements to ensure fulfillment of commitments to NSF. Evaluates progress of awards through review and evaluation of reports and publications submitted by awardees and/or meetings at NSF and during site visits. Contributes to the responsibility for establishing goals and objectives, initiating new program thrusts and phasing out old projects. Recommends new or revised policies and plans in scientific, fiscal, and administrative matters to improve the activities and management of the program.

Qualifications Required: For the Associate Program Director level, applicants must have a Ph.D. or equivalent experience in one of the above disciplines plus four or more years of successful research, research administration, and/or managerial experience.

The salary range, which includes a locality pay adjustment, is from $66,226–$104,336 per annum depending on qualifications and experience. Individuals interested in applying for this vacancy should submit a resume or any application of your choice to the National Science Foundation, Division of Human Resource Management, XXXX Wilson Blvd., Arlington, VA 22230, Attn: XXXXXXXXX-Rotator. In addition, you are asked to complete and submit the attached Applicant Survey form. Submission of this form is voluntary and will not affect your application for employment (the information is used for statistical purposes). Announcements may be accessed electronically on the Web at www.nsf.gov/jobs/.

The National Science Foundation provides reasonable accommodations to applicants with disabilities on a case-by-case basis. If you need a reasonable accommodation for any part of the application and hiring process, please notify the point of contact listed on this vacancy announcement.

NSF IS AN EQUAL OPPORTUNITY EMPLOYER COMMITTED TO EMPLOYING A HIGHLY QUALIFIED STAFF THAT REFLECTS THE DIVERSITY OF OUR NATION.

VACANCY ANNOUNCEMENT NUMBER: XXXXXXXXX

Opening Date: 01/02/2002

Closing Date: Open until further notice

Position: **ASTRONOMER (PROGRAM DIRECTOR)** AD-1330-04/04

Salary: $74,697–$116,414 per year

Promotion Potential: AD-04

Duty Location: 1 vacancy at Arlington, VA

ANNOUNCEMENT NO: XXXXXXXXX

OPEN: 1/2/2002 CLOSE: OPEN UNTIL FILLED

THIS VACANCY HAS BEEN AMENDED TO INCLUDE THE TEMPORARY POSITION.

THIS POSITION MAY BE FILLED ON A TEMPORARY, 1- OR 2- YEAR VISITING SCIENTIST, OR INTERGOVERNMENTAL PERSONNEL ACT (IPA) BASIS. INDIVIDUALS WISHING TO APPLY FOR A PERMANENT APPOINTMENT: SEE VACANCY ANNOUNCEMENT XXXXXXXXX.

Initial assignments under the IPA may be made for a period of up to two years. Individuals eligible for an IPA assignment include employees of State and local government agencies or institutions of higher education, Indian tribal governments, and other eligible organizations in instances where such assignments would be of mutual benefit to the organizations involved. The individual remains an employee of the home institution and cost-sharing arrangements are generally negotiated between NSF and the home institution.

Position Vacant: Astronomer (Program Director), AD-1330-4. Salary ranges from $74,697 to $116,414 per annum.

Promotion Potential: Astronomer (Program Director), AD-4.

Location: Directorate for Mathematical and Physical Sciences, Division of Astronomical Sciences, Optical and Infrared Facilities Unit, Arlington, VA.

Bargaining Unit Status: This position is included in the bargaining unit and will be filled in accordance with the merit staffing provisions of the Collective Bargaining Agreement, Article VIII.

Area of Consideration: All Sources.

THIS POSITION IS OUTSIDE THE COMPETITIVE CIVIL SERVICE

Appointment to this position will be made under the Excepted Authority of the NSF Act. Candidates who do not have civil service status or reinstatement eligibility will not obtain civil service status if selected. Candidates currently in the competitive civil service will be required to waive competitive civil service rights if selected. Usual civil service benefits (retirement, health benefits, life insurance) are applicable for temporary appointments of more than one year. Disabled veterans with 30% service-connected disabilities as well as other applicants with severe disabilities will be considered without regard to the closing date if applications are received prior to final selection.

Duties and Responsibilities:

• Provide expert scientific and technical knowledge in the sub-disciplines of science assigned to the Program.

• Manage Program or Centers' resources with appropriate scientific judgment to insure integrity and consistency in the grants/declination or Centers management process without conflicts-of-interest, to insure balance among appropriate subfields and institutions, and to insure participation by all qualified scientists. Incorporate cross-directorate responsibilities into Program or Center administration.

• Manage a merit review process for evaluation of proposals in the subdisciplines assigned to the Program.

• Advise and assist in the development of short- and long-range plans and in establishing goals and objectives for the Program. Plan the budget for the Program considering past, present and future-year experiences and projections; allocate and distribute resources within the budget; and manage post-award evaluation.

• Represent the Program, Division, and Foundation within the scientific community, with other NSF Division, with other agencies and organizations, and with the public.

Qualifications Required: Applicants must have a Ph.D. or equivalent experience in astronomy or a related field of science, plus at least six years of successful research, research administration, and/or managerial experience beyond the Ph.D. pertinent to the position.

Conditions of Employment: Appointment to this position is contingent upon successful completion of the appropriate background investigation. Satisfactory completion of a one year-trial period is also required.

How to Apply: You may apply for this position with the Optional Application for Federal Employment (OF-612), the older Application for Federal Employment (SF-171), a resume, or other application format of your choice - so long as it contains the necessary information (summarized below). You must also submit a current Performance Appraisal or letter(s) of recommendation from professionals who can comment on your capabilities. In order to ensure full consideration, it is recommended that you submit a supplemental statement which specifically addresses how your background and experience relate to each Quality Ranking Factor listed on this announcement.

You must specify the job announcement number, and title and grade(s) of the job for which you are applying. You should also provide the following information:

- Your country of citizenship.

- Your social security number.

- Information about your education, including (1) high school graduation date and (2) college/university information - your major, and type and year of degree(s). If no degree, show total credits earned and indicate whether they are semester or quarter hours.

- Information about all your work experience related to this job, including job titles, duties and accomplishments, employer's name and phone number, number of hours worked per week, starting and ending dates (month and year), and annual salary. If you held various positions with the same employer, describe each separately. If you have federal civilian experience, indicate the highest grade held, the job series, and dates held.

- The brochure Applying for a Federal Job provides information on the federal job application process; it is available by calling the number listed below. If your application does not provide all the information requested in the vacancy announcement, you may lose consideration for this job.

The National Science Foundation provides reasonable accommodations to applicants with disabilities on a case-by-case basis. If you need a reasonable accommodation for any part of the application and hiring process, please notify the point of contact listed on this vacancy announcement.

Submit all application material to:

> National Science Foundation
> Division of Human Resource Management
> Arlington, VA 22230

Attn: Announcement Number XXXXXXXX.

In addition to the required application materials, you are asked to complete and submit the attached Applicant Survey form. Submission of this form is voluntary and will not affect your application for employment. The information is used for statistical purposes only. ALL FORMS MUST BE RECEIVED BY THE CLOSING DATE OF THIS ANNOUNCEMENT.

NSF IS AN EQUAL OPPORTUNITY EMPLOYER COMMITTED TO EMPLOYING A HIGHLY QUALIFIED STAFF THAT REFLECTS THE DIVERSITY OF OUR NATION.

ADMINISTRATIVE AND MANAGEMENT POSITIONS

VACANCY ANNOUNCEMENT NUMBER: XXXXXXX

Opening Date: 05/06/2002

Closing Date: 06/28/2002

Position: ACCOUNTANT/POLICY ANALYST (TL)
GG-0501-12/13

Salary: $55,694–$86,095 per year

Promotion Potential: GS-13

Duty Location: 1 vacancy at ROCKVILLE, MD

Who May Apply: Open to all qualified persons.

Major Duties:

**PLEASE APPLY AS SOON AS POSSIBLE. SELECTING OFFICIAL MAY REQUEST CERTIFICATE OF ELIGIBLES WITHIN SIXTEEN DAYS OF OPENING DATE OF ANNOUNCEMENT.

**APPLICANTS SHOULD SPECIFY THE GRADE LEVEL(S) FOR WHICH THEY WISH TO BE CONSIDERED. FAILURE TO SPECIFY WILL RESULT IN CONSIDERATION ONLY AT THE HIGHEST GRADE QUALIFIED.

Incumbent serves as Team Leader of the Payments Team responsible for the audit and payment of all types of travel and commercial vouchers, covering services received by NRC under contracts, interagency agreements, purchase orders, training request, Government bills of lading, personal services contracts, and other miscellaneous payments. These payments must be in compliance with the Prompt Payment Act.

Qualifications Required: Applicant must have one year of specialized experience equivalent to the next lower grade, which has equipped the applicant with the particular knowledge, skills, and abilities to successfully perform the duties of the position. Experience is typically in or related to the work of the position described.

PLEASE NOTE: THIS POSITION MAY BE FILLED AS GG-510 ACCOUNTANT (TEAM LEADER) OR GG-501 POLICY ANALYST (TEAM LEADER).

Candidates must have at least one year of specialized experience at the next lower grade level or equivalent.

Basic Qualifications for Accountant: Candidates must have knowledge of accounting principles and standards as evidenced by a four-year degree that included at least 24-semester hours in accounting OR an equivalent combination of college-level education (at least 24-semester hours in accounting courses), training that provided professional accounting knowledge, and accounting experience.

Basic Qualifications for Policy Analyst: Candidates must have at least one year of specialized experience at the next lower grade level or equivalent. Specialized experience is experience that equipped the applicant with the particular knowledge, skills, and abilities to perform successfully the duties of the position, and that is typically in or related to the work of the position to be filled. To be creditable, specialized experience must have been equivalent to at least the next lower grade level.

Knowledge, Skills, and Abilities Required: Candidates should submit a narrative statement on (a) separate page(s) with specific responses to the knowledge, skills, and abilities (KSAs) in this announcement. Failure to submit your narrative response to the KSAs for this job may negatively affect your eligibility and/or rating for this position.

Basis of Rating: Applicants meeting basic eligibility requirements will be rated and ranked on the knowledge, skills, and abilities, and other characteristics (KSAs) required to perform the duties of the position. Please carefully review the KSAs. Include in the write-ups such things as experience in and out of federal service that gave you the specific knowledge, skill, or ability; objectives of your work; and evidence of your success (such as accomplishments, awards received, etc.)

APPLICANTS ARE REQUIRED TO ADDRESS THE RATING FACTORS LISTED BELOW:

1. Comprehensive knowledge of generally accepted federal accounting practices and experience applying GAO, GSA, OMB, and treasury regulations to apply policies, principles and standards, procedures, and systems consistent with federal requirements.

    Example: Describe specific experience, training, and developmental assignments that demonstrate your knowledge of and ability to apply policies and procedures, and interpret, analyze, and apply the various Federal laws, OMB directives, GSA, GAO, and treasury regulations related to federal accounting, travel, and accounts payable activities. Describe the type, scope, and complexity of the activities you have participated in. What were your duties and activities you participated in? Provide specific examples and accomplishments.

2. Knowledge of applying techniques, principles, and procedures regarding processing and recording invoices and travel vouchers.

    Example: Describe specific work experience, training, and developmental assignments that demonstrate your knowledge and ability to apply techniques, principles, regulations, and procedures in processing invoices and travel vouchers. Describe work experience or training in processing and recording invoices and travel vouchers that required you to review and analyze purchase orders, training requests, travel authorizations, statement of work, contracts, automatic clearing house information, electronic funds transfers, interagency agreements, work orders, commitments, obligations, and various financial reports. Provide specific examples and accomplishments.

3. Thorough knowledge of the capabilities, applications, and skills in the use of microcomputers, financial management systems, and associated software to accomplish work assignments.

    Example: Describe your specific experience, education, training, and accomplishments that demonstrate your knowledge of and ability to utilize computer-based systems applications including databases, spreadsheets, and financial systems. What specific software and/or system have you used? What were your duties and responsibilities?

4. Demonstrated skill in presenting information, ideas, and advice in a clear, concise, and logical manner, both orally and in writing.

    Example: Describe specific experience, training, and accomplishments that demonstrate your ability to communicate information both orally and in writing. Describe your experience with furnishing system assistance and advice to staff and training users in the operation of time and labor and payroll systems. Describe the various types and level of individuals you communicate with. What kind of information was provided and for what purpose? Include examples of presentations you have given and the types of original writing you routinely perform. What were your most challenging writing assignments?

5. Demonstrated ability or potential to provide leadership and effectively utilize human resources.

    Example: Describe specific experience, training, and assignments that demonstrate your ability or potential to provide leadership, project management, or supervision as evident by success in areas such as: resolving difficult and complex problems; formulating program goals and objectives; planning long-term and short-term program activities; establishing and controlling procedures and schedules of work products or programs; establishing methods for evaluating the effectiveness of work programs and procedures; providing oversight, guidance, training, and direction to personnel of diverse backgrounds to foster a motivated and effective work atmosphere; and effectively utilizing human resources.

Note: Breadth, recency, and length of experience in the field; training, awards, and commendations; past and current performance; and community or outside professional activities will be considered as they relate to each of the above factors to determine the level of knowledge, skill, or ability of candidates.

Salary Range: $55,694–$86,095 PER ANNUM

IF CLAIMING 5-POINT VETERANS PREFERENCE, YOU MUST ATTACH A COPY OF YOUR DD-214, CERTIFICATE OF RELEASE OR DISCHARGE FROM ACTIVE DUTY, OR OTHER PROOF OF ELIGIBILITY. IF CLAIMING 10-POINT VETERANS PREFERENCE, YOU MUST ATTACH AN SF-15, APPLICATION FOR 10-POINT VETERANS PREFERENCE, PLUS THE PROOF REQUIRED BY THAT FORM.

THE NRC PROVIDES REASONABLE ACCOMMODATIONS TO APPLICANTS WITH DISABILITIES WHERE APPROPRIATE. IF YOU NEED A REASONABLE ACCOMMODATION FOR ANY PART OF THE APPLICATION AND HIRING PROCESS, PLEASE NOTIFY THE DISABILITY PROGRAM COORDINATOR AT 000–000–0000. DETERMINATIONS ON REQUESTS FOR A REASONABLE ACCOMMODATION WILL BE MADE ON A CASE-BY-CASE BASIS.

EXECUTIVE AGENCIES ARE PROHIBITED FROM ACCEPTING OR CONSIDERING APPLICANTS FOR COMPETITIVE APPOINTMENTS FOR POSITIONS BASED ON POLITICAL RECOMMENDATIONS FROM MEMBERS OF CONGRESS, CONGRESSIONAL EMPLOYEES, ELECTED STATE OR LOCAL GOVERNMENT OFFICIALS, AND POLITICAL PARTY OFFICIALS. SUCH OFFICIALS MAY ONLY SUPPLY STATEMENTS REGARDING THE CHARACTER AND RESIDENCE OF THE APPLICANT.

Pay, Benefits, and Work Schedule: All federal employees are required by PL 104-134 to have federal payments made by direct deposit.

This position will be filled on a full-time permanent basis. Upon completing any required probationary period, the position will become permanent.

Conditions of Employment: Under Executive Order 11935, only U.S. citizens and nationals (residents of American Samoa and Swains Island) may compete for civil service jobs. Agencies are permitted to hire noncitizens only in very limited circumstances where there are no qualified-citizens available for the position. As a condition of employment, male applicants born after December 31, 1959, must certify that they have registered with the Selective Service System, or are exempt from having to do so under the Selective Service Law.

A background security investigation will be required for all new hires. Appointment will be subject to the applicant's successful completion of a background security investigation and favorable adjudication. Failure to successfully meet these requirements will be grounds for termination.

Occasional travel may be required.

Other Information: Applications will be accepted from status and nonstatus candidates. Candidates who wish to be considered under both merit promotion and competitive procedures must submit two (2) complete applications. When one (1) application is received, it will be considered under the merit promotion announcement.

This position is in the excepted service. It is excluded from provisions of the career transition assistance program.

Time in grade restrictions must be met by the closing date of the announcement.

Identification of promotion potential in this position does not constitute a commitment or an obligation on the part of management to promote the employee selected at some future date. Promotion will depend upon administrative approval and the continuing need for an actual assignment and performance of higher level duties.

Competitive status is not required for mentally retarded or severely physically disabled applicants eligible for appointment under Section 213.3102 (T) or (U) of Schedule A, and 30 percent or more disabled veterans eligible for appointment under 5 CFR 16.402 (b) (5), and veterans eligible for a Veterans Readjustment Appointment (VRA) under 5 CFR 307.103.

Veterans—Long. You must clearly identify your claim for veterans' preference on your application.

5-POINT PREFERENCE. A 5-point preference is granted to veterans who served prior to 1976 and served at least six months on active duty. Those who served after 1980 and 1982 must have served at least two years on active duty.

A 5-point preference is also granted to veterans who served on active duty during the Gulf War from August 2, 1990 through January 2, 1992. The law grants preference to anyone who is otherwise eligible and who served on active duty during this period regardless of where the person served or for how long. "Otherwise eligible" means that the person must have been released from the service under honorable conditions and must have served a minimum of two years on active duty, or if a reservist, must have served the full period for which called to active duty.

If you are claiming a 5-point veteran preference please provide a DD-214, Certificate of Release or Discharge from Active Duty, or other proof of entitlement. Tentative preference will be granted in the absence of paperwork.

10-POINT PREFERENCE. You may be entitled to a 10-point veteran preference if you are a disabled veteran; you have received the Purple Heart; you are the spouse or mother of a 100 percent disabled veteran; or, you are the widow, widower, or mother of a deceased veteran. If you are claiming 10-point veteran preference, you will need to submit an SF-15, Application for 10-point Veteran Preference, plus the proof required by that form.

Your Social Security number (SSN) is requested under the authority of Executive Order 9397 to uniquely identify your records from those of other applicants who may have the same name. As allowed by law or presidential directive, your SSN is used to seek information about you from employers, schools, banks, and others who may know you. Failure to provide your SSN on your application materials will result in your application not being processed.

Before being hired, you will be required to sign and certify the accuracy of the information in your application if you have not done this using an application form such as the OF-612.

If you make a false statement in any part of your application, you may not be hired; you may be fired after you begin work; or you may be subject to fine, imprisonment, or other disciplinary action.

Employees who received a buyout and subsequently return to positions in federal agencies, whether by re-employment or contracts for personal services, are generally obligated to repay the full amount of the buyout to the agency that paid it.

VACANCY ANNOUNCEMENT NUMBER: XX-XX-XX (READVERTISEMENT)

Opening Date: 06/10/2002

Closing Date: 06/24/2002

Position: ACCOUNTING SPECIALIST
GS-0501-07/11

Salary: $30,597–$58,867 per year

Promotion Potential: GS-11

Duty Location: 1 vacancy at Nashville, TN
                            Eastern Regional Office,
                            Office of the Deputy Regional Director,
                            Branch of Finance, Nashville, TN

GS-11: $45,285–$58,867 per annum

GS-09: $37,428–$48,652 per annum

GS-07: $30,597–$39,779 per annum

Who May Apply: BUREAU-WIDE / NATIVE AMERICAN PREFERENCE ELIGIBLES / CURRENT OR FORMER CAREER STATUS FEDERAL EMPLOYEES

Major Duties: Under the general supervision of the Accounting Officer, the incumbent is responsible for maintaining and controlling all records and documents for timely and accurate processing and encoding through the Federal Finance System. Reviews, analyzes, researches, and processes obligations, modifications, change documents, vendor updates, levy, and income assignments; and check cancellations for appropriate accounting information, documents, appropriations, funds, and programs. Maintains accounts that include the reviewing of the correction of paid documents to verify accounting data and necessary subsequent entries. Completes and reviews transaction coding for input of financial data into automated accounting systems. Provides technical advice, guidance, and information on financial matters and recommends corrective revisions. Assists in the preparation of reports and correspondence regarding bureau organizations, regulatory authority, Congress, vendors and departmental bureaus. Reviews and analyzes various financial reports and researches files and correspondence to accomplish special assignments. Monitors computerized reject reports to identify discrepancies and recommends corrective actions.

Qualifications Required: (OPM Operating Manual, Qualification Standards for Two-Grade Interval Administrative and Management Positions and/or BIA Excepted Standards, GS-0501).

GS-11: One year of specialized experience equivalent to the GS-9 grade level OR Ph.D. or equivalent doctoral degree or three full years of progressively higher level graduate education leading to such a degree or LL.M., if related.

GS-09: One year of specialized experience equivalent to the GS-7 grade level OR master's or equivalent graduate degree or two full years of progressively higher level graduate education leading to such a degree or LL.B. or J.D., if related.

GS-07: One year of specialized experience equivalent to the GS-5 grade level OR one full year of graduate level education or superior academic achievement.

Specialized Experience: Experience that is directly related to the position to be filled and that has equipped the candidate with the particular knowledge, skills, and abilities to successfully perform the duties of the position.

Superior Academic Achievement: Superior Academic Achievement (S.A.A.) must have been gained in a curriculum that is qualifying for the position to be filled. S.A.A. is based on (1) Class standing—applicants must be in the upper third of the graduating class, based on completed courses; or (2) grade-point average—applicants must have a grade-point average of 3.0 or higher out of a possible 4.0 based on four years of education, or as computed based on courses completed during the final two years of the curriculum; or 3.5 or higher out of a possible 4.0 based on the average of the required courses completed in the major field completed during the final two years of the curriculum; or (3) election to membership in a National Scholastic Honor Society—membership in a freshman honor society cannot be used to meet the requirements of this provision.

Basis of Rating: All applicants for this position will be rated and ranked based upon the extent and quality of their experience, training, and/or education as reflected on the application. Applicants will be further evaluated according to the degree to which they possess or have the potential to acquire KSAs, and personal characteristics as listed below. The judgment of qualifications will be based on the material submitted; therefore, it is to the applicant's advantage to give complete and thorough responses and to present information in a neat and orderly fashion. Qualifications and veteran's preference eligibility will be determined on the basis of information submitted.

Knowledges, Skills, and Abilities Required: A supplemental questionnaire may be written on plain paper or addressed within the body of your application or resume describing your qualifications, experience, and/or education related to the following KSAs in the following order:

1.   Knowledge of accounting techniques and procedures to make a thorough analysis involving analytical and accounting inferences (e.g., logical, deduction, conclusion, appropriate, summation, judgment, etc.).

2.   Knowledge of the bureau's computerized Federal Finance System payment and accounting system for processing of financial documents.

3.   Knowledge of cash management, disbursements, prompt payment, federal obligations, and electronic fund transfer laws, regulations, and procedures.

4.   Ability to communicate effectively, both orally and in writing.

Basis of Rating: The information provided in the KSA responses will be heavily relied upon in the rating process. Applicants must prepare a concise narrative addressing EACH of the KSAs listed. Show how your experience and/or education provided you with that KSA. Responses must be separate from the application form.

Native American Preference: Under federal law, all qualified Native American applicants will receive preference over non-Native American applicants, unless the tribe has made a specific waiver of Native American preference. In accordance with the Indian Preference Act of 1934 (25 U.S.C. 472), when filling vacancies priority in selection will be given to Native American candidates who present proof of eligibility for Indian preference. Verification BIA Form 5-4432 must be provided with the application of a candidate who claims Indian preference. Applicants not entitled to Indian preference must be federal employees with competitive status or former federal employees with reinstatement eligibility and must submit latest Personnel Action, Standard Form (SF) 50, as proof.

Department of the Interior (DOI) Career Transition Assistance Plan (CTAP) procedures apply in filling this vacancy. 5 CFR 330, Career Transition Assistance for surplus and displaced federal employees requires the following order of selection for this position:

(a)   At Bureau option, personnel actions listed in 5 CFR 330.606(b).

(b)   Any well-qualified SSP candidate who applies within the local commuting area (Surplus and displaced employees will be given equal consideration).

(c)   At Bureau option, personnel actions are not subject to RPL.

(d)   Qualified RPL candidates in the local commuting area.

(e)   At bureau discretion, any other former displaced well-qualified DOI employee, e.g., a well-qualified RPL candidate who applies from outside the local commuting area.

(f)   Well-qualified ICTAP applicants in the local commuting area.

(g)   Other outside applicants (other agencies, nonstatus, etc.).

Definition of Well-Qualified: To be rated well-qualified for the position, applicants must fully meet the quality-ranking factor identified as KSA #1. NOTICE TO ALL MALE APPLICANTS: Section 1622 of the Defense Authorization Act of 1986, prohibits any male born after December 31, 1959, from being appointed to a position in an executive agency if he has knowingly and willfully failed to register with the Selective Service System. Male applicants born after December 31, 1959, will be required to complete a certification document to confirm their Selective Service registration status, if selected for appointment.

APPLICATIONS FILED UNDER THIS ANNOUNCEMENT WILL BE RETAINED AS PART OF THE MERIT PROMOTION FILE AND WILL NOT BE RETURNED OR DUPLICATED FOR OTHER VACANCIES

Suitability, Clearance, and Requirements: A background security investigation will be required for all new hires. Appointment will be subject to the applicant's successful completion of a background security investigation and favorable adjudication. Failure to successfully meet these requirements will be grounds for termination.

Other: Incumbent is required, as an incidental duty, to operate a government-owned or leased motor vehicle in the performance of duties, therefore, a valid driver's license is required.

Incumbent will be required to file an OGE-450, Confidential Financial Disclosure Report, in accordance with the 5 CFR, Part 2634, Subpart I.

Living and Working Conditions: This position is located in Nashville, TN.

Government quarters are not available.

VACANCY ANNOUNCEMENT NUMBER: XXX-XX-XX-XX

Opening Date:	06/06/2002
Closing Date:	06/20/2002
Position:	ADMINISTRATIVE ASSISTANT GS-0301-07
Salary:	$31,397–$39,772 per year
Duty Location:	2 vacancies at WASHINGTON, D.C. National Business Center Employee and Public Services Division Drug and Security Staff Washington, D.C.

Who May Apply: Open to all qualified persons.

About the National Business Center: The National Business Center (NBC) is a component of the Department of the Interior and serves as a franchise for administrative systems for budget, procurement and contracts, personnel management, finance and accounting, and other general administrative services. For additional information on the Products and Services provided by NBC, please visit our Web site at www.nbc.gov.

This position is located in the NBC, Employee and Public Services Division, Office of the Secretary, U. S. Department of the Interior. NBC is an office within the Department of the Interior responsible for providing administrative services to the Office of the Secretary and other organizational customers within and external to the department.

Incumbent will provide administrative and technical support to the department's drug staff, security staff, an serve as the principal point of contact for all budgetary matters associated with the division's budget. Incumb serves as the focal information point for division administrative activities and programs, and performs a variet of administrative support related to the diverse activities and programs of the division. He/she will provide assistance to the drug/security staffs by screening calls, ordering supplies, scheduling equipment maintenance, and maintaining data files. He/she receives and screens visitors to the drug/security staffs and answers questions as appropriate before forwarding them to other staff members. Screens visitors to refer them to the appropriate the division employee or office. Responsible for preparing budget justifications and performs associated budget execution of the division's allocation, authorizing expenditures in accordance with approved plans and within budgetary constraints.

Prepares budget projections, which are based on actual costs to reflect remaining available budgetary authority. Provides instruction on methods and procedures to obtain services such as training, printing, or procurement of supplies. Analyzes and distributes incoming mail to the appropriate staff members. Researches and assembles background information pertaining to inquires to provide the responsible staff member with a complete package on all requests requiring other than a routine response. Establishes due dates for responses, maintains control logs of pending inquiries, and follows-up to ensure completion of necessary actions. Manages the division's system of records. Ensures files are kept up-to-date at all times. Reviews all outgoing correspondence for proper format, grammar, typographical accuracy, proper coordination, attachments, etc. Ensures that all corrections are made prior to giving to the division chief for signature. Assembles background material for staff members' use, as requested, or in anticipation of a member's need. Prepares reports of program activities by extracting relevant data from office records and files. He/she uses office automation systems and various software packages to accomplish work. Prepares a variety of narrative and statistical material, correspondence, and reports, in final form for division chief's or other staff member's signature. Initiates personnel actions using the FPPS system. Prepares automated time and attendance and personnel reports. Enters and tracks requisitions for products and services; establishes maintenance agreements for equipment and orders office supplies.

Qualifications Required: Applicants must have one year of specialized experience equivalent to the next lower grade level in the federal service. Specialized experience is experience that is typically in or related to the position to be filled and that has equipped the candidate with the particular knowledge, skills, and abilities to successfully perform the duties of the position.

Knowledge, Skills, and Abilities Required:

1   Ability to get along and work with people.

3.   Knowledge of computer software programs.

4.   Experience working in any one of the following fields: budget, personnel, training, security, teaching, health care, etc.

5.   Ability to communicate both orally and in writing.

Basis of Rating: Your experience, education, training, and awards will be reviewed to determine the degree to which you possess the required knowledge, skills, and abilities that are essential for successful job performance. These same factors will be used as the basis for determining the best qualified applicants. You will be given credit for unpaid experience or volunteer work such as community, cultural, social service, and professional association activities on the same basis as paid experience.

Pay, Benefits, and Work Schedule: The National Business Center supports the Family Friendly workplace by offering programs such as flexible work schedules, employee assistance, health and wellness, child/elder care information, job share, work at home, and other programs. Not all programs are available in all locations.

...range for direct deposit of your pay to a financial institution in accordance with the Debt ...ent Act of 1996.

...ion, and relocation expenses for this position will not be paid by the Department of Interior. ...ses associated with reporting for duty in this position will be your responsibility.

...of Employment: If selected, you will be required to submit an OF-306, Declaration for Federal ...ent, prior to entrance on duty.

...ted, male applicants born after December 31, 1959, must certify that they have registered with the ...ctive Service system or exempt from having to do so under Selective Service Law.

...ther Information: If selection is made at a lower grade, promotion(s) up to the full performance level may be made without further competition. However, promotion(s) will depend on the performance of the incumbent and are not guaranteed.

This vacancy announcement may be used to fill similar positions within ninety days.

Individuals who have special priority selection rights under the Agency Career Transition Assistance Program (CTAP) or the Interagency Career Transition Assistance Program (ICTAP) must be well qualified for the position to receive consideration for special priority selection. CTAP and ICTAP eligibles will be considered well-qualified if an applicant has a rating of 85 or higher out of a scale of 100.

U.S. Citizenship is required.

Vacancy Announcement Number: XX-XXX-XXX

Opening Date:	05/28/2002
Closing Date:	06/25/2002
Position:	HUMAN RESOURCES COORDINATOR GS-0301-09/09
Salary:	$37,428–$48,652 per year

Duty Location: 1 vacancy at CADILLAC, MI

Who May Apply: Applications will be accepted from all qualified persons.

This position is also being advertised under the Forest Service Merit Promotion Program in an announcement open to status applicants. The announcement number is R9-779-02G. Status applicants and those eligible for appointment under special authorities may apply under both the government announcement and the demonstration announcement, but will only be considered under the announcement specified on their application. It is important to consider under which (or both) announcements you want to apply and make your choice clear. A status candidate who does not specify which announcement(s) he or she wishes consideration will only be considered under the government announcement. We encourage any applicants who believe they may be eligible under both announcements to consider submitting an application for each announcement. Be sure to write on your application the announcement number to which you are applying. Only one position will be filled.

If a selection is made from WRAPS, a Forest Service placement program for employees in unfunded positions, the announcement will be cancelled.

You may verify receipt of your application by enclosing a self-addressed, postage-paid postcard.

Major Duties: The incumbent performs the full range of personnel management and administrative support for an organization where the personnel problems encountered result from a specific request from a supervisor or employee. Assists managers with recruitment including the development of job advertisements, referral of job candidates, the selection process, and notification of applicants. Coordinates and prepares personnel actions, tracks the status of various personnel actions from origination to conclusion in areas relating to personnel management in order to ensure that suspense dates are met, that employees are paid properly, that employees are at the proper step and within proper leave categories, etc. Prepares and analyzes personnel reports such as affirmative action reports, slot and FTE information, etc.

Qualifications Required: OPM Qualification Standards Operating Manual is available in any federal personnel office or on the OPM Web site www.opm.gov/qualifications/index.htm.

Basic Requirements: One year of experience equivalent to at least the GS-5 level in the federal service OR one full year of graduate level education or superior academic achievement.

If using any or all education to qualify, applicants must submit a copy of official transcripts with the school name and address, semester/quarter hours, degree conferred, major, grade point average, and class ranking.

Specialized experience is described as experience that equipped the applicant with the particular knowledge, skills, and abilities to successfully perform the duties of the position, and that is typically in or related to the work of the position to be filled. To be creditable, specialized experience must have been equivalent to at least the next lower grade level in the normal line of progression for the occupation in the organization.

Combinations of successfully completed education and experience may be used to meet total experience requirements.

For each period of your employment in which you performed a mixture of duties, you must indicate the approximate hours per week spent performing each different type of work.

Basis of Rating: For CTAP and ICTAP, well-qualified means that the applicant is eligible, qualified, and clearly exceeds qualification requirements for the position as demonstrated by either: (1) meeting selective and quality ranking factor levels as specified by the agency; or (2) being rated above minimally-qualified under the agency's specific rating and ranking process.

Promotion panel members, a subject-matter expert, or a personnel specialist will evaluate each candidate's qualifications, including experience, performance, awards, training, and education.

Pay, Benefits, and Work Schedule: All federal employees are required by PL 104-134 to have federal payments made by direct deposit.

FLSA: GS-09 — Exempt

Forest Service day care facilities are not available.

Government housing is not available.

This position is covered by the Master Agreement between the Forest Service and NFFE (National Federation of Federal Employees).

Conditions of Employment: Under Executive Order 11935, only U.S. citizens and nationals (residents of American Samoa and Swains Island) may compete for civil service jobs. Agencies are permitted to hire noncitizens only in very limited circumstances where there are no qualified citizens available for the position.

As a condition of employment, male applicants born after December 31, 1959, must certify that they have registered with the Selective Service System, or are exempt from having to do so under the Selective Service Law.

A background security investigation will be required for all new hires. Appointment will be subject to the applicant's successful completion of a background security investigation and favorable adjudication. Failure to successfully meet these requirements will be grounds for termination.

This position requires completion of a one year probationary period.

Other Information: First consideration will be given to CTAP and ICTAP eligibles.

If claiming 5-point veterans' preference, a DD-214 must be submitted. If claiming 10-point veterans' preference, both a DD-214 and SF-15 must be submitted.

Your Social Security number (SSN) is requested under the authority of Executive Order 9397 to uniquely identify your records from those of other applicants who may have the same name. As allowed by law or presidential directive, your SSN is used to seek information about you from employers, schools, banks, and others who may know you. Failure to provide your SSN on your application materials will result in your application not being processed.

If you make a false statement in any part of your application, you may not be hired; you may be fired after you begin work; or you may be subject to fine, imprisonment, or other disciplinary action.

This agency provides reasonable accommodations to applicants with disabilities. If you need a reasonable accommodation for any part of the application and hiring process, please notify the agency. The decision on granting a reasonable accommodation will be on a case-by-case basis.

Now that you've had the opportunity to read some actual job vacancy announcements, we're sure that you have a better idea of what you'll find in your job search. Each announcement has it's own individual requests and requirements. All you have to do is to remember to read each one carefully, and follow the directions. It's really that simple.

PART III

Useful Information about Civil Service Tests

CHAPTER 5

INTRODUCTION TO FEDERAL EXAMS

In the not so distant past if you wanted to get a Federal Civil Service Job you had to take a test. As you can imagine, this made a lot of people very anxious. In general, people aren't too thrilled about taking exams. If you break out in hives when you see the words, "bring a number two pencil," here's some news that may brighten your day—sit-down examinations are a rarity these days. This change has come about due to the decentralization of the federal hiring process over the last twenty years. Before that the U.S. Office of Personnel Management was responsible for administering examinations and compiling lists of eligible candidates from which managers at various federal agencies could hire employees. These days, hiring for most federal jobs is handled by Delegated Examining Units (DEUs) that have been given this authority by the OPM. DEUs can be found in most federal agencies and are staffed by personnel who are responsible for deciding what assessment tools to use.

There are two types of assessment tools DEUs may administer to job candidates—written tests and unassembled examinations. Written tests aren't given very often now, but some agencies still use them when hiring for certain positions, i.e., the Immigration and Naturalization Service's Border Patrol Agent. Some agencies use written tests when hiring for clerical positions. Formerly, the OPM administered the Clerical and Administrative Support Exam; now individual agencies can decide how to assess potential hires. They have the option of using commercially developed tests, rating schedules/crediting plans (described in the next paragraph), work samples, or structured interviews.

Most often, agencies choose to use unassembled examinations, which aren't actually exams as you know them. They can take the form of ratings schedules. Ratings schedules are lengthy questionnaires that ask questions about a candidate's education and experience. DEUs may look at a candidate's Knowledge, Skills, and Abilities (KSAs) that were submitted with his or her job application. They may also conduct a structured interview or look at a candidate's work sample. DEUs use a crediting plan to arrive at a numerical score for each job applicant. The candidate receives a numerical score based on this information. The DEU then chooses from those with the three highest scores.

It is unlikely you will have to sit down to take an exam in order to get a federal job. In case you do, we have included some information about and some sample questions from the Immigration and Naturalization Service's Border Patrol Agent Examination, one of the few exams still being administered. Since you are more likely to encounter a rating schedule, we are including two of those here. The questions will differ from position to position, and of course there are no correct answers. All you can do is give answers that truthfully show your experience and education. Before we begin, here are some test-taking tips you might want to look at should you have to take a written exam.

TEST-TAKING TIPS

1. Give yourself enough time to prepare for the exam. Start studying weeks ahead of time; study every day; don't cram in the last 24 hours.

2. Arrive for your exam rested and relaxed. Get a good night's sleep before the exam. Leave home early enough so that you are not flustered by traffic or transit delays.

3. Arrive a bit early so that if you are not assigned a seat you can choose one away from drafts or a flickering light.

4. Wear a watch. Bring identification and an admission ticket if one was issued to you.

5. Listen to instructions before the exam begins. Ask questions if there is anything that you do not fully understand.

6. Read directions carefully. Directions that state "Mark choice (D) if all three names being compared are alike" are very different from directions that state "Mark choice (D) if *none* of the three names being compared are alike." Misreading these directions will ruin your score.

7. Read every word of every question. Little words like "not," "most," "all," "every," and "except" can make a big difference.

8. Read all the answer choices before you mark your answer. Don't just choose the first answer that seems correct; read them all to find out which answer is best.

9. Mark your answers by completely blackening the space of your choice. Every answer must be recorded in a space on the answer sheet.

10. Mark only one answer for each question.

11. If you change your mind, erase completely and cleanly. Never cross out an answer.

12. Answer the questions in order. If you are not sure of an answer, eliminate those answers that are obviously wrong and guess from those remaining. Mark the question booklet so that you can return and rethink the guesses if you have time.

13. Check often to be certain that you are marking each question in the right space and that you have not skipped a space by mistake. The answer sheet is scored by a machine. Question 8 must be answered in space 8; question 52 in space 52.

14. Stay awake. Stay alert. Work steadily and carefully using all the time allowed to earn your best possible score.

BORDER PATROL AGENT EXAM

Applicants for the position of Border Patrol Agent must pass an OPM exam and must either speak Spanish or have the ability to learn Spanish. If the candidate feels comfortable speaking and understanding Spanish, he or she may choose to take the Spanish Language Proficiency Test. If the candidate does not know any Spanish or if he or she is not certain of passing the oral exam, the candidate may elect to take a written multiple-choice test of ability to learn a foreign language. This test is called the ALT, or the Artificial Language Test. The ALT must be requested and taken at the same time as the OPM exam. The candidate cannot choose the language aptitude exam after failing the oral Spanish exam.

The main portion of the written exam is the Logical Reasoning Test. Because of the nature of the job, it is necessary to determine which candidates would be able to apply these decision-making skills to real-life situations. The test questions involve reading a paragraph and answering questions that pertain to the information contained in that paragraph. You aren't necessarily being tested on your knowledge of specific information, but instead on your ability to determine the correct answer from the facts that you've been given. To pass the Logical Reasoning Test, you must receive a score of 70 or above.

The next part of the exam is the Spanish Language Proficiency Test. This test consists of two parts. The first part tests your Spanish vocabulary, while the second part is on Spanish grammar. If you speak Spanish, this part shouldn't be difficult. If you don't feel confident in your Spanish-speaking abilities, then you have the option of taking the ALT exam.

The ALT is an exam that can determine your ability to learn a language. Remember, to apply to become a Border Patrol Agent, you don't need to speak Spanish, but you need to prove that you will be able to learn it. It uses an entirely fictitious language, with a grammatical structure, which is similar to Spanish to test this ability. If you intend to take this exam, you can refer to the manual at www.ins.usdoj.gov/graphics/workfor/careers/prep1896.pdf to study for it. This will help you become familiar with some of the grammatical rules before you actually take the exam.

In addition to the written exam, the applicant must also take an oral exam. As part of the basic qualifications determination, candidates must appear before an oral interview panel and demonstrate that they possess the abilities and other characteristics important to Border Patrol Agent positions. Among these competencies are judgement/decision-making, emotional maturity, interpersonal skills, and cooperativeness/sensitivity to the needs of others. The interview will be rated on a pass/fail basis. Candidates must receive a "pass" in all areas in order to continue in the hiring process.

The following are official sample questions for the Border Patrol Agent Exam. They have been taken from material that appears on the Immigration and Naturalization Service Web site. This a multiple-choice exam. It is divided into two or three parts, depending on whether you choose to take the ALT, or just the Spanish Language Proficiency Test. Each part of the exam is separately timed.

When the exam is scored, you will receive credit for every correct answer but suffer no penalty for a wrong answer. That means it is best to answer every question. A space left blank cannot raise your score, but even a wild guess could possibly help you. Choose the correct answer if you can. If not, eliminate obviously wrong answers and choose intelligently from the remaining choices. The official instructions, which will be read to you in the examination room, state: "It will be to your advantage to answer every question in this test that you can, since your score will be number of right answers only. If you don't know the answer to a question, make the best guess you can. You may write in the test booklet if you need to."

The official sample questions that follow will give you a good idea of the kinds of questions that you must answer but remember, they're just samples.

Directions: Each question has five suggested answers, lettered (A), (B), (C), (D), and (E). Decide which one is the best answer to the question. Then, darken completely the space corresponding to the letter that is the same as the letter of your answer. Keep your mark within the space. If you have to erase a mark, be sure to erase it completely. Mark only one answer for each question.

Sample questions 1–3. In each of the next three sample questions, select the one of the five suggested answer choices that is closest in meaning to the word in italics. Then, darken the proper space on the sample answer sheet.

SAMPLE QUESTIONS FOR THE LOGICAL REASONING EXAM

In this part of the exam, you will be expected to read the paragraph very carefully. Using the facts provided or excluded, you will answer some questions. Remember, there may be facts contained within the paragraph that may not always be true, but you are only answering the questions based on the facts that you've been given. You aren't being judged on your previous knowledge, but instead on your ability to reason and reach conclusions based on what you've just read.

Following the paragraph, you will find a lead-in phrase. This phrase asks you to finish a sentence by selecting one of several answers, labeled (A) to (E). The phrases can be either positive or negative. For example, "From the information given above, it can be validly concluded that" or "From the information given above, it CANNOT be validly concluded that." Positive lead-in phrases contain four invalid conclusions and only one valid conclusion. You will need to choose the valid one. Negative lead-in phrases have four valid conclusions and only one invalid conclusion. To answer these correctly, you will need to figure out which answer cannot be validly concluded based on the facts contained in the paragraph.

1. Often, crimes are characterized as either *malum in se*—inherently evil—or *malum prohibitum*—criminal because they are declared as offenses by a legislature. Murder is an example of the former. Failing to file a tax return illustrates the latter. Some jurisdictions no longer distinguish between crimes *malum in se* and *malum prohibitum,* although many still do.

From the information given above, it can be validly concluded that

    (A) many jurisdictions no longer distinguish between crimes *malum in se* and *malum prohibitum.*

    (B) some jurisdictions still distinguish between crimes *malum in se* and *malum prohibitum.*

    (C) some crimes characterized as *malum in se* are not inherently evil.

    (D) some crimes characterized as *malum prohibitum* are not declared by a legislature to be an offense.

    (E) sometimes failing to file a tax return is characterized as *malum in se.*

2. A trucking company can act as a *common carrier*—for hire to the general public at published rates. As a common carrier, it is liable for any cargo damage, unless the company can show that it was not negligent. If the company can demonstrate that it was not negligent, then it is not liable for cargo damage. In contrast, a *contract carrier* (a trucking company hired by a shipper under a specific contract) is only responsible for cargo damage as spelled out in the contract. A Claus Inc. tractor-trailer, acting under common carrier authority, was in a 5-vehicle accident that damaged its cargo. A Nichols Inc. tractor-trailer, acting under contract carrier authority, was involved in the same accident, and its cargo was also damaged.

From the information given above, it can be validly concluded that, in reference to the accident, if

    (A)   Claus Inc. is liable, then it can show that it was not negligent.

    (B)   Claus Inc. cannot show that it was not negligent, then it is not liable.

    (C)   Claus Inc. can show that it was not negligent, then it is not liable.

    (D)   Nichols Inc. is liable, then it cannot show that it is negligent.

    (E)   Nichols Inc. can show that it is not negligent, then it is not liable.

3.   A rapidly changing technical environment in government is promoting greater reliance on electronic mail (e-mail) systems. As this usage grows, there are increasing chances of conflict between the users' expectations of privacy and public access rights. In some investigations, access to all e-mail, including those messages stored in archival files and messages outside the scope of the investigation, has been sought and granted. In spite of this, some people send messages through e-mail that would never be said face-to-face or written formally.

*From the information given above, it **CANNOT** be validly concluded that*

    (A)   some e-mail messages that have been requested as part of investigations have contained messages that would never be said face-to-face.

    (B)   some messages that people would never say face-to-face are sent in e-mail messages.

    (C)   some e-mail messages have been requested as part of investigations.

    (D)   e-mail messages have not been exempted from investigations.

    (E)   some e-mail messages contain information that would be omitted from formal writing.

4.   Phyllis T. is a former federal employee who was entitled to benefits under the federal Employee Compensation Act because of a job-related, disabling injury. When an eligible Federal employee has such an injury, the benefit is determined by this test: If the beneficiary is married or has dependents, benefits are 3/4 of the person's salary at the time of the injury; otherwise, benefits are set at 2/3 of the salary. Phyllis T.'s benefits were 2/3 of her salary when she was injured.

From the information given above, it can be validly concluded that, when Phyllis T. was injured, she

    (A)   was married but without dependents.

    (B)   was not married and had no dependents.

    (C)   was not married but had dependents.

    (D)   was married and had dependents.

    (E)   had never been married.

5.   Some 480,000 immigrants were living in a certain country in 1999. Although most of these immigrants were not employed in professional occupations, many of them were. For instance, many of them were engineers and many of them were nurses. Very few of these immigrants were librarians, another professional occupation.

From the information given above, it can be validly concluded that, in 1999, in the country described above,

    (A)   most immigrants were either engineers or nurses.

    (B)   it is not the case that some of the nurses were immigrants.

    (C)   none of the engineers were immigrants.

    (D)   most of those not employed in professional occupations were immigrants.

    (E)   some of the engineers were immigrants.

6. Police officers were led to believe that many weapons sold at a certain gun store were sold illegally. Upon investigating the lead, the officers learned that all of the weapons sold by the store that were made by Precision Arms were sold legally. Also, none of the illegally sold weapons were .45 caliber.

From the information given above, it can be validly concluded that, concerning the weapons sold at the store,

   (A) all of the .45 caliber weapons were made by Precision Arms.
   (B) none of the .45 caliber weapons were made by Precision Arms.
   (C) some of the weapons made by Precision Arms were .45 caliber weapons.
   (D) all of the .45 caliber weapons were sold legally.
   (E) some of the weapons made by Precision Arms were sold illegally.

7. Impressions made by the ridges on the ends of the fingers and thumbs are useful means of identification, since no two people have the same pattern of ridges. If finger patterns from fingerprints are not decipherable, then they cannot be classified by general shape and contour or by pattern type. If they cannot be classified by these characteristics, then it is impossible to identify the person to whom the fingerprints belong.

*From the information given above, it **CANNOT** be validly concluded that, if*

   (A) it is possible to identify the person to whom fingerprints belong, then the fingerprints are decipherable.
   (B) finger patterns from fingerprints are not decipherable, then it is impossible to identify the person to whom the fingerprints belong.
   (C) fingerprints are decipherable, then it is impossible to identify the person to whom they belong.
   (D) fingerprints can be classified by general shape and contour or by pattern type, then they are decipherable.
   (E) it is possible to identify the person to whom fingerprints belong, then the fingerprints can be classified by general shape and contour or pattern type.

8. Explosives are substances or devices capable of producing a volume of rapidly expanding gases that exert a sudden pressure on their surroundings. Chemical explosives are the most commonly used, although there are mechanical and nuclear explosives. All mechanical explosives are devices in which a physical reaction is produced, such as that caused by overloading a container with compressed air. While nuclear explosives are by far the most powerful, all nuclear explosives have been restricted to military weapons.

From the information given above, it can be validly concluded that

   (A) all explosives that have been restricted to military weapons are nuclear explosives.
   (B) no mechanical explosives are devices in which a physical reaction is produced, such as that caused by overloading a container with compressed air.
   (C) some nuclear explosives have not been restricted to military weapons.
   (D) all mechanical explosives have been restricted to military weapons.
   (E) some devices in which a physical reaction is produced, such as that caused by overloading a container with compressed air, are mechanical explosives.

ANSWERS AND EXPLANATIONS:

1. **The correct answer is (B).** Some jurisdictions still distinguish between crimes *malum in se* and *malum prohibitum*. This question is concerned with classification of crimes into sets—that is, with the classification of crimes as either *malum in se* or *malum prohibitum*. The last phrase in the last sentence tells us that many jurisdictions make the distinction between these two categories of crimes. Choice (B) follows from that sentence, because if many jurisdictions make the distinction, some jurisdictions make the distinction. From the fact that many jurisdictions make the distinction, it cannot be inferred that many do not make the distinction. Therefore, choice (A) is incorrect.

   Choices (C), (D), and (E) are based on erroneous definitions of the two classes of crimes. The paragraph tells us that all crimes characterized as *malum in se* are inherently evil.

   Choice (C) is false because it cannot be the case that SOME crimes characterized as *malum in se* are NOT inherently evil. The paragraph also tells us that all crimes characterized as *malum prohibitum* are declared as offenses by a legislature. Choice (D) is false because it cannot be the case that SOME crimes characterized as *malum prohibitum* are NOT declared by a legislature to be an offense. In the paragraph, we are told that filing a tax return late is *malum prohibitum*, rather than *malum in se*. Choice (E) is incorrect because it cannot be the case that failing to file a tax return is *malum in se*.

2. **The correct answer is (C).** If Claus Inc. can show that it was not negligent, then it is not liable. The second sentence states the liability rule for common carriers: all common carriers are liable for cargo damage unless they can show that they are not negligent; if they can show that they are not negligent, then they are not liable for cargo damage. Claus Inc. is a common carrier, and accordingly this rule applies to it. From this rule it follows that if Claus Inc. can show it was not negligent, then it is not liable, choice (C). Choice (A) contradicts this rule by claiming that when Claus Inc. is liable it can show that it was not negligent. Choice (B) contradicts this rule by claiming that Claus Inc. is not liable even when it cannot show that it is not negligent. Choices (D) and (E) concern Nichols Inc., a contract carrier. However, the terms of the Nichols Inc. contract were not disclosed in the paragraph, so neither response is supported.

3. **The correct answer is (A).** Some e-mail messages that have been requested as part of investigations have contained messages that would never be said face-to-face. This is an example of a test question with a negative lead-in statement. It asks for the conclusion that is **NOT** supported by the paragraph. That means that four of the statements are valid conclusions from the paragraph while one is not. Choice (B) is a valid conclusion because it restates a fact given in the last sentence of the paragraph. Choice (E) is valid because it restates the other fact in the last sentence of the paragraph. The next-to-last sentence in the paragraph is the source of both choice (C) and choice (D). Both of these choices restate information in that sentence, based on the fact that access to e-mail messages was sought and granted. This leaves only the first option, choice (A). This is the only choice that does **NOT** represent a valid conclusion, because even though we know from the paragraph that there is a group of e-mail messages that are requested in investigations and also that there is a group of messages that contain information that people would not say face-to-face, there is nothing that says that these groups overlap. We simply do not know.

4. **The correct answer is (B).** Phyllis T. was not married and had no dependents. This question concerns an either/or situation. The paragraph states that benefits under the Federal Employees Compensation Act are awarded at one level (3/4 of salary) if a beneficiary is married or has dependents when injured and at another level (2/3 of salary) if this is not true. Phyllis T. is eligible for benefits under the Act. The paragraph states that Phyllis T.'s benefit level was 2/3 of her salary. Given this benefit level, it is clear that Phyllis T. did not meet either of the conditions for the 3/4 level. Therefore, choices (A), (C), and (D) cannot be correct. Choice (A) states that she was married, choice (C) states that she had dependents, and choice (D) states that she both was married and had dependents. Choice (E) goes beyond the facts given because prior marriages are not listed as a

factor relating to this benefit. The one correct conclusion is that Phyllis T. did not meet either requirement to qualify for the higher benefit level (3/4 of salary), so choice (B) is the correct answer to the question.

5. **The correct answer is (E).** Some of the engineers were immigrants. Choice (E) is correct because it restates the third sentence in terms of the overlap between immigrants and engineers in the country described in the paragraph. Choice (A) says that most immigrants are engineers or nurses, which are professional occupations. However, the second sentence says that most immigrants are not employed in professional occupations, so choice (A) is false. Choice (B) is false because it denies that there is any overlap between immigrants and nurses, even though this overlap is clear from the third sentence of the paragraph. Choice (C) is false because it denies the overlap between immigrants and engineers. Because the paragraph does not give complete information about the non-professionals (immigrant and non-immigrant) in the country described in the paragraph, Choice (D) is invalid.

6. **The correct answer is (D).** All of the .45 caliber weapons were sold legally. The second and last sentences are the two main premises in the paragraph. These two sentences give information about three categories of weapons: weapons made by Precision Arms, weapons sold legally, and .45 caliber weapons. The last sentence states that none of the illegally sold weapons were .45 caliber. This means that none of the .45 caliber weapons were sold illegally. Notice that this new statement is a double negative. In affirmative form, the statement means that all of the .45 caliber weapons were sold legally, choice D. The information that all of the .45 caliber weapons were sold legally (last sentence), combined with the information that all of the weapons made by Precision Arms were sold legally (second sentence), allows us to draw no valid conclusions about the relationship between the .45 caliber weapons and the weapons made by Precision Arms. There is insufficient information about the entire group of weapons sold legally to know whether the group of .45 caliber weapons and the group of weapons made by Precision Arms overlapped entirely, choice (A), partially, choice (C), or not at all, choice (B). Choice (E) contradicts the second sentence and is, therefore, invalid.

7. **The correct answer is (C).** If fingerprints are decipherable, then it is impossible to identify the person to whom they belong. This question asks for the response option that CANNOT be validly concluded from the information in the paragraph. The only option that cannot be validly concluded is choice (C), therefore it is the correct answer. Choice (C) is invalid because the paragraph does not provide enough information to conclude whether or not it would be possible to identify the person to whom the fingerprints belong from the mere fact that the fingerprints are decipherable. Choice (A) refers to a condition where it is possible to identify the person to whom fingerprints belong. Based on the final sentence in the paragraph, this condition of fingerprints means that the fingerprints could be classified by general shape and contour or by pattern type. Based on the second sentence, the ability to classify the fingerprints means that the fingerprints are decipherable. Since choice (B) refers to a condition in which finger patterns from fingerprints are not decipherable, we know from the second sentence that, in that circumstance, they cannot be classified by general shape and contour or by pattern type. From the final sentence in the paragraph, we can infer that since they cannot be classified by these characteristics, then it is impossible to identify the person to whom the fingerprints belong. According to the second sentence, fingerprints cannot be classified by general shape and contour or by pattern type when they are not decipherable. Therefore, if fingerprints can be classified by general shape and contour or by pattern type, then the fingerprints must be decipherable, choice (D). According to the third sentence, it is impossible to identify the owner of a set of fingerprints when the fingerprints cannot be classified by general shape and contour or by pattern type. Therefore, if it is possible to identify the person to whom fingerprints belong, then the fingerprints must be able to be classified by general shape and contour or pattern type, choice (E). Notice that choices (D) and (E) are valid based on the same type of reasoning. The first and second state-

ments of the second sentence were made opposite and reversed in choice (D), and the first and second statements of the final sentence were made opposite and reversed in choice (E).

8. **The correct answer is (E).** Some devices in which a physical reaction is produced, such as that caused by overloading a container with compressed air, are mechanical explosives. The third sentence states the overlap between all mechanical explosives and devices in which a physical reaction is produced, such as that caused by overloading a container with compressed air. From this, we can safely conclude that some devices in which a physical reaction is produced, such as that caused by overloading a container with compressed air, are mechanical explosives. Choice (A) is incorrect because the paragraph does not provide sufficient information to validly conclude that all explosives that have been restricted to military weapons are nuclear weapons. It may be that some types of explosives other than nuclear weapons also have been restricted to military weapons. Choices (B) and (C) are incorrect because they contradict the paragraph. Choice (B) contradicts the third sentence, and choice (C) contradicts the last sentence. Choice (D) is incorrect because the paragraph provides no information about whether or not mechanical explosives are restricted to military weapons.

THE ARTIFICIAL LANGUAGE TEST (ALT)

If you choose to take the Artificial Language Test (ALT), instead of the Spanish Language Proficiency Exam, you will take this exam, after a break, on the same day as you take the OPM exam just described above. The ALT is an *artificial* language exam. You must demonstrate your ability to learn a foreign language by manipulating vocabulary and grammar in an *artificial* language.

You will be presented with a booklet describing the artificial language; the booklet will include two vocabulary lists. One list, presented alphabetically by English word, gives the English word and its artificial language equivalent (Example: alien = huskovy). The other list is alphabetized by artificial language and gives the English equivalent of each artificial language word (Example: friggar = to work). The booklet includes a glossary of grammatical terms. Grammatical terms have the same meaning in both English and the artificial language. (Example: An *adjective* is a word that describes a noun.) Finally, the booklet sets out grammar rules for the artificial language. (Example: The feminine singular of a noun, pronoun, and adjective is formed by adding the suffix *ver* to the masculine singular form.)

The exam contains four different types of questions, with 50 questions in all. The parts are *not* separately timed. You are allowed 1 hour and 45 minutes to study the accompanying booklet and to answer the questions. The ALT is a test of your ability to reason and to manipulate the vocabulary and grammar of a foreign language. It is not a memory test. It does not test your ability to remember vocabulary or language. You may keep the booklet open in front of you and refer to it frequently as you answer the questions. You do not need to memorize any information.

The Office of Personnel Management (OPM) does not provide official sample questions for the ALT. The exam description below can give you a feeling for the phrasing and style of questions, but without a vocabulary and grammar list you cannot even attempt to answer these unofficial sample questions.

The first part consists of questions 1–20. In this part, you must correctly identify translated words. For example, you may be given an English sentence such as "He injured the man,"

followed by a sentence in the artificial language such as " Yer Zelet wir huskoy." You must

$$1 \qquad 2 \qquad\qquad 3$$

then mark choice (A) if only #1 is translated correctly, choice (B) if only #2 is correct, choice (C) if only #3 is correct, choice (D) if two or more are correct, and choice (E) if none are correct.

The second part consists of questions 21–30. In this part, you must choose which of five choices correctly translates an underlined word or group of words from English into the artificial language.

Example: There is the <u>lost boy</u>.

- (A) bex kapkoy,
- (B) wir kapvoy,
- (C) hex kapvoy,
- (D) wir kapkoy,
- (E) bex kapyok.

The third part, questions 31–42, puts a slightly different spin on translation into the artificial language. You are given an incomplete sentence in the artificial language and must complete it with the correctly translated English word, being conscious not only of the vocabulary word but also the grammatical form.

> **Example:** Synet hex avekoy (man).
>
> (A) ekapiko,
> (B) ekapiver,
> (C) kopiak,
> (D) ekapiak,
> (E) pokiver.

The fourth part, questions 43–50, requires you to correct a sentence in the artificial language. You must change the form of the italicized word or words in the sentence according to instructions given in parentheses.

> **Example:** Yer *bongar* wit broukon (present tense).
>
> (A) bongaro,
> (B) bonagar,
> (C) bongarara,
> (D) bongo,
> (E) bongit.

THE SPANISH LANGUAGE PROFICIENCY TEST

The Spanish Language Proficiency Test is divided into two parts. The first part consists entirely of *vocabulary* questions; the second part is divided into three sections, each section dealing with a different type of *grammar* question. The following pages contain four examples of each type of question included in the Spanish Language Proficiency Test.

SAMPLE QUESTIONS

PART I

Read the sentence and then choose the most appropriate synonym for the underlined word.

1. Es muy *complicado* pilotar mi avión.

   (A) fácil
   (B) difícil
   (C) divertido
   (D) compilado
   (E) comparado

The correct answer is (B). The word *complicado* means complicated. In the context of the sentence, it refers to something that is hard to do. Hence, choice B, *difícil* (difficult), is the best synonym. Choice (A), *fáci* (easy), is opposite in meaning to *complicado*. Choice (C), *divertido,* has the same beginning syllable (*di-*) as the correct answer, but its meaning (amusing) is completely different. The basic meanings of choices (D) and (E) (compiled and compared, respectively) are completely different from the meaning of *complicado,* although both *compilado* and *comparado* are phonetically similar to it.

2. Es fácil *comprender* lo que el agente está diciendo.

   (A) responder
   (B) comprobar
   (C) entender
   (D) pretender
   (E) desentender

The correct answer is (C). The word *comprender* means to understand something after watching, listening to, or reading it. Hence, choice (C), *entender* (to understand), is the best synonym. Choice (E), *desentender*, is the exact opposite of the correct answer; in fact, it is *entender*, but with a negative prefix added to it, thus giving it the meaning of "to misunderstand." Choices (A), (B), and (D) (to respond, to verify, and to pretend) are completely unrelated to the meaning of *comprender.*

3. Hay que esclarecer todo el proceso.

   (A) encontrar
   (C) aclarar
   (B) concentrar
   (D) empeorar
   (E) aplastar

The correct answer is (C). The word *esclarecer* means "to clarify." Hence, choice (C), *aclarar* (to clarify), is the best synonym. Choices (A), (B), (D), and (E) (to find, to concentrate, to worsen, and to crush) are completely unrelated to the meaning of *esclarecer.*

4. Hemos otorgado concesiones especiales a los países en vías de desarrollo.

   (A) privilegios
   (B) determinaciones
   (C) estipendios
   (D) cortesías
   (E) ofrendas

The correct answer is (A). The word *concesiones* means concessions, rights, or privileges that have been granted. Hence, choice (A), *privilegios* (privileges) is the best synonym. Choices (B), (C), (D), and (E) (determinations, stipends, courtesies, and offerings) are completely unrelated to the meaning of *concesiones*.

PART II

Section I

Read each sentence carefully. Select the appropriate word or phrase to fill each blank space.

1. Me gusta entrar _____ la puerta que está _____ de la oficina.

    (A) a, sobre
    (B) en, desde
    (C) con, bajo
    (D) en, al lado
    (E) por, detrás

The correct answer is (E). Choices (A), (B), (C), and (D) all use incorrect prepositions.

2. La agente me _____ la correspondencia cuando yo no _____ en casa.

    (A) traido, estoy
    (B) traer, estuviera
    (C) trajo, estaba
    (D) traerá, habré estado
    (E) habrá traido, estar

The correct answer is (C). Both verbs represent the correct past tense in the indicative mood (preterite indefinite *trajo* and preterite imperfect *estaba*). In choices (A), (B), (D), and (E), the wrong forms of the verb have been used.

3. Los oficiales _____ usan la sala de reuniones para discutir asuntos _____.

    (A) sumariamente / difícil
    (B) frecuentemente / variadas
    (C) normalmente / diversos
    (D) rara vez / personal
    (E) ocasionalmente / unilateral

The correct answer is (C). The adverb *normalmente* ("normally") correctly modifies the verb *usan* ("[they] use"), and the plural, masculine adjective *diversos* ("diverse") agrees in gender and number with the noun it modifies ("asuntos"). In choices (A), (D), and (E), there is no agreement in number between adjective and noun. In choice (B), there is no agreement in gender between adjective and noun.

4. _____ a los detenidos y _____ al tanto de los resultados.

    (A) Visita / pónlos
    (B) Visite / ponerlos
    (C) Visitaré / ponga
    (D) Habré visitado / pondré
    (E) Visitando / había puesto

The correct answer is (A). The two imperative verb forms [tú] *visita* and [tú] *pónlos* are the correct choices. In choices (B), (C), (D), and (E), there is no agreement between the two main verbs.

Section II

Read each sentence carefully. Select the one sentence that is correct.

1. (A) Todos los agentes coincidieron del sospechoso cuando entrarían por la puerta.
   (B) El sospechoso que entró fue señalado en la puerta con los agentes coincidiendo.
   (C) Todos los agentes señalaron al mismo sospechoso cuando entró por la puerta.
   (D) Todos los agentes coincidió en señalar al sospechoso cuando entrarán por la puerta.

The correct answer is (C). It has the proper sentence structure (subject, verb, direct object) and contains no errors. Choices (A), (B), and (D) contain various errors, including incorrect prepositions, illogical structures, or incorrect verb forms; hence, none of them can be the correct answer.

2. (A) La inmigración ilegal y el contrabando suponen un gran problema para muchos países.
   (B) La inmigración ilegal y el contrabando supongo un problema grande para muchos países.
   (C) Muchos países con gran problemas suponían la inmigración ilegal y el contrabando.
   (D) La inmigración ilegales y el contrabando suponen un gran problema para muchos países.

The correct answer is (A). It has the proper sentence structure (subject, verb, direct object, indirect object) and contains no errors. Choices (B), (C), and (D) contain various errors, including incorrect terms, illogical structures, or incorrect verb forms; hence, none of them can be the correct answer.

3. (A) Como el agente sabía que andando es bueno para la salud, andaría unos veinte minutos antes de iniciar el entrenamiento oficial.
   (B) Como el agente sabía que andar es bueno para la salud, anduvo unos veinte minutos antes de iniciar el entrenamiento oficial.
   (C) Andaría unos veinte minutos como andar es bueno sabía el agente antes de iniciar el entrenamiento oficial.
   (D) Que andar es bueno para la salud unos veinte minutos antes de había iniciado el entrenamiento oficial el agente sabía que andaría.

The correct answer is (B). It has the proper sentence structure (subject, verb, direct object) and contains no errors. Choices (A), (C), and (D) contain various errors, including incorrect terms, misplaced clauses, or disagreement of verb tenses; hence, none of these responses can be the correct answer.

4. (A) Aunque hay países donde existen varias agrupaciones de derechos humanos que se preocupan por velar sobre las garantías individuales y que resultan muy efectivas en ciertas sociedades en que su esfera de influencia es muy limitada o casi nula.
   (B) Existen varias agrupaciones internacionales de derechos humanos que se preocupan por velar sobre las garantías individuales y que resultan muy efectivas en ciertas sociedades, aunque hay países en que su esfera de influencia es muy limitada o casi nula.
   (C) Existen de derechos humanos varias agrupaciones internacionales que se preocupan por velar sobre las garantías individuales, aunque hay países en que su esfera de influencia que resultan muy efectivas en ciertas sociedades es muy limitada o casi nula.
   (D) Hay países en que existen varias agrupaciones internacionales de derechos humanos y que resultan muy efectivas en ciertas sociedades aunque que se preocupan por velar sobre las garantías individuales en que su esfera de influencia es muy limitada o casi nula.

The correct answer is (B). It has the proper sentence structure (subject, verb, direct object, indirect object) and contains no errors. Choices (A), (C), and (D) contain misplaced clauses; hence, none of these responses can be the correct answer.

Section III

Read each sentence carefully. Select the correct word or phrase to replace the underlined portions of the sentence. In those cases in which the sentence needs no correction, select choice (E).

1. Los agentes detectaron el contrabando antes de <u>abrir</u> la maleta.

   (A) abriendo
   (B) abrirá
   (C) abriremos
   (D) abrió
   (E) No es necesario hacer ninguna corrección.

The correct answer is (E). The infinitive form of the verb, *abrir*, must be used after the preposition *de*. Incorrect forms of the verb have been used in the other responses; namely, choice (A) (gerund), choice (B) (future imperfect), choice (C) (future imperfect), and choice (D) (preterite indefinite).

2. Es necesario tener <u>todo las</u> documentos de identificación en regla.

   (A) todos las
   (B) todo el
   (C) todas las
   (D) todos los
   (E) No es necesario hacer ninguna corrección.

The correct answer is (D). *Todos los* is plural in number and masculine in gender, and is thus in agreement with *documentos*. Choices (A), (B), and (C) have either the wrong gender or the wrong number.

3. Los manuales hemos <u>abarcado</u> un sinnúmero de posibilidades y hemos abreviado el tiempo que se necesita para completar los trámites.

   (A) abarcando / abreviando
   (B) abarcados / abreviados
   (C) abarcó / abrevió
   (D) abarcan / abrevian
   (E) No es necesario hacer ninguna corrección.

The correct answer is (D). The two verbs in the third person plural [*abarcan* (cover) and *abrevian* (shorten)] agree with the masculine plural subject *manuales* (manuals). Choices (A) and (B) use incorrect verb forms (gerund and participle). In choices (C) and (E), there is no agreement between verbs and subject.

4. Los que <u>abastecen</u> las cocinas de las unidades de rescate <u>anoche</u> trajeron magníficas provisiones.

   (A) habían abastecido / lentamente
   (B) abasteciendo / no
   (C) abastecieran / mañana
   (D) abastezco / arriba
   (E) No es necesario hacer ninguna corrección.

The correct answer is (E). The present indicative verb *abastecen* ([they] supply) agrees with the preterite indefinite *trajeron* ([they] brought) after the correctly selected adverb *anoche* ("last night"). In choice A, the adverb of manner *lentamente* (slowly) is incorrect. Choices (B) and (C) use the wrong verb form. Choice (D) does not have agreement in number between subject and verb.

SAMPLE RATING SCHEDULES

AGRICULTURAL MARKETING SPECIALIST (GS-05/07)

Mark only 1 response for each question.

EDUCATIONAL BACKGROUND AND WORK EXPERIENCE
This section asks you to describe your educational background, your work, and other experiences in specific factors that relate to job performance. ALL QUESTIONS MUST BE ANSWERED. Record your answers in (Section 25).

1. From the descriptions below, select the letter that describes the education or experience you have that demonstrates your ability to perform Fruit & Vegetable Marketing Specialist work. If your highest level of education is not described below, choose the letter that describes experience or lower level education you do have. Mark only 1 response.

    (A) I have completed a four-year course of study leading to a bachelor's degree or I possess a bachelor's degree.

    (B) I have completed education beyond the bachelor's degree, e.g., graduate study, master's degree, Ph.D., in a field that provided the knowledge, skills, and abilities necessary to do the work. Such fields include marketing, economics, business administration, agriculture, agricultural economics, agricultural business, accounting, statistics, mathematics, commerce, transportation, or in one of the specialized commodity fields, if required.

    (C) I have at least one year of work experience merchandising agricultural products that involved trading, transportation, processing regulations, storage, inspection, grading, or standardization of pertinent agricultural commodities; or developing, surveying, and promoting markets for U.S. commodities in foreign areas and developing pricing policies; or marketing research or analysis of business practices, consumption patterns, processing, wholesaling; or developing new processes, forms, agreements, requirements; or insuring compliance with regulatory laws to prevent unfair trade practices regarding agricultural products; or improving marketing facilities, equipment, packaging, handling, work methods or transportation of agricultural products.

    (D) My work primarily involved following procedures with detailed and explicit guidelines and performing duties such as typing, filing, or maintaining records.

    (E) I have three years of experience that demonstrated effective oral and written communication; ability to analyze problems to identify significant factors, gather pertinent data, and recognize solutions; and the ability to plan and organize work.

    (F) I have at least three years of post-high school education and at least three months of experience as described in (C).

    (G) I have less than four years of post-high school education or a bachelor's degree and less than the experience described in (E), but I have a combination of education and the type of experience described in (E).

    (H) My education and/or experience are not reflected in any of the above statements.

2. From the descriptions below, select the letter that describes the education or experience you have that demonstrates your ability to perform (GS-7), Fruit & Vegetable Marketing Specialist work. If your highest level of education is not described below, choose the letter that describes experience or lower level education you do have. Mark only 1 response.

(A) I have a bachelor's degree AND superior academic achievement which is defined as one of the following: (1) ranked in the upper 1/3 of the graduating class in the college, university or major subdivision; (2) earned election to a national scholastic honor society; (3) earned a grade point average (GPA) of 3.0 or higher out of a possible 4.0 based on the average of all completed undergraduate courses;(4) earned a grade point average of 3.0 or higher out of a possible 4.0 based on the average of all undergraduate classes completed during my final two years; (5) earned a GPA of 3.5 or higher out of a possible 4.0 based on the average of all completed undergraduate courses in my major field of study; or (6) earned a GPA of 3.5 or higher out of a possible 4.0 based on the average of all undergraduate courses in my major field of study completed during my final two years.

(B) I have one full year of graduate level study, or possess a master's or higher degree, e.g., Ph.D., in a field that provided the knowledge, skills, and abilities necessary to do the work. Such fields include marketing, economics, business administration, agriculture, agricultural economics, agricultural business, accounting, statistics, mathematics, commerce, transportation, or in one of the specialized commodity fields, if required. One year of full-time graduate education is considered to be the number of credit hours that the school attended has determined to represent one year of full-time study. If the information cannot be obtained from the school, 18 semester hours should be considered as satisfying one year of full-time study at the school attended.

(C) I have at least one year of work experience merchandising agricultural products that involved trading, transportation, processing regulations, storage, inspection, grading, or standardization of pertinent agricultural commodities; or developing, surveying, and promoting markets for U.S. commodities in foreign areas and developing pricing policies; or marketing research or analysis of business practices, consumption patterns, processing, wholesaling; or developing new processes, forms, agreements, requirements for agricultural products; or insuring compliance with regulatory laws to prevent unfair trade practices; or improving marketing facilities, equipment, packaging, handling, work methods or transportation for agricultural products. This experience was equivalent in duties and level of responsibility to at least the GS-5 grade level in the federal service.

(D) I have at least one year of work experience following procedures with detailed and explicit guidelines and performing duties such as typing, filing, or maintaining records.

(E) I have less than the full amount of graduate education described in (B) and less than the amount of experience described in (C), but I have a combination of the type of graduate education described in (B) and the type of experience described in (C). (To combine education and experience, first determine your total qualifying experience as a percentage of the experience required; then determine your graduate education as a percentage of the education required; and then add the two percentages. The total percentages must equal at least 100 percent to qualify.)

(F) My education and/or experience are not reflected in any of the above statements.

3. Do you have a bachelor's degree and have you maintained a grade-point average (GPA) of 3.5 or higher on a 4.0 scale for all undergraduate course work or do you have a bachelor's degree and graduated in the upper 10 percent of your baccalaureate graduating class or of a major university subdivision?

   (A) Yes
   (B) No

4. Please fill in "A" for this question.

   (A) A

5. Please fill in "A" for this question.

   (A) A

   The following questions ask you to describe your educational background, your work, and other experiences in specific areas that relate to successful job performance. You are to choose one answer to each question from among the alternatives presented. Then, record your answers in Section 25 on Form C beginning at Item 6.

   Do not mark more than one answer for each question. Multiple answers will not be counted. Do not omit answers unless instructed to do so. Other omissions may decrease your score.

6. During high school (grades 9-12), I made the semester honor roll:

   (A) never
   (B) once or twice
   (C) three or four times
   (D) five or six times
   (E) seven or eight times

7. The high school grade I most often received was

   (A) A
   (B) B
   (C) C
   (D) D or lower
   (E) I do not remember.

IF YOU DID NOT ATTEND COLLEGE, PLEASE SKIP TO ITEM 9.

8. The college grade I most often received was:

   (A) A
   (B) B
   (C) C
   (D) D or lower
   (E) I do not remember.

9. In the past three years the number of different paying jobs I have held for more than two weeks is:

   (A) 7 or more
   (B) 5-6
   (C) 3-4
   (D) 1-2
   (E) None

10. I have been employed in work similar to that of the job covered by this examination:
    (A) I have never been employed in a similar job.
    (B) Less than 1 year
    (C) 1-2 years
    (D) 3-4 years
    (E) Over 5 years

11. In the past three years, my primary work experience has been in:
    (A) professional or administrative occupations
    (B) clerical or sales occupations
    (C) service occupations
    (D) trades or labor occupations
    (E) Not employed in the past three years

12. On my present or most recent job, my supervisor rated me as:
    (A) outstanding
    (B) above average
    (C) average
    (D) below average
    (E) Not employed or received no rating

13. In the past three years, the number of jobs I have been fired from is:
    (A) 5 or more
    (B) 3 to 4
    (C) 2
    (D) 1
    (E) None

14. The number of civic or social organizations (which have regular meetings and a defined membership) that I belong to is:
    (A) None
    (B) 1
    (C) 2 or 3
    (D) 4 to 6
    (E) 7 or more

15. In organizations to which I belong, my participation is best described as which of the following?
    (A) Do not belong to any organizations.
    (B) I am not very active.
    (C) I am a regular member but not an office holder.
    (D) I have held at least one important office.
    (E) I have held several important offices.

16. My previous supervisors (or teachers if not previously employed) would most likely describe my basic math skills as:
    (A) superior
    (B) above average
    (C) average
    (D) below average
    (E) do not know

ACCOMPLISHMENTS

In this part, you will respond to questions about experiences you have had that are related to the requirements of the job for which you are applying. Please answer YES or NO to each question. Begin marking your responses to the items for this part in Section 25 on Form C beginning at Item 17. Fill in (A) for YES or (B) for NO. Answer all questions to the best of your ability. Do not answer YES unless you can provide specific examples or documentation as proof that you have had this type of experience. You may be asked to provide such evidence or documentation at a later stage in the selection process. Your responses are subject to verification through background checks, job interviews, or any other information obtained during the application process. Any exaggeration of your experience or any attempt to conceal information can result in your being removed from a federal job and in barring you from seeking federal employment in the future. Use the following guidelines to answer these questions:

(1) Many questions refer to work experiences. The word *work* refers to all experiences gained through school, paid employment, military service, voluntary work, and through activities done for professional, charitable, church, community, social, or other organizations, unless otherwise stated.

(2) Some questions ask for experience in a specific type of setting. For example, if the question says "Have you done paid work that involved . . ." then only respond YES if your experience was gained in a paid job.

(3) Do not include personal or home-related experiences unless the question specifically mentions them.

(4) Some questions ask about customers or clients. Customers or clients include any individuals who used or received the products or services that you provided, including individuals inside or outside of your organization. Keep in mind that you may have worked with customers or clients in a variety of settings including those listed in guideline number 1 above.

(5) Some questions ask you if you received a grade of B or above on schoolwork. If you were not graded on an A, B, C, D, F scale, use the equivalent of a B or above, that is, an above average grade, on the type of scale on which you were graded. Remember to fill in (A) for YES or (B) for NO.

(A) Yes

(B) No

17. Have you successfully done work where your primary responsibility was to help others work out their problems (for example, worked as a therapist)?

18. Have you successfully taught a writing course or worked as a professional journalist, editor, or writer?

19. Have you written procedures or instructions that others have followed successfully (for example, instruction manuals, survey instructions, training materials, etc.)?

20. Have you successfully done work that regularly involved being on duty by yourself, or completing nonroutine assignments with minimal or no close supervision?

21. Have you often been asked to proofread or edit the writing of others for content, punctuation, spelling, and grammar?

22. Have you made decisions that turned an unprofitable business into a profit-making operation?

23. Have you successfully done work that frequently required you to present nontechnical information at briefings, meetings, conferences, or hearings?

24. Have you taken the initiative to learn new skills or acquire additional knowledge that improved your performance at work or school or in leisure activities?

25. Have you successfully provided quality service to many different customers or clients with whom you interacted only briefly (for example, worked as a receptionist, bank teller, cashier, or waiter/waitress)?

26. Have you participated in post-high school activities that helped you improve your negotiation or persuasion skills (for example, college debate team, training classes, workshops, or seminars)?

27. Have you received a grade of B or above on oral presentations made for school courses, taken since high school, that did not focus on oral communication skills (for example, history, or sociology), or for any oral presentations made for high school?

28. Have you successfully done work that required you to keep enough cash on hand or maintain an adequate stock of supplies, equipment, or merchandise?

29. Have you received formal recognition for your ability to work well with others (for example, received a letter of recommendation or appreciation, or an excellent performance appraisal rating)?

30. Have you successfully done work that regularly required you to modify plans to accommodate unexpected assignments or to respond to changing workloads, priorities, or deadlines?

31. Have you successfully completed a complex research project that included collecting and analyzing information and reporting conclusions or recommendations?

32. Have you successfully planned or monitored a large-scale project or program that involved several steps that were carried out over an extended period of time?

33. Have you devised a strategy to overcome a major setback that successfully enabled you to complete a project on time or within budget?

34. Have you successfully done work that regularly involved making decisions about disclosure of sensitive or confidential information?

35. Have you successfully done work that regularly involved discussing sensitive information with others, or interviewing or surveying people, either in person or by telephone, to gather information they were reluctant to give?

36. Have you successfully taught a course that focused on interpersonal skills (for example, customer relations, or counseling)?

37. Do you regularly monitor your progress toward achieving your career goals (for example, by initiating discussions about your career goals with your supervisor, employee counselor, or mentor)?

38. Have you successfully done work that regularly involved deciding how to handle disorderly people or situations?

39. Have you participated in training classes, workshops, or seminars outside of school that helped you improve your self-management skills (for example, time management, goal setting, or career development)?

40. Have you successfully done work where you were responsible for determining appropriate treatment or rehabilitation programs (for example, worked as a probation/parole officer, social worker, or counselor)?

41. Have you successfully done work that involved making personnel decisions (for example, who to hire, promote, or discipline) or deciding how to allocate equipment, materials, or staff)?

42. Have you successfully remained friendly and polite while briefly interacting with many different clients or customers (for example, worked as a receptionist, bank teller, cashier, waiter/waitress, or sales clerk)?

43. Have you successfully determined space layouts or assignments for equipment, furniture, or displays?

44. Have you successfully completed an apprenticeship in a trade or craft?

45. Have you successfully remained courteous and tactful while enforcing laws or policies or helping customers, clients, or members of the public who were hostile or upset, not including handling customer complaints (for example, worked in a crisis center, worked as a police officer, parole officer, or park ranger)?

46. Have you successfully learned a hobby or leisure activity requiring extensive study or use of complex directions (for example, constructing stereo or computer systems, building a car, or making stained glass objects)?

47. Have you done work that involved writing brochures, press releases, or speeches?

48. In college, did you have an overall undergraduate grade point average of (3.0) or higher on a (4.0) scale, belong to an honor society, or graduate with honors? (Answer NO to this question if you did not attend college.)

49. Have you successfully done work that regularly involved deciding how best to use the strengths of team members (for example, deciding who to assign to various projects, which player to put in each position, etc.)?

50. Have you successfully done work where your primary responsibility was to handle customers' problems or complaints, or where you were required to deal with customer complaints that could not be resolved by lower level employees?

51. Have you successfully resolved conflicts among group or team members while acting in a leadership role for the group?

52. Have you broken a sales record or a similar record, regularly exceeded quotas or similar productivity standards, or received formal recognition for doing work that surpassed what was expected (for example, received a certificate of appreciation or bonus)?

53. Have you received a grade of B or above in school courses, taken since high school, with a strong emphasis on interpersonal skills (for example, customer relations or counseling)?

54. Have you successfully reviewed and evaluated forms, applications, documents, or other information, not including contract proposals or bids, to make determinations (for example, to determine approval or denial of loans, or eligibility for claims)?

55. Have you formally taught, instructed, or trained others in educational or occupational settings and received favorable feedback about your ability to do so?

56. Have you developed a formal mechanism to learn more about a problem (for example, developed a survey, conducted interviews or focus groups)?

57. Have you successfully done work that regularly involved planning, prioritizing, scheduling, and monitoring work for ten or more people?

58. Have you submitted articles or similar types of written work that were published in a professional, trade, or scholarly journal or in a nationally recognized newspaper or magazine?

59. Have you received a grade of B or above on essays or reports written for high school classes?

60. Do you have a professional license or certificate issued by a state or other official or professional licensing board indicating your mastery of a specialized body of knowledge (for example, cosmetology, real estate, or certified public accounting)?

61. Have you successfully owned or managed a business, or done paid work as a contractor or consultant, where business depended on establishing and maintaining good customer relations?

62. Have you successfully done work where you regularly completed routine work assignments with minimal supervision?

63. Since high school, have you received a grade of B or above in oral communication classes (for example, speech, public speaking, or theater) or participated in activities that improved your oral communication skills (for example, training classes, workshops, seminars, debate team, or speech club)?

64. Have you earned a degree in an area of study related to oral communication (for example, speech communication, broadcast journalism, etc.)? (Answer YES to this question if you anticipate receiving this degree within the next nine months.)

65. Have you performed home repairs that involved determining the specific problem, determining how to make the repair, and successfully completing the repair (for example, fixed a leaking faucet or reshingled a roof)?

66. Have you successfully done work that regularly involved interacting with customers, clients, coworkers, or supervisors who were especially difficult to get along with?

67. Have you successfully done work that regularly involved interacting with or counseling people with special needs or problems (for example, hospital patients, psychiatric patients, prisoners, or people who are elderly or disabled)?

68. Have you made presentations where you successfully persuaded someone to do something (for example, support a project, accept your recommendations or purchase a product or service)?

69. Have you successfully done work that regularly involved interacting or coordinating with people outside of your immediate work group (for example, people from other offices, departments or organizations)?

70. Have you successfully coordinated work, school, and/or family responsibilities under especially difficult circumstances (for example, you and your spouse worked full-time while raising young children, you went to school full time and worked more than 20 hours per week, or you worked full time while caring for an elderly parent)?

71. Have you received formal recognition for solving a work-related problem (for example, received an award or a letter of commendation)?

72. Have you written articles or similar types of work that have been included in a school newspaper, community newsletter, or similar type of publication?

73. Have you successfully done work that regularly involved negotiating with customers or clients to modify products or to resolve problems or disputes?

74. Have you successfully done work that constantly required you to work under difficult time constraints?

75. Have you successfully done paid work that regularly involved troubleshooting and resolving problems with equipment or systems (for example, appliances, vehicles, machinery, computer or electrical systems)?

76. In high school, did you have an overall grade point average of 3.0 or higher on a 4.0 scale, belong to an honor society, or graduate with honors?

77. Have you received favorable feedback about your ability to provide oral instructions or on-the-job training to others, or about your ability to instruct or coach others in athletic, leisure, or community activities?

78. Have you successfully provided good customer service while constantly working under difficult time constraints (for example, worked in a fast-food restaurant or worked as a stockbroker)?

79. Have you successfully done work that regularly involved listening carefully to others to understand a need, problem, or situation (for example, investigative work or counseling)?

80. Have you worked on several major assignments or projects at the same time with minimal supervision and completed the work on time or ahead of schedule?

81. Have you received formal recognition for your oral communication skills (for example, received certification from Toastmasters International, won a speech contest or debate tournament, etc.)?

82. Have you successfully negotiated with faculty, staff, advisors, etc., as an active member of the student council in high school or college?

83. Have you successfully persuaded others to volunteer time, money, or resources to a cause, or recruited others to join an organization (for example, college, fraternity, or military)?

84. Have you designed or developed something, on your own initiative, to help you or other employees better complete assignments (for example, designed a training manual)?

85. Have you successfully persuaded management, other members of your group, customers, or clients to accept a proposal?

86. Have you successfully resolved disagreements among a group of peers in a goal-oriented setting (for example, sports team, work group, theater group, or cheerleading squad)?

87. Have you successfully completed a large-scale project (lasting several months or longer) on or ahead of schedule with minimal supervision?

88. Have you successfully done work that regularly involved conducting quality checks or following up with customers or clients to ensure satisfaction with a product or service?

89. Is your highest level of formal education a bachelor's degree or higher?

    (Answer YES to this question if you anticipate receiving a bachelor's degree within the next 9 months.)

90. Have you successfully worked closely with a client over an extended period of time to complete a project or resolve a problem?

91. Have you successfully done work where your supervisor regularly relied on you to make decisions while he or she was in meetings or out of the office?

92. Have you successfully solved problems that occurred because of a critical emergency or a disruption of a life-saving operation, with very few resources or guidelines (for example, solved problems related to a natural disaster, or a power outage in a hospital)?

93. Have you successfully done work that regularly involved answering questions, gathering nonsensitive information, or providing assistance to others, either in person or by telephone?

94. Have you successfully done work that required you to interact with people at many levels in an organization?

95. Have you successfully done work that regularly involved interacting with people, other than your co-workers, from a foreign country or from different ethnic or cultural backgrounds?

96. Have you owned and successfully managed your own profit-making business?

97. Have you successfully done work where one of your primary responsibilities was to solve customer problems (for example, provided support services for customers with software problems)?

98. Have you been requested to take on additional responsibilities because of your ability to manage your own work effectively?

99. Have you successfully done work that involved writing technical or legal reports, or translating technical or other complex material into language that was more easily understood?

100. Have you identified and solved a problem with a procedure, product, or service that benefited the organization (for example, saved the organization time or money, increased sales, or reduced errors)?

101. Have you successfully done work that regularly involved persuading customers or clients to purchase a product or service?

102. Have you successfully completed a long-term project outside of work where you were solely responsible for doing the work (for example, completed a thesis, wrote a book that was published, prepared a horse for competition that won a ribbon, or restored an antique car)?

103. Have you successfully negotiated bargaining unit contracts?

104. Have you received favorable feedback about your interpersonal skills when serving as a leader, instructor, or supervisor for academic, religious, community, sports, leisure, or work activities?

105. Have you successfully remained polite and tactful while doing work where one of your primary responsibilities was to handle customer problems or complaints (for example, worked as a customer service representative)?

106. Have you successfully done work that involved deciding which supplies, equipment, or merchandise to purchase for a group or organization?

107. Have you successfully done work that regularly required you to make quick decisions where the consequences were critical (for example, worked as a 911 operator or on an ambulance squad)?

108. Since high school, have you received a grade of B or above in writing courses (for example, composition, creative writing, or journalism) or on essays, reports, or term papers written for school courses that were not focused on writing skills (for example, history, geography, or psychology)?

109. Have you successfully done work that regularly involved planning, prioritizing, scheduling, and monitoring work for fewer than ten people?

110. Have you successfully done work that regularly involved composing letters or writing reports containing several short paragraphs, such as investigation reports, accident reports, or performance evaluations?

111. Have you completed assignments on time and maintained an overall grade point average of 3.0 or higher on a 4.0 scale in post-high school courses while carrying a full course load?

112. Have you successfully done work that regularly involved informally providing oral explanations of technical information or other complex information, such as regulations, policies, or procedures?

113. Have you successfully planned activities for nonwork groups (for example, athletic teams, professional associations, or church groups)?

114. Have you successfully written reports that presented facts, findings, logical conclusions, and persuasive arguments (for example, wrote a thesis, briefing papers, policy papers, or complex research papers)?

115. Have you received formal recognition for your written work (for example, received an award, letter of commendation, or excellent performance appraisal rating)?

116. Have you successfully done work that required extensive on-the-job training?

117. Have you successfully done work that required you to identify what a customer or client needs?

118. Have you learned a hobby or leisure activity well enough that you have been asked to do it for others on a voluntary basis?

119. Have you successfully planned for and started a new business or opened a new store?

120. Have you successfully completed a highly structured, formal training program, not including an apprenticeship for a trade or craft, that required you to learn a complex body of information (for example, training for jobs in insurance, law enforcement, or real estate)?

121. Have you successfully dealt with a disruption to regular operations in a way that allowed for completion of the work or continuation of a noncritical service?

122. Is your highest level of formal education some college, but no bachelor's degree, or completion of technical, trade, or business school training? (Answer NO to this question if you anticipate receiving a bachelor's degree within the next nine months.)

123. Have you successfully done work that regularly involved planning, prioritizing, and monitoring your own work?

124. Have you successfully done work that often required you to accommodate last minute requests from customers or clients or to provide quality service in situations where timeliness is critical (for example, worked as a courier or travel agent or worked in newspaper publishing)?

125. Have you successfully taught self-management skills (for example, time management, goal setting, or career development)?

126. Have you successfully planned an event such as a conference, fund-raiser?

127. Have you successfully done work that regularly required you to lead or facilitate briefings, meetings, or conferences, or formally present technical or other complex information to others?

128. Have you successfully done work where your primary responsibility involved interacting with current or potential customers or clients for the purpose of selling a product or service?

129. Have you served on a decision-making board or committee (for example, student governing board, planning board, or homeowners' association board)?

130. Have you successfully done work that regularly involved answering questions, demonstrating a product or service, or providing assistance to customers, clients, or the public?

131. Have you successfully negotiated with your subordinates to find mutually acceptable solutions for poor performance or inappropriate work behaviors (for example, absenteeism or tardiness)?

132. Have you written a play, script, or novel that was sold, published, or produced?

133. Have you submitted articles or similar types of written work that were published in a local newspaper, nationally distributed newsletter, or similar type of publication?

134. Have you learned a hobby or leisure activity well enough that others have paid you to do it?

135. Have you successfully done work that only occasionally involved helping others work out their problems (for example, worked as a resident advisor in a dorm or camp counselor)?

136. Have you received a grade of B or above in school courses, taken since high school, that focused on negotiation skills (for example, conflict resolution, labor relations, or mediation)?

137. Have you successfully done work that regularly involved determining appropriate products or services for customers or clients?

138. Have you suggested or made changes to products or procedures that resulted in better meeting customer needs?

139. Have you received a grade of B or above in school courses, taken since high school, that emphasized problem solving (for example, logic or computer programming)?

140. Have you used study or review techniques that helped you learn material more effectively?

141. Have you participated in training classes, workshops, or seminars outside of school that improved your performance at work?

142. Have you successfully done work that regularly involved verifying the accuracy of information or the relevance of information to a problem or a situation (for example, investigative work)?

143. Have you successfully completed a small-scale project (lasting several days or weeks) on or ahead of schedule with minimal supervision?

144. Have you successfully done work that regularly involved using negotiation or persuasion to help others avoid trouble or conflict or make positive changes in their lives (for example, worked for a crisis hotline, a resident advisor, or substance abuse counselor)?

145. Have you participated in training classes, workshops, or seminars outside of school that helped you improve your customer service skills?

146. Have you successfully provided quality service to people with special needs or problems (for example, worked in a hospital, halfway house, or special education program)?

147. Have you successfully done work that regularly required you to determine resource requirements or monitor the use of resources (for example, staff, space, equipment, supplies, or materials)?

148. Have you been given additional responsibilities because of your ability to organize and complete your regular work more quickly than expected?

149. Have you successfully negotiated with another person sharing the same resources (for example, negotiated for employees, space, or equipment)?

150. Have you successfully negotiated contracts, leases, or prices for services, supplies, equipment, or property?

151. Have you received formal recognition for providing good service to customers or clients (for example, received an award, a letter of commendation, an excellent performance appraisal rating, etc.)?

152. Have you successfully done work that involved reviewing various contract proposals or contract bids to determine which one to select?

153. Have you received favorable feedback for oral presentations you have given to management or other officials, or to the public (for example, for speaking at religious services or performing in theatrical productions)?

154. Have you taught yourself skills that improved your performance in school or at work (for example, taught yourself typing, computer skills, or a foreign language)?

155. Have you successfully done work that regularly involved relaying messages to coworkers, or providing information or giving simple instructions to customers or the public, either in person or by telephone (for example, worked as a receptionist or dispatcher)?

156. Have you successfully done work that only occasionally required you to present information at briefings, meetings, conferences, or hearings?

ADMINISTRATIVE SERVICE ASSISTANT (GS-05/06/07)

1. Do you meet the minimum qualification requirements for GS-5?

    (A) I meet the minimum qualification requirements for GS-5 as described in the vacancy announcement section under "QUALIFICATION REQUIREMENTS"
    (B) I do not meet the minimum qualification requirements for GS-5.

2. Do you meet the minimum qualification requirements for GS-6?

    (A) I meet the minimum qualification requirements for GS-6 as described in the vacancy announcement section under "QUALIFICATION REQUIREMENTS"
    (B) I do not meet the minimum qualification requirements for GS-6.

3. Do you meet the minimum qualification requirements for GS-7?

    (A) I meet the minimum qualification requirements for GS-7 as described in the vacancy announcement section under "QUALIFICATION REQUIREMENTS"
    (B) I do not meet the minimum qualification requirements for GS-7.

4. For each task in the following group, choose the statement from the list below that best describes your experience and/or training. Darken the oval corresponding to that statement in Section 25 of the Qualifications and Availability Form C. Please select only one letter for each item.

    (A) I have not had education, training, or experience in performing this task.
    (B) I have had education or training in performing the task but have not yet performed it on the job.
    (C) I have performed this task on the job. My work on this task was monitored closely by a supervisor or senior employee to ensure compliance with proper procedures.
    (D) I have performed this task as a regular part of a job. I have performed it independently and normally without review by a supervisor or senior employee.
    (E) I am considered an expert in performing this task. I have supervised performance of this task or I am normally the person who is consulted by other workers to assist them in doing this task because of my expertise.

4. Perform complete procurement transactions for a variety of standard, non-standard, and technical supplies, materials, and services through fixed-price contracts.
   Ⓐ Ⓑ Ⓒ Ⓓ Ⓔ

5. Follow cross-servicing agent's procedures for entry of purchase orders into an automated procurement database.
   Ⓐ Ⓑ Ⓒ Ⓓ Ⓔ

6. Correct obligations and documents and amend information and data previously entered into the National Finance Center's mainframe computer.
   Ⓐ Ⓑ Ⓒ Ⓓ Ⓔ

7. Monitor and verify that invoices received for procurement actions are accurate and correct and reflect accurately the desired prices on the previously prepared purchase orders and prints hard-copy of purchase orders for external distrubution to vendors.
   Ⓐ Ⓑ Ⓒ Ⓓ Ⓔ

8. Recommend payment or non-payment according to whether terms of the purchase contract have been met.
   Ⓐ Ⓑ Ⓒ Ⓓ Ⓔ

9. Prepare requisitions for supplies, equipment, publications, forms, and services.
   Ⓐ Ⓑ Ⓒ Ⓓ Ⓔ

10. Maintain files for staff.
    Ⓐ Ⓑ Ⓒ Ⓓ Ⓔ

11. Receive and refer telephone calls to the director and staff.
    Ⓐ Ⓑ Ⓒ Ⓓ Ⓔ

12. Make travel arrangements for air travel.
    Ⓐ Ⓑ Ⓒ Ⓓ Ⓔ

13. Type letters, memoranda, reports, documents using a personal computer.
    Ⓐ Ⓑ Ⓒ Ⓓ Ⓔ

14. Operate a high-speed printer to produce paper documents from previously scanned electronic images, including initiating communication links between the print server and the printer.
    Ⓐ Ⓑ Ⓒ Ⓓ Ⓔ

15. Custom bind very large documents.
    Ⓐ Ⓑ Ⓒ Ⓓ Ⓔ

16. Remove faulty materials, from machines that have caused malfunctions, and corrects error situation.
    Ⓐ Ⓑ Ⓒ Ⓓ Ⓔ

17. Observe input and output material for creases, tears, printing defects, or other similar conditions.
    Ⓐ Ⓑ Ⓒ Ⓓ Ⓔ

18. Monitor the equipment panel lights to detect machine malfunctions and error situations.
    Ⓐ Ⓑ Ⓒ Ⓓ Ⓔ

19. Perform minor routine maintenance functions on all reproduction equipment, such as replenishing paper, staple supplies, changing tonor cartridges, and cleaning glass.

    Ⓐ   Ⓑ   Ⓒ   Ⓓ   Ⓔ

20. Process requisitions for procurement of printing of large jobs.

    Ⓐ   Ⓑ   Ⓒ   Ⓓ   Ⓔ

21. Maintain control records for production or cost purposes and produce necessary reports.

    Ⓐ   Ⓑ   Ⓒ   Ⓓ   Ⓔ

PART IV

Appendices

APPENDIX A

IMPORTANT CIVIL SERVICE EMPLOYMENT CONTACTS

MAJOR FEDERAL AGENCIES CONTACT INFORMATION

Central Intelligence Agency (CIA)
Office of Public Affairs
Washington, DC 20505
703-482-0623
www.odci.gov

Environmental Protection Agency
401 M St. SW
Washington, DC 20460
202-260-2090
www.epa.gov

Federal Bureau of Investigation (FBI)
J. Edgar Hoover Building
935 Pennsylvania Ave. NW
Washington, DC 20535-0001
202-324-3000
www.fbi.gov

Federal Communications Commission
445 12th Street, SW
Washington, DC 20554
1-888-225-5322 (1-888-CALL-FCC)
TTY: 888-TELL-FCC (835-5322)
E-mail: fccinfo@fcc.gov
www.fcc.gov

Federal Deposit Insurance Corporation (FDIC)
550 17th St. NW
Washington, DC 20429
1-877-275-3342 (1-877-ASK-FDIC), press 1, then press 4
E-mail: jobs@fdic.gov
www.fdic.gov

Federal Emergency Management Agency
500 C St. SW
Washington, DC 20472
202-566-1600
E-mail: opa@fema.gov
www.fema.gov

Federal Highway Administration
400 7th St. SW
Washington, DC 20590
202-366-4000
www.fhwa.dot.gov

Federal Trade Commission
CRC-240
Washington, DC 20580
202-326-2222
www.ftc.gov

Food & Drug Administration
5600 Fishers Lane
Rockville, MD 20857
1-800-INFO-FDA
www.fda.gov

General Services Administration
1800 F Street, NW
Washington, DC 20405
202-501-0705
E-mail: public.affairs@gsa.gov
www.gsa.gov

Health Resources & Services Administration
U.S. Dep't. of Health & Human Services
Parklawn Building
5600 Fishers Lane
Rockville, MD 20857
F1-888-ASK-HRSA
E-mail: comments@hrsa.gov
www.hrsa.gov

Immigration and Naturalization Service
425 I Street, NW
Washington, DC 20530
202-514-2000
www.ins.gov

Library of Congress
101 Independence Avenue, SE
Washington, DC 20540
202-707-5000
www.lcweb.loc.gov

National Aeronautics & Space Administration
300 E Street, SW
Washington, DC 20546-0001
202-358-0000
E-mail: comments@hq.nasa.gov
www.nasa.gov

National Science Foundation
4201 Wilson Blvd.
Arlington, VA 22230
703-292-5111
E-mail: info@nsf.gov
www.nsf.gov

Securities and Exchange Commission
450 5th St. NW
Washington, DC 20549
202-942-7040
www.sec.gov

Social Security Administration
6401 Security Blvd.
Baltimore, MD 21235
1-800-772-1213
www.ssa.gov

U.S. Consumer Product Safety Commission
Washington, DC 20207-0001
301-504-0990
E-mail: info@cpsc.gov
www.cpsc.gov

Appendix B

Webliography of Federal Employment Web Sites

JOB LISTINGS

■ **Government and Law Enforcement Jobs** (jobsearch.about.com/msubgov.htm)—An annotated list of Web sites that list jobs with federal, state, and local governments and law enforcement agencies, from the About.com Guide to Job Searching.

■ **govtjobs.com** (www.govtjobs.com)—A list of jobs in the public sector.

■ **HRS Federal Job Search** (www.hrsjobs.com)—A subscription job search and e-mail delivery service, which also has a lot of free information.

■ **Jobs in State Government** (usgovinfo.about.com/blstjobs.htm)—An index of state Web sites that list government employment opportunities, with sites ranging from About.com Guide to U.S. Government Info/Resources.

■ **U.S. Postal Service: Human Resources** (www.usps.com/employment)—A list of vacancies in management, supervisory, administrative, professional, and technical positions.

■ **USAJOBS** (www.usajobs.opm.gov)—The official site for worldwide federal employment listings from the U.S. Office of Personnel Management, with full text job announcements, forms, and answers to frequently asked questions.

APPLICATIONS AND OTHER FORMS

■ **Electronic Forms** (www.usajobs.opm.gov/forms.htm)—All forms and applications relating to federal employment, from the Office of Personnel Management.

GENERAL INFORMATION

- **Federal Salaries and Wages** (www.opm.gov/oca/payrates/index.htm)—Rates from the U.S. Office of Personnel Management Web site.

- **Public Service Employees Network** (www.pse-net.com)—A guide to government employment, including job listings.

- **The U.S. Office of Personnel Management Web Site** (www.opm.gov)—Tons of information on all aspects of federal employment, with an index and a search feature to make navigation easier.

ONLINE PUBLICATIONS

- **Federal Jobs Digest Online** (www.jobsfed.com)—An online version of this well-known publication that provides job listings, federal employment news, and advice on how to get hired.

- **FederalTimes.com** (www.federaltimes.com)—News of interest to those in the federal government.

- **Federal Employees News Digest** (www.fendonline.com)—Online service for federal employees, with free registration.

- **GovExec.com** (www.govexec.com)—An online publication from *Government Executive Magazine*, bringing news to federal executives and managers.

FEDERAL OCCUPATIONS THAT REQUIRE EXAMINATIONS

Test requirements are for competitive and outside-the-register appointments only, unless otherwise specified. This list does not reflect special examining provisions. Note that Administrative Careers With America (ACWA) examinations refer to positions that meet the criteria for ACWA.

SERIES	TITLE/POSITION(S)	GRADE(S)	ACWA	WRITTEN	PERFORMANCE
				TYPE OF EXAM	
011	Bond Sales Promotion	5/7	•		
018	Safety and Occupational Health Management	5/7	•		
019	Safety Technician	2/3		•	
023	Outdoor Recreation Planning	5/7	•		
025	Park Ranger	5/7	•		
028	Environmental Protection Specialist	5/7	•		
029	Environmental Protection Assistant	2/3/4		•	
072	Fingerprint Identification	2/3/4		•	
080	Security Administration	5/7	•		
082	U.S. Marshal	5/7		•	
083	Police	2		•	
083	Park Police	5		•	
083a	Police (Secret Service)	4/5		•	
085	Security Guard	2		•	
086	Security Clerical and Assistance	2/3/4		•	
105	Social Insurance Administration	5/7	•		

			TYPE OF EXAM		
SERIES	**TITLE/POSITION(S)**	**GRADE(S)**	**ACWA**	**WRITTEN**	**PERFORMANCE**
106	Unemployment Insurance	5/7	•		
132	Intelligence	5/7	•		
134	Intelligence Aide and Clerk	2/3/4		•	
142	Manpower Development	5/7	•		
181	Psychology Aide and Technician	2/3		•	
186	Social Services Aide and Assistant	2/3		•	
187	Social Services	5/7	•		
189	Recreation Aide and Assistant	2/3		•	
244	Labor Management Relations Examining	5/7	•		
249	Wage and Hour Compliance	5/7	•		
301	Misc. Administration and Program	5/7	•		
302	Messenger	2/3/4		•	
303	Misc. Clerk and Assistant	2/3/4		•	
304	Information Receptionist	2/3/4		•	
305	Mail and File	2/3/4		•	
309	Correspondence Clerk	2/3/4		•	
312	Clerk-Stenographer	3/4/5		•	•
312	Reporting Stenographer	5/6			*
312	Shorthand Reporter	6/7/8/9			*
318	Secretary	3/4		•	
319	Closed Microphone Reporting	6/7/8/9			*
322	Clerk-Typist	2/3/4		•	•
326	Office Automation Clerical and Assistance	2/3/4		•	•
332	Computer Operation	2/3/4		•	
334	Computer Specialist	5/7	•	(for alternative B only)	
335	Computer Clerk and Assistant	2/3/4		•	
341	Administrative Officer	5/7	•		
343	Management and Program Analysis	5/7	•		
344	Management and Program Clerical and Assistance	2/3/4		•	
346	Logistics Management	5/7	•		
350	Equipment Operator	2/3/4		•	

			TYPE OF EXAM		
SERIES	**TITLE/POSITION(S)**	**GRADE(S)**	**ACWA**	**WRITTEN**	**PERFORMANCE**
351	Printing Clerical	2/3/4		•	
356	Data Transcriber	2/3/4		•	•
357	Coding	2/3/4		•	
359	Electric Accounting Machine Operator	2/3/4		•	
382	Telephone Operating	2/3/4		•	
390	Telecommunications Processing	2/3/4		•	
391	Telecommunications	5/7	•		
392	General Telecommunications	2/3/4		•	
394	Communications Clerical	2/3/4		•	
404	Biological Science Technician	2/3		•	
421	Plant Protection Technician	2/3		•	
455	Range Technician	2/3		•	
458	Soil Conservation Technician	2/3		•	
459	Irrigation System Operation	2/3		•	
462	Forestry Technician	2/3		•	
501	Financial Administration and Program	5/7	•		
503	Financial Clerical and Assistance	2/3/4		•	
525	Accounting Technician	2/3/4		•	
526	Tax Technician	5/7	•		
530	Cash Processing	2/3/4		•	
540	Voucher Examining	2/3/4		•	
544	Civilian Pay	2/3/4		•	
545	Military Pay	2/3/4		•	
560	Budget Analysis	5/7	•		
561	Budget Clerical and Assistance	2/3/4		•	
570	Financial Institution Examining	5/7	• (except for FDIC positions)		
592	Tax Examining	2/3/4		•	
593	Insurance Accounts	2/3/4		•	
621	Nursing Assistant	2/3		•	
636	Rehabilitation Therapy Assistant	2/3		•	
640	Health Aide and Technician	2/3		•	

SERIES	TITLE/POSITION(S)	GRADE(S)	ACWA	WRITTEN	PERFORMANCE
				TYPE OF EXAM	
642	Nuclear Medicine Technician	2/3		•	
645	Medical Technician	2/3		•	
646	Pathology Technician	2/3		•	
647	Diagnostic Radiologic Technologist	2/3		•	
648	Therapeutic Radiologic Technologist	2/3		•	
649	Medical Instrument Technician	2/3		•	
651	Respiratory Therapist	2/3		•	
661	Pharmacy Technician	2/3		•	
667	Orthotist and Prosthetist	3		•	
673	Hospital Housekeeping Management	5/7	•		
675	Medical Records Technician	2/3/4		•	
679	Medical Clerk	2/3/4		•	
681	Dental Assistant	2/3		•	
683	Dental Lab Aide and Technician	2/3		•	
685	Public Health Program Specialist	5/7	•		
698	Environmental Health Technician	2/3		•	
704	Animal Health Technician	2/3		•	
802	Engineering Technician	2/3		•	
809	Construction Control	2/3		•	
817	Surveying Technician	2/3		•	
818	Engineering Drafting	2/3		•	
856	Electronics Technician	2/3		•	
895	Industrial Engineering Technician	2/3		•	
950	Paralegal Specialist	5/7	•		
958	Pension Law Specialist	5/7	•		
962	Contact Representative	3/4		•	
962	Contact Representative	5/7	•		
963	Legal Instruments Examining	2/3/4		•	
965	Land Law Examining	5/7	•		
967	Passport and Visa Examining	5/7	•		
986	Legal Clerk and Technician	2/3/4		•	
987	Tax Law Specialist	5/7	•		
990	General Claims Examining (One-grade interval)	4		•	

SERIES	TITLE/POSITION(S)	GRADE(S)	TYPE OF EXAM ACWA	WRITTEN	PERFORMANCE
990	General Claims Examining (Two-grade interval)	5/7	•		
991	Workers' Comp. Claims Examining	5/7	•		
993	Social Insurance Claims Examining	4		•	
993	Railroad Retirement Claims Examining	5/7	•		
994	Unemployment Comp. Claims Examining	5/7	•		
996	Veterans Claims Examining	5/7	•		
998	Claims Clerical	2/3/4		•	
1001	General Arts and Information	2/3/4		•	
1001	General Arts and Information	5/7	• (except fine arts positions)		
1016	Museum Specialist and Technician	2/3		•	
1021	Office Drafting	2/3		•	
1035	Public Affairs	5/7	•		
1046	Language Clerical	2/3/4		•	
1082	Writing and Editing	5/7	•		
1083	Technical Writing and Editing	5/7	•		
1087	Editorial Assistance	2/3/4		•	
1101	General Business and Industry	2/3/4		•	
1101	General Business and Industry	5/7	•		
1101	International Trade Analyst	5/7	•		
1102	Contracting	5/7	•		
1103	Industrial Property Management	5/7	•		
1104	Property Disposal	5/7	•		
1105	Purchasing	2/3/4		•	
1106	Procurement Clerical and Technician	2/3/4		•	
1107	Property Disposal Clerical and Technician	2/3/4		•	
1130	Public Utilities Specialist	5/7	•		
1140	Trade Specialist	5/7	•		
1140	International Trade Specialist	5/7		•	
1145	Agricultural Program Specialist	5/7	•		
1146	Agricultural Marketing	5/7	•		
1146	Grain Marketing Specialist	5/7		•	
1147	Agricultural Market Reporting	5/7	•		

			TYPE OF EXAM		
SERIES	TITLE/POSITION(S)	GRADE(S)	ACWA	WRITTEN	PERFORMANCE
1150	Industrial Specialist	5/7	•		
1152	Production Control	2/3/4		•	
1160	Financial Analysis	5/7	•		
1163	Insurance Examining	5/7	•		
1165	Loan Specialist	5/7	•		
1169	Internal Revenue Officer	5/7	•		
1170	Realty	5/7	•		
1171	Appraising and Assessing	5/7	•		
1173	Housing Management	5/7	•		
1176	Building Management	5/7	•		
1311	Physical Science Technician	2/3		•	
1316	Hydrologic Technician	2/3		•	
1341	Meteorological Technician	2/3		•	
1371	Cartographic Technician	2/3		•	
1374	Geodetic Technician	2/3		•	
1411	Library Technician	2/3/4		•	
1412	Technical Information Services	5/7	•		
1421	Archives Specialist	5/7	•		
1421	Archives Technician	2/3/4		•	
1521	Mathematics Technician	2/3		•	
1531	Statistical Assistant	2/3/4		•	
1541	Cryptanalysis	2/3		•	
1702	Education and Training Technician	2/3		•	
1715	Vocational Rehabilitation	5/7	•		
1801	Civil Aviation Security Specialist	5/7	•		
1801	Center Adjudications Officer	5/7	•		
1801	District Adjudications Officer	5/7	•		
1802	Compliance Inspection and Support	2/3/4		• (except Detention Enforcement Officer positions)	
1810	General Investigating	5/7	•		
1811	Criminal Investigating	5/7	•		
1811	Treasury Enforcement Agent	5/7		•	

			TYPE OF EXAM		
SERIES	**TITLE/POSITION(S)**	**GRADE(S)**	**ACWA**	**WRITTEN**	**PERFORMANCE**
1812	Game Law Enforcement	5/7	•		
1812	Special Agent (Wildlife)	7		•	
1816	Immigration Inspection	5/7	•		
1831	Securities Compliance Examining	5/7	•		
1854	Alcohol, Tobacco, and Firearms Inspection	5/7	•		
1863	Food Inspection	5/7		•	
1864	Public Health Quarantine Inspection	5/7	•		
1884	Customs Patrol Officer	5/7		•	
1889	Import Specialist	5/7	•		
1890	Customs Inspection	5/7	•		
1896	Border Patrol Agent	5/7		• (and language proficiency)	
1897	Customs Aid	2/3/4		•	
1910	Quality Assurance	5/7	•		
1981	Agricultural Commodity Aid	2/3		•	
2001	General Supply	5/7	•		
2003	Supply Program Management	5/7	•		
2005	Supply Clerical and Technician	2/3/4		•	
2010	Inventory Management	5/7	•		
2030	Distribution Facilities and Storage Management	5/7	•		
2032	Packaging	5/7	•		
2050	Supply Cataloging	5/7	•		
2091	Sales Store Clerical	2/3/4		•	
2101	Transportation Specialist	5/7	•		
2101	Airway Transportation System Specialist (Department of Transportation Federal Aviation Administration)	5/7		•	
2102	Transportation Clerk and Assistant	2/3/4		•	
2110	Transportation Industry Analysis	5/7	•		
2125	Highway Safety	5/7	•		
2130	Traffic Management	5/7	•		
2131	Freight Rate	2/3/4		•	

SERIES	TITLE/POSITION(S)	GRADE(S)	ACWA	WRITTEN	PERFORMANCE
2135	Transportation Loss and Damage Claims Examining	2/3/4		•	
2150	Transportation Operations	5/7	•		
2151	Dispatching	2/3/4		•	
2152	Air Traffic Control	5/7		•	

(optional above 7)

* Mandatory for competitive appointment and in-service placement

APPENDIX D

GLOSSARY OF CIVIL SERVICE TERMS

When you're reading the announcement and filling out your application, you need to understand the government's hiring terminology. Take a few minutes to familiarize yourself with the words listed below. These are very common terms used repeatedly, both in the announcements and in any correspondence or conversation you may have with the federal civil service.

Career status—To be considered a *status employee*, a federal employee must have served for at least three consecutive years in a permanent position.

Certificate of Eligibles—This refers to the list of eligible candidates that results from responses to a vacancy announcement and an application process.

Competitive service—Most positions in the federal government that are subject to Title 5, U.S. Code, meaning that candidates compete for entrance with other non-status applicants.

Continuously open positions—Positions that are open for an indefinite period. These positions, however, may be closed by the agency at any time.

Eligibles—Refers to qualified applicants.

Excepted service—Most positions in the legislative and judicial branches, and some in the executive branch, which are not in the *competitive service*.

Federal Wage System—The classification used for trade and labor jobs in the federal government.

FWS—See *Federal Wage System*.

General Schedule—The classification for white-collar jobs in the federal government.

Grade—Each pay category; *WG* is used to indicate pay categories for *Federal Wage System* (WS) jobs, while *GS* is used to indicated categories for *General Schedule* jobs.

Schedule and also *Grade*.

...ge salary—Used to determine retirement benefits, this term refers to the average ...est basic pay over any three years of consecutive service.

...nily—Grouping of occupations in the *Federal Wage System* that are related in either ...arity of functions performed, transferability of knowledge and skills, or similarity of mate-... or equipment worked on.

Merit Promotion System—This system helps determine whether current employees will be promoted within the federal government's competitive service.

Occupation—Includes all jobs at the various skill levels in a particular kind of work.

Occupational groups—Related occupations in the *General Schedule (GS)* that are grouped together within the same multiple of 100, i.e., GS-100, 200, and 300.

OF-612—The Optional Application for Federal Employment.

Pay comparability—Federal salaries, by law, are based on a comparison with private-sector jobs.

Probationary period—A trial period before a new employee becomes permanent.

Rating and ranking—Job candidates are evaluated and placed on a *Certificate of Eligibles* in score order.

Register—A list of qualified applicants for a specific occupation.

Reinstatement eligibility—This provision allows former federal employees to apply for jobs that are open to *status employees*.

Senior Executive Service—Top management in federal agencies.

Series—All jobs in a subgroup of an *occupational group* that are related by subject matter, basic knowledge, and skill requirements. Includes jobs at various skill levels.

Status employee—An employee with *career status* is eligible to apply for other federal jobs based on current service or reinstatement eligibility.

Temporary appointment—An appointment that lasts one year or less and has a specific expiration date.

Term appointment—An appointment that lasts for over one year and up to four years.

Veterans preference—Veterans receive preference points that are added to their scores when competing for federal jobs.

WG—See *Grade*.

Within-Grade Step Increases—Pay increases indicated by 10 steps within each *grade*. Steps are based on performance and time in grade.

APPLYING FOR A FEDERAL JOB

**United States
Office of
Personnel
Management**

OF 510
(September 1994)

JOB OPENINGS

For job information 24 hours a day, 7 days a week, call **912-757-3000**, the U.S. Office of Personnel Management (OPM) automated telephone system. Or, with a computer modem dial **912-757-3100** for job information from an OPM electronic bulletin board. You can also reach the board through the Internet (Telnet only) at FJOB.MAIL.OPM.GOV.

APPLICANTS WITH DISABILITIES

You can find out about alternative formats by calling OPM or dialing the electronic bulletin board at the numbers above. Select "Federal Employment Topics" and then "People with Disabilities." If you have a hearing disability, call **TDD 912-744-2299**.

HOW TO APPLY

Review the list of openings, decide which jobs you are interested in, and follow the instructions given. **You may apply for most jobs with a resume, the** *Optional Application for Federal Employment***, or any other written format you choose.** For jobs that are unique or filled through automated procedures, you will be given special forms to complete. (You can get an *Optional Application* by calling OPM or dialing our electronic bulletin board at the numbers above.)

WHAT TO INCLUDE

Although the Federal Government does not require a standard application form for most jobs, we do need certain information to evaluate your qualifications and determine if you meet legal requirements for Federal employment. If your resume or application does not provide all the information requested in the job vacancy announcement and in this brochure, you may lose consideration for a job. Help speed the selection process by keeping your resume or application brief and by sending only the requested material. Type or print clearly in dark ink.

Here's what your resume or application must contain

(in addition to specific information requested in the job vacancy announcement)

JOB INFORMATION

❏ Announcement number, and title and grade(s) of the job you are applying for

PERSONAL INFORMATION

❏ Full name, mailing address *(with ZIP Code)* and day and evening phone numbers *(with area code)*
❏ Social Security Number
❏ Country of citizenship *(Most Federal jobs require United States citizenship.)*
❏ Veterans' preference *(See reverse.)*
❏ Reinstatement eligibility *(If requested, attach SF 50 proof of your career or career-conditional status.)*
❏ Highest Federal civilian grade held *(Also give job series and dates held.)*

EDUCATION

❏ High school
    Name, city, and State *(ZIP Code if known)*
    Date of diploma or GED
❏ Colleges or universities
    Name, city, and State *(ZIP Code if known)*
    Majors
    Type and year of any degrees received
    (If no degree, show total credits earned and indicate whether semester or quarter hours.)
❏ Send a copy of your college transcript only if the job vacancy announcement requests it.

WORK EXPERIENCE

❏ Give the following information for your paid and nonpaid work experience related to the job you are applying for.
    (Do not send job descriptions.)
    Job title *(include series and grade if Federal job)*
    Duties and accomplishments
    Employer's name and address
    Supervisor's name and phone number
    Starting and ending dates *(month and year)*
    Hours per week
    Salary
❏ Indicate if we may contact your current supervisor.

OTHER QUALIFICATIONS

❏ **Job-related** training courses *(title and year)*
❏ **Job-related** skills, for example, other languages, computer software/hardware, tools, machinery, typing speed
❏ **Job-related** certificates and licenses *(current only)*
❏ **Job-related** honors, awards, and special accomplishments, for example, publica–tions, memberships in professional or honor societies, leadership activities, public speaking, and performance awards *(Give dates but do not send documents unless requested.)*

> **THE FEDERAL GOVERNMENT IS AN EQUAL OPPORTUNITY EMPLOYER**

VETERANS' PREFERENCE IN HIRING

❑ If you served on active duty in the United States Military and were separated under honorable conditions, you may be eligible for veterans' preference. To receive preference if your service began after October 15, 1976, you must have a Campaign Badge, Expeditionary Medal, or a service-connected disability. For further details, call OPM at **912-757-3000**. Select "Federal Employment Topics" and then "Veterans." Or, dial our electronic bulletin board at **912-757-3100**.

❑ Veterans' preference is not a factor for Senior Executive Service jobs or when competition is limited to status candidates (current or former Federal career or career-conditional employees).

❑ To claim 5-point veterans' preference, attach a copy of your DD-214, *Certificate of Release or Discharge from Active Duty*, or other proof of eligibility.

❑ To claim 10-point veterans' preference, attach an SF 15, *Application for 10-Point Veterans' Preference*, plus the proof required by that form.

OTHER IMPORTANT INFORMATION

❑ Before hiring, an agency will ask you to complete a *Declaration for Federal Employment* to determine your suitability for Federal employment and to authorize a background investigation. The agency will also ask you to sign and certify the accuracy of all the information in your application. **If you make a false statement in any part of your application, you may not be hired; you may be fired after you begin work; or you may be fined or jailed.**

❑ If you are a male over age 18 who was born after December 31, 1959, you must have registered with the Selective Service System (or have an exemption) to be eligible for a Federal job.

❑ The law prohibits public officials from appointing, promoting, or recommending their relatives.

❑ Federal annuitants (military and civilian) may have their salaries or annuities reduced. All employees must pay any valid delinquent debts or the agency may garnish their salary.

PRIVACY AND PUBLIC BURDEN STATEMENTS

The Office of Personnel Management and other Federal agencies rate applicants for Federal jobs under the authority of sections 1104, 1302, 3301, 3304, 3320, 3361, 3393, and 3394 of title 5 of the United States Code. We need the information requested in this brochure and in the associated vacancy announcements to evaluate your qualifications. Other laws require us to ask about citizenship, military service, etc.

❑ We request your Social Security Number (SSN) under the authority of Executive Order 9397 in order to keep your records straight; other people may have the same name. As allowed by law or Presidential directive, we use your SSN to seek information about you from employers, schools, banks, and others who know you. Your SSN may also be used in studies and computer matching with other Government files, for example, files on unpaid student loans.

❑ If you do not give us your SSN or any other information requested, we cannot process your application, which is the first step in getting a job. Also, incomplete addresses and ZIP Codes will slow processing.

❑ We may give information from your records to: training facilities; organizations deciding claims for retirement, insurance, unemployment or health benefits; officials in litigation or administrative proceedings where the Government is a party; law enforcement agencies concerning violations of law or regulation; Federal agencies for statistical reports and studies; officials of labor organizations recognized by law in connection with representing employees; Federal agencies or other sources requesting information for Federal agencies in connection with hiring or retaining, security clearances, security or suitability investigations, classifying jobs, contracting, or issuing licenses, grants, or other benefits; public or private organizations including news media that grant or publicize employee recognition and awards; and the Merit Systems Protection Board, the Office of Special Counsel, the Equal Employment Opportunity Commission, the Federal Labor Relations Authority, the National Archives, the Federal Acquisition Institute, and congressional offices in connection with their official functions.

❑ We may also give information from your records to: prospective nonfederal employers concerning tenure of employment, civil service status, length of service, and date and nature of action for separation as shown on personnel action forms of specifically identified individuals; requesting organizations or individuals concerning the home address and other relevant information on those who might have contracted an illness or been exposed to a health hazard; authorized Federal and nonfederal agencies for use in computer matching; spouses or dependent children asking whether an employee has changed from self-and-family to self-only health benefits enrollment; individuals working on a contract, service, grant, cooperative agreement or job for the Federal Government; non-agency members of an agency's performance or other panel; and agency-appointed representatives of employees concerning information issued to an employee about fitness-for-duty or agency-filed disability retirement procedures.

❑ We estimate the public burden for reporting the employment information will vary from 20 to 240 minutes with an average of 40 minutes per response, including time for reviewing instructions, searching existing data sources, gathering data, and completing and reviewing the information. You may send comments regarding the burden estimate or any other aspect of the collection of information, including suggestions for reducing this burden, to the U.S. Office of Personnel Management, Reports and Forms Management Officer, Washington, DC 20415-0001.

Send your application to the agency announcing the vacancy.

Form Approved: OMB 3206-0219   50510-101   NSN 7540-01-351-9177

*U.S. Government Printing Office: 1995 — 393-606/20008

NOTES

NOTES

NOTES

NOTES

Your everything education destination...
the *all-new* Petersons.com

petersons.com

When education is the question, **Petersons.com** is the answer. Log on today and discover what the *all-new* Petersons.com can do for you. Find the ideal college or grad school, take an online practice admission test, or explore financial aid options—all from a name you know and trust, Peterson's.

www.petersons.com

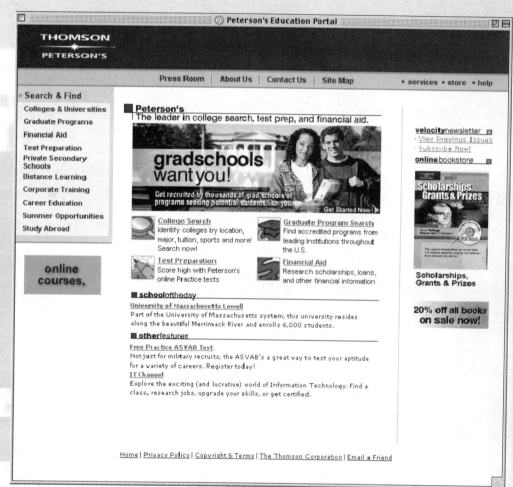